Farewell to the Bloody Shirt

Farewell to the Bloody Shirt

NORTHERN REPUBLICANS & THE
SOUTHERN NEGRO, 1877–1893

STANLEY P. HIRSHSON

introduction by

DAVID DONALD

Indiana University Press
Bloomington

SECOND PRINTING 1966

COPYRIGHT © 1962 BY INDIANA UNIVERSITY PRESS
MANUFACTURED IN THE UNITED STATES OF AMERICA
LIBRARY OF CONGRESS CATALOG CARD NUMBER:
62-8975

TO MY FATHER

Contents

Introduction

THE PRESENT racial crisis in the United States had its origins in the years following the Civil War. One of the Northern objectives in that conflict had been to secure the freedom of the Negro, and, in the minds of many Republican Radicals, it had the additional purpose of insuring his equality before the law. During the Reconstruction period there were hopeful beginnings in the ex-Confederate states which looked toward making the former slave a first-class citizen.

The years following the end of Radical Reconstruction in the South, however, marked an unhappy reversion in Southern attitudes toward the Negro. Though not completely disfranchised until the 1890's, the Negro voter, as Professor C. Vann Woodward has pointed out, was "often coerced, defrauded, or intimidated." He was relegated to a permanent place of economic inferiority. Lynching rose to new, staggering heights. Everywhere in the South this period was marked by "race conflict and violence, brutality and exploitation."

Professor Stanley P. Hirshson's book is a fine scholarly study of the political background of these developments. It is not, except incidentally, a tract for our times. Though obviously hostile to racial discrimination, Dr. Hirshson is less concerned with denouncing that system than with understanding how it came into being. Nor is his book a history of the Negro. Recognizing that the colored man was a helpless pawn during these troubled years, he concentrates instead upon the powerful social and political forces beyond the Negro's control which shaped his destiny.

The Negro realized that he could not realistically look to the Southern white man for aid in securing his basic legal rights. Though there was much talk during these years about the Southerner as the natural benefactor of the colored race, the Negro was rightly cynical about such theories. He saw how abortive was the one hopeful attempt to bring about interracial harmony during the Populist movement, and he recognized that the ex-Confederate states were controlled by Bourbon Democrats, inflexibly opposed to the extension of political, economic, or social equality to his race. Even a moderate, thoughtful Bourbon like L. Q. C. Lamar of Mississippi said frankly that "Negro government was necessarily ignorant, and ignorant government was necessarily vicious and bad" and added "that the white people of the South would continue to govern their states."

Unable to help himself and unable to secure protection from the Southern whites among whom he lived, the Negro looked for assistance to the Republican party, the party of Abraham Lincoln and emancipation, which had presumably guaranteed his rights through the Thirteenth, Fourteenth, and Fifteenth amendments to the Constitution. Dr. Hirshson's book is a superb analysis of the reasons why such protection was not granted.

Professor Hirshson makes it abundantly evident that during these post-Reconstruction decades Republican attitudes toward the Negro question were shaped less by humanitarian concern than by selfish political considerations. Gone was the reforming zeal which had animated such Radical Republicans as Charles Sumner, Thaddeus Stevens, and George W. Julian. In men like John Sherman, James G. Blaine, and Chester A. Arthur

humanitarianism burned with but a flickering flame. For them
—as for too many of their present-day successors of both
parties—the Negro vote was not a cause but an opportunity.
As the abolitionist Thomas Wentworth Higginson astutely observed in 1884, the Negroes throughout the period were being
"used merely as pawns or dice in a game played by political
tricksters."

Mr. Hirshson's elaborate analysis makes clear for the first
time the motives behind the shifting Republican attitudes
toward the Negro in the 1870's and 1880's. Fundamentally the
problem confronting Republican strategists was the fact that
the Democrats were the party in the permanent majority; indeed, it could be argued that since the days of Andrew Jackson the Democrats had normally had a majority of popular
votes in presidential elections and that only exceptional circumstances—such as the nomination by the Whigs of a famous,
uncommitted military leader in 1848; the division of the Democratic party in 1860; or the disfranchisement of Southern whites
in 1868—ever permitted their opponents to attain the Presidency. The elections in the post-Reconstruction years were
especially close. The cumbersome electoral machinery did not
always permit the Democrats to win the Presidency, but they
had a plurality of the popular votes in 1876, 1884, 1888, and
1892; even in 1880 the Republicans won by the hair-breadth
plurality of less than 10,000 votes.

In these circumstances the basic Republican problem was
to break down Democratic centers of strength, and they naturally turned toward the Solid South, fifteen states which cast
not one Republican electoral vote from 1880 to 1892. Two possible courses seemed open. One was the policy, which had
already been tried during the Reconstruction years, of building a Republican party in the South based largely upon the
Negro vote. To bring about this result—in which the Negroes,
of course, saw the best chance of protecting their rights—there

would have to be Federal intervention in Southern elections, to prevent intimidation by the whites and to secure fair play. And in order to secure Northern backing for such a program, there would also have to be much harping upon the alleged crimes and treasons of the Southern whites, a practice generally known as "waving the bloody shirt." Throughout this postwar period, as Mr. Hirshson demonstrates, there were Republicans who advocated this policy. Some few were motivated by a genuine concern for the plight of the Negro; more were actuated by a belief that only Negro votes in the South could be relied upon to be Republican. The way to enlarge the Republican party in the South, argued William E. Chandler, "is not by forming white Republican clubs but by enforcing the fifteenth amendment."

An opposing school of Republican thought, which receives prominent attention in Mr. Hirshson's pages, believed that the Negro was politically undependable and proposed the establishment of a white-dominated Republican party in the Southern states. Mugwump reformers, who thought the Negro race was innately inferior and believed that Negro participation in government inevitably led to further corruption as in the Reconstruction days, hoped to unite the best people—meaning whites—of North and South in a respectable Republican party. More influential were certain key Northern economic interests. Advocates of protective tariffs thought they could find support among the rising Southern manufacturing interests, and merchants of such Southern-oriented cities as Cincinnati feared that continued advocacy of Negro rights would alienate their profitable Southern markets. Like their opponents, these Republican groups could claim to be following party tradition, for most of them looked longingly back to the days before the Civil War, when conservative business interests of North and South had worked amiably together in the old Whig party.

Dr. Hirshson's book is a detailed account of the rivalry between these two conflicting schools of Republican thought, the outcome of which determined the basic pattern of race relations which persists in most of the South to this day. From a close examination of the private and unpublished correspondence of the period and from a wide sampling of the contemporary newspapers, he has been able to document these alternating winds of doctrine as they swept the Republican banner first one way and then the other. This is, consequently, an important contribution to the political history of a neglected era.

Mr. Hirshson's study is also an exemplary case history of the actual workings of American politics. Realistically he shows that issues have generally been misunderstood and overrated in our political histories. Doubtless the "Negro issue," for example, aroused basic emotions in Northern voters during this period, but as Mr. Hirshson quietly points out, the politicians were cynically opportunistic about it, advocating Negro rights when it was politically convenient and abandoning them when it was expedient. The politicos, as the New York *Post* observed, "never discoursed upon the suppression of the suffrage of the South, except as an argument for keeping themselves in power, and as a reason why the country should not be disgusted or enraged by the gross abuses in administration which the Republican party practiced, permitted, or connived at."

At the same time Mr. Hirshson's book is a contribution to the sociology of American political parties, an instructive analysis of the tension between the economic base of a political organization and its institutional needs. The Republican party of the post-Civil War decades, as is well known, was an organization dominated by big business and responsive to mercantile and industrial pressures. Dr. Hirshson shows how these interests solidly lined up behind the project of forming a white Republican party in the South; most of them agreed with the spokesman of the iron industry that "we need not longer . . . wave the 'bloody shirt,' but rather, as vastly more politic, press the tariff issue upon our Southern brethren." So potent and persuasive, indeed, was this argument that Presidents Hayes, Arthur, and Harrison successively experimented with its implementation. But the striking fact is that these economic pressures upon party leaders were, in the long run, less effective than the institutional exigencies of the organization— the need to get elected. Despite all the adjurations of the businessmen, Republican politicians, when they feared defeat, reverted to waving the bloody shirt, both to consolidate their Northern following and to enlist the one sure Republican element in the South, the Negro.

Finally, Mr. Hirshson's narrative is a revelation of the role that irrational forces play in American political life. Although there were many throughout the South who agreed with Congressman William C. Oates of Alabama, who remarked, "Sometimes I feel I am more of a Republican than a Democrat," and though there were many in the North who thought that the Southern states "ought to be in the republican party, where they belong by heredity and by natural affinity," the striking fact is that this realignment of American political parties never took place. Partly the Southern whites were frightened off by recurrences of the old pro-Negro sentiment among their Northern colleagues, such as the Lodge force bill; even more, they were prisoners of the racial attitudes and prejudices of their own section.

Mr. Hirshson's study ends with the 1890's. With the growth of the Northern and Western population, the rise of the city, and the nationalizing of American business, the Republican party after 1892 unexpectedly found that it had become the party of the permanent majority, and it no longer needed assistance from either Southern Negroes or Southern whites. Abruptly Republicans dropped all interest in the Southern question. The final burial of the Lodge bill ended for a generation the Negro's chance for acceptance as a full citizen in American society and made inevitable the acceptance of Booker T. Washington's "Atlanta Compromise."

DAVID DONALD

Preface

FUNDAMENTALLY, this book is concerned with how and why the Republican party, which after the Civil War passed numerous laws and set up many organizations to aid the Southern Negro, deserted the colored man by the 1890's. It deals with the positions taken by Northern Republicans on the race question between 1877 and 1893 and with the groups which influenced party chieftains on this subject. It is not a history of the freedmen, of Republicanism in the South, or of alleged Democratic atrocities in that region. Prominent Northern and Southern Negroes and major Democrats are included in this work solely when they affected or spoke about the ideas of well-known Republicans. Nor is this a study of the reaction of either Northern or Southern voters to Republican policies. Only upon a few essential occasions has an effort been made to determine how the public received Republican plans.

For a competent study of Republicanism in the South during these years the reader is referred to Professor Vincent P. De Santis's important book, *Republicans Face the Southern Question.*[*] The present manuscript was completed before the pub-

* Vincent P. De Santis, *Republicans Face the Southern Question, The New Departure Years, 1877–1897* (Baltimore: Johns Hopkins Press, 1959).

lication of Dr. De Santis's book, but, in any case, the two works in no way duplicate one another. Professor De Santis has written a study of the Republican party in the South, while this book is an analysis of Northern Republican attitudes toward the Southern Negro. The major themes and ideas presented in each work are unique; the two books, having different aims, supplement and amplify one another and are in no sense competitors.

Illustrative of the factionalism and the lack of unity within American political parties, the story of the struggle within the Republican organization from 1877 to 1893 over Negro rights is, in its broadest sense, the story of the forces which worked to extinguish the bitterness and sectional distrust created by the Civil War. By 1893 the race question as a political issue was dead and national solidarity was, to a large extent, achieved, but at the expense of the Southern Negro. Without Northern political friends and defenders for the first time in generations, the freedmen soon fell more completely than ever under the dominance of the Redeemers. Thus Northern merchants, Eastern industrialists, and Mugwumps, while binding the nation together, helped clear the path for the emergence of Jim Crow.

I am indebted to many people for their aid and encouragement during the writing of this book. From Professor David Donald of Princeton University I received invaluable assistance. He examined the manuscript at least a dozen times and offered so many suggestions that it would require another volume of this size merely to list them. Both this book and I are much the richer for having had the sage counsel of this truly outstanding scholar.

My debt to other prominent historians and political scientists is also great. Professor William E. Leuchtenburg of Columbia University went over the manuscript with unusual care and improved almost every page of it. Professors David B. Truman and Dwight C. Miner of Columbia, Chilton Williamson of Barnard College, and John Higham of the University of Michigan also provided numerous suggestions and made me realize that the Negro question was inextricably connected with the struggle between the Republican and Democratic parties for control of the national government.

Librarians throughout the country helped me in a variety of ways. I am particularly obligated to Mr. Watt P. Marchman of the Rutherford B. Hayes Library; Mr. Claude Cook and Mrs. Opal Mae Williams of the Iowa State Department of History and Archives; Dr. C. Percy Powell of the Manuscripts Division of the Library of Congress; Dr. Howard Gottlieb of the Historical Manuscripts Division of the Yale University Library; Miss Margaret A. Flint of the Illinois State Historical Library; Dr. James Rodabaugh of the Ohio State Historical Society; Dr. Josephine Harper of the Wisconsin State Historical Society; Dr. F. Clever Bald of the Michigan Historical Collections; Dr. William Petersen and Dr. Mildred Throne of the Iowa State Historical Society; Mr. Robert Hill of the New York Public Library; and Mr. Charles Shetler of the West Virginia University Library.

I should also like to thank Mr. George Cabot Lodge for permission to see and to quote from the Henry Cabot Lodge Papers and Mr. Winthrop Aldrich for granting me access to the Nelson W. Aldrich Papers.

STANLEY P. HIRSHSON

1

A President, a Policy, and a Party

I

FAR FROM furnishing a solution to the race question, the end of the Civil War raised new problems for the South. Slavery was gone and so was much of the old way of life. The status of both white and colored men remained to be redefined.

The Radicals, a powerful Northern Republican group, insisted that their party should determine the South's new make-up. In 1866, when President Andrew Johnson sponsored a plan of Reconstruction which enabled the prewar leaders of the South to rise again to power, the Radicals skillfully enlisted the aid of social reformers anxious to safeguard the freedmen and of businessmen who supported Republican economic policies and defeated him.[1] The next year they divided ten of the eleven former Confederate states into five military districts, each ruled by a major general. With the enfranchisement of over 700,000 Negroes the entire South fell under Radical domination.[2]

Republicans did not stop here. Constantly reminding the nation that they had saved the Union from rebels, they sponsored between 1865 and 1876 a series of acts and constitutional amendments designed to aid the colored man and to insure his rights: the Thirteenth, Fourteenth, and Fifteenth Amendments formally abolished slavery and enfranchised the Negro; the Freedmen's Bureau bills of 1865 and 1866 set up an organization to care for the colored people; the Civil Rights laws of 1866 and 1875 guaranteed social privileges to all men in public places; and the Force and Ku Klux Klan acts of 1870 and 1871 provided machinery to enforce the recent amendments and to break up organized white resistance to Radical decrees.[3]

Despite these measures the South gradually slipped from Republican hands. By 1876 the party controlled only Florida, Louisiana, and South Carolina, the other Southern states having been recaptured by the Redeemers, or white Bourbon Democrats. As the presidential canvass of that year got under way, Republicans were challenged by a Democratic organization which for the first time in years seemed to be an equal match.[4]

Republican campaign tactics during 1876 differed little from those consistently employed since 1866. Burdened with the blame for the depression which had relentlessly plagued the country since 1873 and for a series of scandals which had shaken public confidence in the administration of President Ulysses S. Grant, party leaders decided that, as in 1866, 1868, and 1872, the bloody shirt was their strongest argument.[5]

The Republican national convention in June acted in accord with this plan. Demanding that the President and Congress do all in their power to enforce the war amendments, the nation's Republicans promised to protect the rights of all men.[6]

Inspired by this strong assertion, a host of Republican campaigners systematically revived Civil War passions. Vice-Presidential candidate William A. Wheeler of New York urged

Northern voters: "Let your ballots protect the work so effectually done by your bayonets at Gettysburg, and on many a field of strife." [7] In an interview with the New York *Tribune* a week before the election he called the Southern issue the most important of the canvass, charged that the Bourbons were unrepentant and did not really accept the war settlement, and stressed that force was the only language the former rebels understood. In this very campaign, Wheeler pointed out, the Democratic nominees for governor in Louisiana, North Carolina, and South Carolina were ex-Confederates. If the Redeemers captured control of the nation, they would raid the federal treasury and use Northern money to construct vast internal improvements projects.[8] Joining in, Robert G. Ingersoll told a gathering of Union veterans:

Every man that endeavored to tear the old flag from the heaven that it enriches was a Democrat. Every man that tried to destroy this nation was a Democrat. . . . The man that assassinated Abraham Lincoln was a Democrat. . . . Soldiers, every scar you have on your heroic bodies was given you by a Democrat.[9]

Other prominent Republicans agreed. Speaking to the Lincoln Battalion of the Boys in Blue, Representative James A. Garfield insisted that the Democracy represented "secession, disunion, slavery and all that went to make disunion and slavery horrible in the eyes of men and in the eyes of God." Republicanism, on the other hand, meant "an indivisible Union, [and] the principles of freedom and equal rights to all men without regard to race and property." The sectional issue would remain an important force in politics as long as the Redeemers created "bloody shirts by killing unoffending citizens," the Congressman argued. Senator Oliver P. Morton of Indiana was sure that the Democrats could carry the South only "by a bloody revolution which no more deserves the name of election than the murder of the Christians by the Turks." He observed that the killing "of a few days since of ten negroes in Hamburg, South Carolina, under circumstances of extraordinary atrocity is but the opening of the Democratic campaign in that state." And Senator James G. Blaine of Maine believed that the government of the United States was duty bound to enforce the Fourteenth and Fifteenth Amendments. Republicans would not stand by idly and permit the Constitution to be "trampled under foot and made of no effect." [10]

Although he did little campaigning himself, Rutherford B. Hayes, the Republican presidential aspirant, pushed this theme forward. His letter of acceptance demanded protection for all men. There could be no enduring peace, he stressed, if the rights of the Negro were disregarded. The war amendments must be observed.[11] During the heat of the canvass, Hayes took an even firmer stand. He advised Blaine that "Our strong ground is the dread of a solid South, rebel rule, etc., etc. I hope you will make these topics prominent in your speeches. It leads people away from 'hard times,' which is our deadliest foe." [12]

These tactics did not enable the Republicans to carry the election immediately. The results of the November balloting were in doubt for months. The first returns showed that Samuel J. Tilden, the Democratic candidate for president, had amassed 184 electoral votes, one short of the total necessary for victory, and Hayes only 166, but the final verdict depended upon disputed tallies in Florida, Louisiana, and South Carolina.[13]

After the election, Hayes was deeply concerned with its effects upon the Negro. Certain that he had been defeated, he lamented:

I don't care for myself; and the party, yes, and the country, too, can stand it, but I do care for the poor colored men of the South. . . . The result will be that the Southern people will practically treat the constitutional amendments as nullities and then the colored man's fate will be worse than when he was in slavery, with a humane master to look after his interests. That is the only reason I regret the news as it is.[14]

While the dispute over the presidency raged, Hayes was subject to constant pressure from the Stalwarts, or Republican machine politicians. Prominent men of this group urged him to adopt a strong Southern policy, like that employed by Grant. Zachariah Chandler, chairman of the Republican National Committee, wanted Hayes to safeguard the rights of all persons. William E. Chandler of New Hampshire, who had been laboring diligently to make Hayes president, hated "to think that this work we have been doing before and since the election, has only been keeping a political party in power. I must believe that it has a higher purpose—that of protecting the colored man and saving the Nation from great peril." [15]

Unlike the Stalwarts, Hayes's closest advisers, just as concerned with the fate of the freedmen, saw the best protection for them not in force but in an alliance with former Southern Whigs interested in internal improvements. Far from believing that their course amounted to deserting the Negro, the candidate's friends argued that it would save the colored man. Garfield hoped to see the day when "the constitutional rights of the negro shall be as safe in the hands of one party as it is in the other; and that thus in the south as in the north men may seek their party associates on the great commercial and industrial questions rather than on questions of race and color." William Henry Smith of the Western Associated Press believed that with Whig support Hayes could build "up a conservative Republican party in the South that shall effectively destroy the color line & save the colored people." Supporting this fresh approach to the problem was Joseph Medill of the Chicago *Tribune*, who did "not think any price too high at which we can purchase the lives and peaceful protection of the poor colored people, and peace for the South." [16]

Forced to choose between the harsh policy of the Stalwarts and the revisionism of his associates, Hayes by early 1877 decided to adopt the latter view. Abandoning sectionalism, he told Congressman Jacob D. Cox of Ohio in January that the Negro could be aided only if important white Southerners could be induced to join the Republican party. The next month Hayes expressed a desire to initiate "such a policy . . . as will cause sectionalism to disappear, and that will tend to wipe out the color line." [17]

While the Republicans were discussing the fate of the Negro, members of both parties set up a bipartisan fifteen-man electoral commission to solve the election crisis. By an eight-to-seven vote the group accepted the tallies favoring the Republican candidate. Then on February 27, 1877, after negotiations between Northern Republicans and Southern Democrats, friends of Hayes announced that he had agreed to recognize the Redeemer government in Louisiana headed by Francis T. Nicholls, who in turn pledged to respect the rights of men of both races. On March 2, just two days before he took office, Hayes was declared the victor by Congress.[18]

Actually, powerful economic forces helped map out the settlement of 1877. A lobby headed by Thomas Scott, president of the Pennsylvania Railroad, and Grenville M. Dodge, the railroad engineer and former Representative from Iowa, was able to get many Southern Congressmen to accept the election of Hayes by convincing them that the completion of the Texas and Pacific Railroad from East Texas to the West Coast, considered essential to the South, depended upon a Republican victory. In return for electing Hayes, the Redeemers received assurances from the candidate's friends that he would quickly withdraw all the Federal troops from the South, thus allowing the Republican governments of Louisiana and South Carolina to fall, would appoint at least one Bourbon to the cabinet, and would make generous appropriations for Southern internal improvements.[19]

Following through with these arrangements, Hayes in his inaugural address clearly indicated that he was about to remove the army from the South. Insisting that local governments could best handle the race question, he asked loyal men everywhere to work with him and requested federal appropriations for Southern education. In accord with his recent statements he promised to promote the interests of both white and Negro persons and to abolish the color line in politics, "to the end that we may have not merely a united North or a united South, but a united country."[20]

Soon after, the announcement of Hayes's cabinet created a furor. Blaine, John A. Logan of Illinois, Roscoe Conkling of New York, and Simon Cameron of Pennsylvania were annoyed because two enemies of theirs, Carl Schurz and William M. Evarts, had respectively been made Secretary of the Interior and Secretary of State. Moreover, the President, living up to his bargain with the South, chose David M. Key, a former Confederate officer from Tennessee, for Postmaster General. The machine politicians tried to prevent confirmation of these men, but Southern Democrats came to the administration's rescue and helped secure Senatorial approval of the nominations.[21]

The machine politicians were dumfounded. "Hayes has sold us all out," Logan wrote from Washington, "and the base ingratitude shown by Hayes to those that elected him has disgusted all people here."[22] Although a short while before he had advocated pulling the troops out of the South,[23] Blaine, incensed by the cabinet selections, attacked the new administration when the Senate debated the claim of William Pitt Kellogg, a Louisiana Republican, to a seat. Accusing the President of deserting Stephen B. Packard and Daniel H. Chamber-

lain, the Republican governors of Louisiana and South Carolina, he argued that Kellogg had been elected by the same votes
which had put Hayes in the White House.[24] Senator Timothy
O. Howe of Wisconsin considered the new cabinet "very distasteful to the old Republican party." The administration's
course "may give peace to the State of Louisiana, but it is quite
likely to breed war within the Republican party and endanger
the safety of the Republicans in that state." [25] Even Garfield
noted that "below the surface of approval there is much hostile
criticism and a strong tendency to believe that Hayes' policy
will be a failure. Blaine thinks the differences between the
North and South are too deep to be bridged over by the proposed methods." [26]

At the very outset of his administration, then, Hayes split his
party. Adopting a Southern policy which, to succeed, required
the support of as many Republican leaders as possible, the
President, instead of trying to work with the machine politicians, refused even to talk to them. A man who as a presidential
candidate had urged the use of bloody shirt tactics, Hayes
belatedly joined the ranks of the reformers.

Despite the great opposition to him within his own party,
the President refused to budge. Early in March he informed
a delegation of South Carolina colored men that he wanted to
solve the race question so that Southern Republicans would
no longer need army protection. He felt the use of force to
uphold governments was repugnant and un-American.[27] A
short time after, the President said that Negroes would "find
me their friend, but we need to win other friends for them
among men who, because of the color line, are now regarded
as their enemies; and we must in some judicious way divide
the Democratic party of the South and make the Republican
party better than it is." [28]

After thinking the Southern problem through for a month,
Hayes finally acted. Spurred on by Evarts, Key, and Schurz,[29]

the President, upon receiving assurances from the Democratic gubernatorial candidate, Wade Hampton, that the Negro would be protected, finally withdrew the troops from South Carolina on April 10, 1877. Two weeks later, he fulfilled his earlier promise to Southerners and did the same thing in Louisiana.[30] The period of military Reconstruction was at an end, and so too was the solidarity shown by the Republican party during the campaign of 1876.

II

During the time between the election and the withdrawal of the troops the nation's commercial interests strongly supported all moves to end sectional rancor. Still suffering from the depression which had begun in 1873, they longed for peace and the growth of intersectional trade. Indifferent rather than hostile to the Negro, businessmen had nothing in particular against the colored race, but they did believe that prosperity could not return unless Southern governments were stable. Desiring profits more than anything else, they demanded a speedy settlement of the presidential question and a return to the peaceful conditions under which commerce best thrived.[31]

Early in the crisis businessmen put great pressure upon Congress. The Chicago, Detroit, Philadelphia, New York, Cincinnati, Kansas City, and Burlington, Iowa, Boards of Trade and the Pittsburgh Chamber of Commerce urged that the troubles disturbing trade be ended.[32] Moreover, one hundred and fifty eminent New Yorkers, representing "a large proportion of the financial and commercial interests of the city," petitioned Congress for a solution "in the spirit of moderation and conciliation." Among the Republican signers were William E. Dodge, the copper king; Theodore Roosevelt, Sr., the glass merchant; John Jacob Astor; and Brown Brothers and Company, Drexel, Morgan and Company, and J. & W. Seligman, banking firms. Prominent Philadelphia Republicans, such as merchant John

Wanamaker, banker Anthony J. Drexel, and publisher Henry C. Lea, and merchants in Cincinnati and Newark also implored Congress to act before trade was irreparably damaged.[33]

Commercial journals just as strongly favored a compromise solution to the political muddle. The New York *Shipping and Commercial List,* by no means overtly anti-Negro, believed that sectional reconciliation would greatly stimulate business. Similarly, the *Commercial and Financial Chronicle* said passage of the Electoral Commission bill would "be received in all business circles with thanksgiving." It suggested that the measure be retitled "A bill to relieve the distressing uncertainty overhanging industrial enterprise and to quiet anxiety." [34]

Important Republicans were quick to note the commercial attitude. Garfield observed that the businessmen of the country, apathetic to the Negro's plight, cared "more for results than for methods—more for an escape from present evils than for a time enduring rule of action." [35] Hamilton Fish, Grant's Secretary of State, was positive that the nation's economy would be wrecked unless sectional differences were soon patched up:

What is our present condition? [he asked] the industries of the country are depressed, business and trade in all their branches are stagnant. Values are diminished. Capital is idle, and unproductive and with its natural timidity and caution, fearful of investment, abstains from affording to the unemployed labor of the country, the opportunity, so beneficial to both capital and labor, for which each is anxious, but which is withheld mainly because of the doubt and fear of disturbance that may follow from a contested decision of the result of the election. The country wants peace, quiet, and harmony between all the sections. It wants a cessation of the political acerbities which arose from not yet remote excitements and passions but which now ought to subside and to be put aside with the vents which gave rise to them.[36]

Some Republicans complained that merchants were all too ready to abandon the colored man. To Congressman Lucien

Bonaparte Caswell of Wisconsin any compromise was a "surrender of the rights reserved to the people," but he was sure
that a settlement unfavorable to the Negro would soon be
agreed upon, "for members of Congress are of the impression
that the people wish to revive business *at any* political sacrifice." Wisconsin's Senator Angus Cameron called "All this fine
talk about peace, the prosperity of the country, etc. . . . the
merest bosh." [37] Noting that as in 1861 commercial interests
were now easily frightened, Representative George Frisbie
Hoar of Massachusetts remembered that "It was the tramp of
men from the valley and hillside hurrying to the defense of an
imperilled country which showed the timid souls in the city
that there was something worth fighting for besides bonds and
stocks and even quotations at the exchange." He laughed at
threats by traders that they would take matters into their own
hands unless the political muddle was quickly cleared up.[38]

Speaking for businessmen, the New York *Daily Bulletin,*
the forerunner of the *Commercial Bulletin,* had harsh words
for Republicans like Hoar and Caswell. The desires of merchants should come first, it asserted. "It is the 'commercial interests' that underlie all the other interests of the country. Let
the 'commercial interests' by all means make their influence felt
now as it has often been at critical periods heretofore," the
paper advised, "and no apprehension need be felt that the result
will not be as it was then, the maintenance of peace and harmony which are so essential to the prosperity and progress of
the country." [39]

After the inauguration, the insensibility of merchants to
Negro rights was once more shown. Traders asked Hayes to end
the Southern question forever by removing the troops from
Louisiana and South Carolina. On March 8, a spirited gathering
of Wall Street bankers, brokers, and merchants implored the
administration to follow through on its plans for the South and
for civil service reform. Sponsoring the meeting were Repub-

licans like John Jay, the former abolitionist; Jacob M. Vermilye, president of the Merchants' Bank; John A. Stewart, president of the United States Trust Company; Samuel B. Ruggles, the lawyer; William A. Booth of Booth and Edgar, sugar importers; and James W. Beekman, the philanthropist.[40] Likewise, a group of New York financiers, led by Brown Brothers, wrote Evarts demanding that the army be withdrawn from the South.[41]

In other sections of the North commercial groups were just as unconcerned with the fate of Southern Republicans. The Cotton and Merchants Exchanges of St. Louis held a joint meeting and passed a series of resolutions calling for the end of bayonet rule in the South. The Cleveland and Minneapolis Boards of Trade, the Cincinnati Chamber of Commerce, Chicago bankers and merchants, and Philadelphia businessmen did the same.[42]

Northern commercial newspapers reinforced these appeals. In late March the New York *Commercial Advertiser* noted that prominent New Orleans merchants had recently sent Hayes over one hundred letters complaining that precarious conditions made it impossible for them to conduct business. In Charleston, the paper went on, over $2,000,000 destined for investment in rice and cotton was idly lying in banks because loan brokers refused to extend credit until the army left the state. A dozen of the largest rice plantations along the Savannah River had already been abandoned by their bankrupt owners. The *Commercial and Financial Chronicle* warned that it was "a prodigious error to regard the condition of South Carolina and Louisiana with indifference as if they were foreign provinces, and not to see that their suffering is our suffering. One member cannot be hurt without hurting the whole body, and anarchy and virtual confiscation in New Orleans and Columbia have reacted upon all business interests everywhere." Only when the South was left alone would business revive.[43]

Occasional murmurs were still heard against the commercial

desire to realign the sections at the expense of the Negro. Soon after Hayes took office, Cyrus Clay Carpenter, former governor of Iowa, feared that this was going to be another "sloppy" administration. "When I think of the speech made by the President the night after the election," he wrote, "when he believed himself defeated, in which he described his painful regret at the result to be his sympathy for the poor black voter at the south, and contrast it with *the serene* state of mind in which all the rebels and copperheads who visit the White-House seem to leave that sacred shrine, I cant quite reconcile these things with a belief in the loveliness of the future." He predicted that "before many winters, patriots of sturdy stuff, and who believe that the sacrifices of the rebellion meant something besides unrestricted commercial comity between the north and the south, would be longing for another hour of Grant. I hope I am wrong about these things but I fear." [44]

III

For a year after Hayes completed his bargain with the South Republicans vigorously debated his course. As time went on, the President became increasingly unpopular; assaults upon him and his Southern program by important members of his own party became more and more frequent.

A series of violent attacks upon the administration during the spring of 1877 illustrated the growing spirit within the party. In an open letter Blaine extended his "profoundest sympathy" to Chamberlain and Packard, both of whom, he felt, were upholders of "civil liberty and constitutional government." Again he insisted that Packard's claim to office was "as valid as that which justly and lawfully seated Rutherford B. Hayes in the presidential chair." [45] An even sharper denunciation came late in April from former Senator Benjamin F. Wade, who had seconded Hayes's nomination for president at the national convention the previous June:

You know with what untiring zeal I labored for the emancipation of the slaves of the South [he wrote] and to procure justice for them, before and during the time I was in Congress, and I supposed Governor Hayes was in full accord with me on this subject. But I have been deceived, betrayed, and even humiliated by the course he has taken to a degree that I have not the language to express. During the first month of his administration we find him closeted with two of the worst and most malignant enemies of the colored race that can be found in all that slave-cursed region, and there consulting with these malefactors how best he can put these colored people under the iron heel of their most bitter enemies, and reduce them to a condition unfortunately worse than before they were made free. I feel that to have emancipated these people and that to leave them unprotected would be a crime as infamous as to have reduced them to slavery when they were free. And for Hayes to do this to the men who had at the hazard of their lives given him the votes without which he never could have had the power to do this terrible injustice! No doubt he meditates the destruction of the party that elected him.

A contemplation of all this fills me with amazement and inexpressible indignation. My only consolation is that history informs me that better men than I ever pretended to be have of like manner been deceived. Some have attempted to excuse him by saying that he 'means well,' but hell is paved with just such good intentions.[46]

Eastern abolitionists were especially disgruntled. Samuel J. May, "God's Choir Boy," protested against what he thought was the surrender of the Negro to the Redeemers.[47] Wendell Phillips demanded that Evarts, Schurz, and Key be replaced by Blaine, Morton, and Benjamin Butler. Unaware of the roles played by Dodge and Scott, he charged that Jay Gould, who desired presidential support for his Southern Pacific Railroad, had engineered the compromise of 1877.[48]

The administration's supporters were few. At an April meeting of the Republican National Committee, William Chandler, Logan, and George C. Gorham, the secretary of the Senate, bitterly assailed the betrayal of Louisiana and South Carolina party members. Congressman Charles Foster, who represented the Ohio district in which Hayes lived, alone upheld the President, warning that it was suicidal to break with him.[49]

Only two Stalwarts, Morton and Grant, defended Hayes. Satisfied by the appointment of his lieutenant, Richard Thompson, as Secretary of the Navy, Morton in a public letter argued that the President had adopted the new course because military intervention had proven a total failure. He believed that Hayes's program would greatly strengthen the Southern wing of the Republican party. Agreeing, Grant admitted that he would have acted as Hayes did if he had been in office longer.[50]

To counter the strong opposition the President repeatedly asserted that his program was the only one which could better the lot of the Southern Negro. In April he told the New York *Tribune* that it would "secure peace between the sections and between the races or parties of the South." Eventually "the rights, interests, and safety of the colored people" would be guaranteed. A month later in another interview Hayes vowed that he would never desert the emancipated race. Arguing that he had always been a defender of the Negro, he recalled that in his boyhood he had sympathized with antislavery leaders such as Wendell Phillips and William Lloyd Garrison. He was still confident that his plans would succeed and that many former Whigs in the South would become Republicans.[51]

Perhaps the strangest aspect of the bitter struggle between Hayes and the machine politicians is that each side was convinced that only its program could bolster the Republican party in the South and aid the Negro. Desiring the same ends, the two factions argued principally about the means of achieving these goals. But despite the confidence which both the administration and its enemies expressed in their positions, the plan of each was just as inadequate as the scheme of the other. The harsh methods of the spoilsmen had not succeeded under

Grant, while the President and his followers could not point to a single gain their policy had made for the party in the former Confederate states. In their eagerness to establish an organization capable of controlling large areas of the South, both groups were unrealistic and overestimated the potentialities of their programs.

IV

During the summer and fall of 1877 the intraparty fight went on. Hoping to show former Southern Whigs that he was friendly toward them, the President selected Redeemers for Southern offices. Besides choosing Democrats for the postmasterships of Louisville, Petersburg, and Memphis, he gave Bourbons in Arkansas, Texas, South Carolina, Georgia, and Alabama a substantial share of the patronage. In Tennessee two Democrats were placed in the federal marshal's office, while a Georgia Redeemer became the United States marshal. One-third of the Southern appointees during the first five months of the Hayes administration were Bourbons.[52]

Rejected by the President, Republican machine politicians from both the North and South fought back. They repeatedly denounced Hayes. Speaking at Woodstock, Connecticut, on Independence Day with Blaine at his side, former Governor Daniel H. Chamberlain of South Carolina compared the President's treachery to that of James Buchanan in the days before the outbreak of the Civil War.[53] William E. Chandler lamented, "I almost ruined myself getting in Hayes—and what have we to show for it? [Secretary of the Treasury] John Sherman abandoning Louisiana!!! The party broken in pieces, and every federal officeholder degraded."[54] Elisha W. Keyes, the Wisconsin political boss, neatly summed up his views: "Give me the 'Bloody Shirt' in preference to 'Carl Shirt.' "[55]

A series of Republican state conventions revealed how deeply the President's Southern and civil service policies had split the party. In Iowa opposition to Hayes was widespread. Shortly before the convention there, former Congressman James F. Wilson announced that he would not follow an administration which had deserted Southern Republicans. Just as bitter was Senator Samuel J. Kirkwood, who pointed to the harsh treatment given Republican members of the South Carolina state legislature by the Democratic majority as proof of the Redeemers' failure to keep their pledges.[56] Moreover, political boss James S. Clarkson of Des Moines denounced Hayes regularly in his paper, the *Iowa State Register*, and in protest resigned from the postmastership of the city.[57]

These Stalwarts dominated the Iowa gathering. At their request Packard, the living proof of the President's treachery in Louisiana, spoke to the state's Republicans. After that, the Radicals, with Wilson as chairman of the convention and Clarkson controlling the resolutions committee, easily beat down two attempts to sustain the administration. Clarkson then secured the unanimous adoption of planks demanding that the rights of all men in the South be protected and promising to "fight the good fight to the end." [58]

Disputes in other states yielded varying results. Anti-Hayes forces carried Maine. When former governor Joshua L. Chamberlain introduced a resolution expressing faith in the administration, Charles A. Boutelle, a close friend of Blaine and editor of the Bangor *Whig and Courier*, countered with an amendment pointing out that Governors Packard of Louisiana and Chamberlain of South Carolina had been elected by the same votes as Hayes and that they had been betrayed. With Blaine as peacemaker, the convention eventually adopted a compromise which ignored the President but which condemned the virtual disfranchisement of Negroes in six Southern states.[59] The Pennsylvania story was different. The Stalwarts, led by J. Donald Cameron, were unable to prevent the endorsement of Hayes, but they did succeed in obtaining passage of a statement recognizing that honest differences of opinion existed within the party.[60] Similarly, New Jersey Radicals, headed by ex-Secretary of the Navy George M. Robeson and his South Jersey adherents, could not stop Newarkers from lauding Hayes,[61] while Ohio Republicans followed Garfield, the chairman of their gathering, in supporting the administration.[62]

The most publicized controversy occurred in New York between Roscoe Conkling, who hated Hayes, and George William Curtis, who favored him. When the state convention refused to endorse the administration,[63] fifty-one of New York City's most prominent Republican merchants, industrialists, and reformers called a rally to show they supported the President. Lifelong Republicans like William E. Dodge, William A. Booth, and James A. Roosevelt, the banker, refused to contribute to their party's campaign fund because of the Stalwart attacks upon the administration.[64]

Faced with these feuds, Hayes hoped a series of tours would build support for his policies. On Memorial Day he journeyed to Tennessee, where he decorated the graves of both Union and Confederate soldiers. The next month the President took Evarts, Schurz, Key, and Attorney General Charles A. Devens with him to Boston. Especially eager to gauge the Yankee reaction to the Postmaster General, Hayes introduced him as "a gentleman from East Tennessee who believes as you do in a united country and equal rights." [65]

The favorable response to the Boston trip induced the President to make an excursion to upper New England. In August he used the centennial anniversary of the Revolutionary War battle of Bennington as an excuse to visit Vermont and New Hampshire. Again Evarts, Key, and Devens went along. In speech after speech Hayes reiterated his desire to protect the constitutional rights of all citizens and to re-establish peaceful relations between the North and the South.[66] Upon returning to Washington the President expressed satisfaction with the results of his journey. "I tried to impress the people with the importance of harmony between different sections, States, classes and races," he wrote, "and to discourage sectionalism and class prejudice." [67]

The next month Hayes, Evarts, and Key embarked upon a good-will trip through Ohio, Kentucky, Tennessee, Georgia, and Virginia. At Louisville early in the tour Wade Hampton joined the official party. Throughout the rest of the journey the President and the Governor stood together as a symbol of national unity; in a number of cities they spoke from the same platform. At Nashville Hayes reiterated his devotion to the Constitution and the war amendments, but optimistically observed "that the majority of the people of the South—the white people of the South—have no desire to invade the rights of the colored people." In Chattanooga the President related to a deputation of Negroes that their welfare had been uppermost in his mind when he had worked out his policy. He had always been confident that if the bayonets were removed from the South the lot of the colored man would improve considerably. At Atlanta Hayes told the many Negroes in his audience: "After thinking it over, I thought your rights and interests would be safer if this great mass of intelligent white men were let alone by the General Government." He consoled them with the news that "for no six months since the war has there been so few outrages and invasions of your rights." [68]

Both Hayes and William Henry Smith, his most trusted adviser, were overjoyed at the results of the Southern visit. "Received everywhere heartily," Hayes observed. "The country is again one and united. I am very happy to be able to feel that the course taken has turned out so well." Smith believed "The trip South has been the greatest success as it has been the most pleasant surprise of the year." To him the President's speeches were "admirable in their directness and unexceptionable in taste." [69]

Some Republicans were not as pleased. Important papers like the Washington *National Republican,* the Newark *Daily Advertiser,* and the New York *Tribune,* all of which had originally supported Hayes, noted that oppressed party members in Mississippi, Georgia, and South Carolina had not even bothered to draw up tickets for the local elections in 1877. Pointing to incidents such as the victory of Matthew C. Butler, the hero of the Hamburg massacre the year before, in the South Carolina race for the United States Senate, they concluded that the Bourbons had learned nothing and forgotten nothing.[70]

Moreover, by the fall of 1877 Hayes's agreement with the South had collapsed completely. Violating their bargain with the administration, Southern Congressmen refused to vote with the Republicans when organizing the House of Representatives which assembled in October. In retaliation the President a short time later came out against a subsidy for the Texas and Pacific Railroad.[71]

In the new House, Hayes was very unpopular. Of the nearly twenty Republican Congressmen who met at John Sherman's house one night to discuss the Southern question Jacob D. Cox alone endorsed the President's course. After the conference, Garfield recorded that "The tendency of part of our party to assail Hayes and denounce him as a traitor and a man who was going to Johnsonize the party was very strong and his defenders were comparatively few." [72]

Few Republican Senators had any use for Hayes, either. Only Henry L. Dawes of Massachusetts, Stanley Matthews of Ohio, and Hoar, now in the upper house, liked him.[73] At a caucus early in November practically everyone agreed that the administration had accomplished nothing in the South, but the Senators decided to send a delegation, led by George F. Edmunds, to talk to Hayes anyway. Undaunted by the breakdown of his schemes and completely unaware of his unpopularity, the chief executive told the visitors that he was certain eight Southern states, including North Carolina, Florida, Tennessee, and possibly Mississippi, would be Republican by 1880. He was elated because the bishops of the Southern branch of the Methodist Church had recently endorsed his course and believed that many former Southern Whigs would soon join the Republican organization. Reporting back to the caucus, Edmunds called the President a dreamer who was incapable of realizing that his course had lost the entire South for the party.[74]

In his first annual message of December 3, 1877, the chief executive stuck to the views he had expressed to the Senators. He called the results of his policy "significant and encouraging" and insisted that harmony was fast replacing lawlessness in the South. Ignoring the fact that no major elections had taken place in the South during 1877, Hayes stated that the past year had been the quietest in memory. He implored Southerners to treat Negroes liberally and humanely and signified that he would take steps to safeguard the rights of all citizens if his present policy failed.[75]

Soon after the message was read, William Chandler launched the most detailed and most devastating of all the condemnations of Hayes. Despite his work in making the Ohioan president, Chandler had been treated by the administration as just another spoilsman. Word of his outright rejection quickly spread through Republican circles. "The New Hampshire men tell me," wrote Angus Cameron, "that he [Hayes] has refused and point-blank to give William E. Chandler any office." [76] In retaliation Chandler issued the first of the series of attacks which were collectively published in pamphlet form as the *Letters of Mr. William E. Chandler Relative to the So-Called Southern Policy of President Hayes.* Arguing that Hayes had been nominated on a platform emphasizing protection of "human rights and lawful governments at the South," he said that the candidate's letter of acceptance and campaign statements had supported this stand. "The bloody shirt, as it is termed, was freely waved and Governor Hayes himself urged public men to put forward, as our best argument, the dangers of 'rebel rule and a solid South.'" The New Hampshire Republican then maintained that in February, 1877, Hayes's representatives, in violation of all previous utterances and party platforms, had struck a bargain with Bourbon leaders during a Washington conference at the Wormley Hotel. In return for making their chieftain president, the Republicans had promised that Hayes would remove the garrisons from Louisiana and South Carolina and would appoint Bourbons to his cabinet and to important Southern posts. The President had lived up to this sell-out by withdrawing the troops, by appointing a Southern Postmaster General, and by naming Democrats to be the district attorney for South Carolina and the marshals of Tennessee and Georgia. Chandler charged that Hayes's treachery had had disastrous results: the Negro had been abandoned; the entire Radical policy of Reconstruction had been overthrown; the Southern wing of the party had virtually been destroyed; and the courts, the last refuge of freedom, had been surrendered to the Redeemers.[77]

Important Republicans welcomed Chandler's letters. Zachariah Chandler believed they contained "a ringing, slashing and yet truthful statement that will open the eyes of some people. The drifting policy must be abandoned or the party is lost in the boundless sea of irresolution and contempt." Support also came from William Lloyd Garrison. Because of Hayes, he wrote, the Ku Klux Klan so completely controlled the South that any attempt to resuscitate Republicanism in the former Confederate states would lead to a new and bitter Civil War. To him Chandler's argument was unanswerable. Even Whitelaw Reid thought the New Hampshire man had come "uncomfortably close" to proving that a bargain had been negotiated.[78]

Stalwart denunciations of Hayes did not end here. In March, 1878, Senator Timothy O. Howe of Wisconsin joined in. Egged on for weeks by Hannibal Hamlin of Maine, Blaine, Conkling, and Don Cameron, he carefully weighed all the advantages and disadvantages involved and then decided to go ahead.[79] In a three-hour Senate address Howe charged that even Tilden would have been better than Hayes. After repeating the old argument that if Packard had not been elected neither had Hayes, he denounced Schurz and civil service reform.[80]

A short while later, Conkling had his say. In a New York *World* interview which covered an entire page he accused the administration of surrendering to the Redeemers. At the present time the President's closest advisers were Senators John B. Gordon and Benjamin Hill of Georgia and Lucius Q. C. Lamar of Mississippi, "while the cold shoulder is given to the oldest and best of our Republican leaders." According to Conkling, Hayes "has an inordinate conceit of his own powers, and in spite of the fact that he can command no votes at the South seems possessed of the delusion that he is able to create a party of his own there." [81]

Hayes and his official family shrugged off these attacks. Schurz was sure that "If such men as Howe and Blaine would only go on a little longer, they would succeed in making the Administration positively popular." [82] The President told some friends that the opposition did not disturb him and that the only thing that still kept the South solid was radical talk by the Stalwarts. As soon as the Redeemers were convinced that they had nothing to fear from the North they would become Republicans. The race issue, the chief executive continued, was really dead and should be replaced by new, live questions. Unless the Republican party realized that Americans desired cordial relations between the sections, it would lose the people's favor.[83]

By the summer of 1878 of those Republican leaders outside the administration only William Henry Smith agreed. Hayes, he believed, was "fulfilling the pledges made by the Republican party in National convention in 1876. . . . The people of the South, both white and colored, bless him for establishing peace between the races." True, carpetbaggers, greedy politicians, and sentimentalists still opposed the President, but "it is only a question of time when there will arise a really powerful Republican party in the South numbering in its ranks the intelligence, the culture, the wealth, the Protestantism of the Southern white people, who will give protection and support to the colored people in their midst." [84]

But by now almost all the rest of Hayes's followers were convinced that he had failed. Garfield observed that "the President's 'Southern policy' is rapidly breaking down. He is losing friends every hour, and unless some favorable turn in the current occurs, he will be left almost without a supporter among the Republican Congressmen." Richard Smith of the Cincinnati *Gazette* admitted that he had made a mistake the previous year in urging Hayes to adopt the new course. The South was still as errant as ever and there was no sign that a rejuvenated Republican organization was emerging. Hamilton Fish, another early follower of Hayes, perhaps best summed up the general feeling: "Mr. Hayes has failed to carry the South, even when falling in with their measures. It is lamentable that with such good impulses as he has, and such a pure character and purpose, he has made a wreck of the Republican party." [85]

2

Disillusionment and Unity

I

THE SECOND half of the Hayes administration differed radically from the first. By the end of 1878 practically all major Republicans realized that the President's Southern policy had collapsed and that only a Solid North could prevent the Democrats from controlling the nation. United, they hereafter freely attacked the Redeemers.

Administration leaders themselves were first disillusioned by Southern atrocities during the campaign of 1878. The most widely publicized incident occurred in Sumter County, South Carolina, in which 17,805 Negroes and 7,463 whites lived. Although the Democrats frightened a number of Republican speakers away from a political rally, a small group of Stalwarts, led by an eighty-year-old man, met anyway, but they were repeatedly interrupted by the firing of cannons. When the Republicans refused to let Democrats address their rally, a riot broke out and only fast action by two Bourbon leaders prevented a Negro massacre. A second episode took place in Williamsburg, where the Redeemers broke up a colored gathering and warned a state senator that he would be killed if he did not leave town within ten days.[1]

Events like these convinced Attorney General Charles Devens that something must be done. He ordered the district attorneys of Louisiana, Alabama, and South Carolina to enforce the election laws and urged them to arrest the Bourbon leaders, "rather than the mere followers." [2]

Despite Devens's firmness, the attempts to prosecute Southerners proved farcical. In the key case arising out of the Sumter affair, the men accused of instigating the trouble frightened the Republican plaintiff into providing bail for them when they threatened to bring retaliatory suits against him. After that, the Democrats interfered with Republican meetings at will.[3]

As a result of Southern oppression of the Negro, the attitude of Northern Republicans stiffened considerably during 1878. The previous year state conventions had taken a variety of positions on Hayes's program: Massachusetts, Minnesota, and Ohio had enthusiastically endorsed it; Pennsylvania and Wisconsin had recognized that disagreements plagued the party but had refused to commit themselves; Maine and New York had also avoided taking a stand after rejecting resolutions supporting the President; and Iowa, the hotbed of Stalwartism, had almost unanimously censured the administration. Now the story was far different. While Massachusetts and Minnesota still had faith in Hayes, Maine, New York, Ohio, Pennsylvania, and Iowa condemned the Redeemers.[4]

Among those shocked by the Bourbon cruelties were the Republican supporters of a mild policy. The Springfield *Daily Republican* complained that "the whites are committing outrages which no cloak of charity can be stretched to cover. They deserve, and must receive, the emphatic condemnation of the North, and the continued silence of Wade Hampton will go far toward depriving him of that enviable national reputation which his conservative and statesmanlike course hitherto was fast winning him." The *Nation* asked: "What Democratic gain by breaking up negro meetings can equal the damage done by supplying material to the 'bloody shirt' agitators at the North?" [5]

For the first time since being inaugurated Hayes was disturbed. When a New York *Times* correspondent called the President's attention to the Sumter riot, to the many acts of terrorism perpetrated in Tensas and the other Republican parishes of Louisiana, to the violently anti-Negro articles in South Carolina newspapers, and to the recent murder of an inoffensive Negro at a Hicksford, Virginia, political meeting by a Democratic member of the state legislature, Hayes acknowledged that these were certainly discomforting signs. But he pointed out that they were the first atrocities to have occurred during his administration and insisted that the real test of his program would take place on election day. The President promised he would spare no effort to execute the laws efficiently, endorsed Devens's recent actions, and indicated that the Justice Department had already sent new and more positive instructions to marshals and district attorneys in South Carolina and Louisiana. Hayes also revealed that he was closely in touch with the situation and was keeping a personal record of all Southern incidents. [6]

While holding out some hope for the success of his policies, the President privately indicated that he was worried by affairs in the South. He told a trusted friend, James M. Comly, the former editor of the Columbus *Ohio State Journal*, that conditions in the section were very "ugly in many ways—but even there we are making progress." [7]

Election day saw the shattering of Republican hopes. Capturing only three seats in the House and none in the Senate— a reduction of six places in the lower chamber and of one in the upper—the Southern wing of the party virtually disap-

peared. Republican strength declined sharply in both white
and Negro areas. Only sixty-two of the 294 Southern counties
with colored majorities went Republican, compared to 125
in 1876. And of the 155 counties whose population was less
than five per cent Negro, the Republicans carried only nine,
three less than in 1876.[8]

Republican journals throughout the North charged that the
Democrats had used fraud and murder to win the election. The
Chicago *Tribune* related that in Caddo Parish, Louisiana, over
seventy-five colored men had been killed on election day *"and
the unburied bodies of many of them are being preyed upon
by animals."* The Portland *Oregonian* claimed that ballot boxes
all over the South had been stuffed with tissue ballots so thin
that the average election receptacle could hold an enormous
number of them. Moreover, many Bourbon election officials
had illegally substituted Democratic votes for Republican and
had submitted false counts. Republicans who observed and
objected to these unlawful practices had often been arrested
for perjury. The New York *Tribune* recalled that in Abbeville
County, South Carolina, where there were twice as many
Negroes as whites, the Republican candidates in 1874 had been
given a majority of 1,500 votes and that two years later the
Democrats had won by but 200. Yet in 1878 only three Republican ballots were cast in the entire county. The story in Fairfield
County, which contained three Negroes for every white, was
the same. Four years before, it had gone Republican by two to
one and in 1876 had given Hayes a plurality of over 800 votes.
"This month," growled the *Tribune*, "Fairfield County returns
not one Republican vote." The Springfield *Daily Republican*
pointed out that 90,000 South Carolinians had cast Republican
ballots in 1876 and only four thousand in 1878.[9] The *Independent* accurately reflected the general attitude:

The facts which, both before and since the elections, have come to
the knowledge of the public leave no doubt as to the purpose and

policy of the white Democracy of the Southern States. The general design has been to root out and destroy the Republican party at the South, and present a solid Democratic South, not only in respect to the state governments, but also in respect to members of Congress, and prospectively in respect to the Presidential election of 1880.[10]

The results upset many prominent Republicans, too. Under Devens's direction and at the insistence of the cabinet, federal marshals arrested twenty-two South Carolina citizens for intimidating Negroes.[11] Robert G. Ingersoll warned the Bourbons that "If the Republican party is not allowed to succeed in the South, the Democratic party certainly will not be allowed to live in the North." [12] Blaming the administration more than the Democrats, William E. Chandler complained "that the dead negroes unburied and eaten by the hogs in Louisiana streets were the victims of Hayes' unmanly eagerness to exercise brief authority in the White House and grasp and lay up $45,000 annually for four years. Their murders are at his door and he has been the betrayer of innocent blood." [13]

Even the President realized that he had been deceived. In an interview with the Washington *National Republican* he announced that "the time for discussion had passed." It was "now too late for anything but the most determined and vigorous action." He had inaugurated his Southern policy "with an earnest desire to conciliate the Southern leaders, to round off the sharp angles of sectional difference, and to soften the asperities of political strife." Unfortunately, the Redeemers had not lived up to their share of the bargain. *"In fact,"* he went on, *"I am reluctantly forced to admit that the experiment was a failure.* The first election of importance held since it was attempted has proved that fair elections with free suffrage for every voter in the South are an impossibility under the existing condition of things." Hayes stressed that he had no desire to stir up sectionalism, but he was determined to protect the

Negro. He blamed the Southern people in general, not leaders
like Hampton and Governor Francis T. Nicholls of Louisiana,
for the atrocities. State officials simply could not control the
ruffians. So significant were these remarks that important papers
like the Chicago *Tribune* and the New York *Tribune* reprinted
them in full on their front pages.[14]

Although disagreeing with Hayes on a few minor points,
Secretary of State William M. Evarts endorsed these views.
He told the *National Republican* that the chief executive had
believed the Redeemers when they had vowed they would safeguard the rights of all citizens. Realizing his error, Hayes would
vigorously enforce the Constitution in the future. Evarts predicted that any Southern appointee reluctant to obey instructions from Washington would be removed. He was thankful
that violations of the law were largely localized in South Carolina and Louisiana, but he regretted that legal manipulations
and all white juries often reduced the powers of the federal
government in the South and made it possible for the guilty
to escape. Unlike Hayes, the Secretary blamed the Bourbon
leaders for the collapse of the administration's policy. He insisted, however, that Hayes had never really been as friendly
with the Democrats as the Stalwarts had said. In reality, only
two of them had been given high federal offices: one had been
made a United States marshal in Georgia and another had
been sent to Brazil as a minister. The Secretary of State, so
hopeful a year ago, now doubted whether his generation would
see the emergence of a new, tolerant Southern attitude.[15]

The turn of events elated Stalwart leaders, who considered
the sectional cry a key political weapon. Senators Zachariah
Chandler and J. Donald Cameron told the President that the
South was still recalcitrant and must be punished. They welcomed the news that Hayes and Devens agreed.[16]

Spurred on by the Stalwarts, Hayes made his annual message
of December 2, 1878, a far cry from his inaugural. He pointed

out that fraud and intimidation had been common in Louisiana and South Carolina during the recent election and recommended that Congress examine carefully the claims of each member to his seat and determine whether any Representatives had been illegally elected. Vowing to protect all Americans, Hayes asked for larger appropriations to enforce the election acts.[17]

On the same day the Attorney General, in his report to Congress, strongly condemned the Bourbons. He revealed that they had stuffed ballot boxes and committed political murders in South Carolina, Texas, Louisiana, and Virginia. Devens recommended that the federal election laws be strengthened and that his department be given additional funds.[18]

Senator James G. Blaine, Hayes's chief enemy in 1877, now followed the administration's lead. Long waiting for the right opportunity to blast the Bourbons and to enhance his own political fortunes,[19] he asked that a Senate committee be set up to determine whether the constitutional rights of any citizen had been violated in the recent canvass and stipulated that the group draw up additional legislation to safeguard such privileges.[20]

A few days later, while explaining his resolution, Blaine attacked the South. Newspaper reports, he said, "represent the elections in some of the Southern States to have been accompanied by violence; in not a few cases reaching the destruction of life; to have been controlled by threats that awed and intimidated a large class of voters; to have been manipulated by fraud of the most shameless and shameful description." The Senator depicted the canvass in South Carolina as "a series of skirmishes . . . in which the polling-places were regarded as forts to be captured by one party and held against the other." Where the Redeemers were in danger of losing, they resorted to frauds and tissue ballots. Stressing that the South was allotted thirty-five Congressmen and thirty-five electoral votes because of its colored population, Blaine argued that the key issue was "whether the white voter of the North shall be equal to the white voter of the South in shaping the policy and fixing the destiny of the country; whether, to put it still more baldly, the white man who fought in the ranks of the Union Army shall have as weighty and influential a vote in the Government of the Republic as the white man who fought in the ranks of the rebel army." He noted that only eight of the seventeen Congressmen from South Carolina, Mississippi, and Louisiana, which had a combined population of 1,035,000 whites and 1,224,000 colored people, actually represented Caucasians. In contrast, the seventeen Congressmen from Iowa and Wisconsin were elected by 2,247,000 white voters.[21]

Democratic Senator Allan Thurman of Ohio ridiculed Blaine's logic. He accused the Plumed Knight of trying "to arouse sectional hatred in one portion of this Union against an almost defenseless people in another portion of the Union." Blaine was merely assuming that Negroes were Republicans and could not prove that they were disfranchised. The present political problem in the South stemmed from the attempts of Republicans during Reconstruction to control the section through Negro-dominated Loyal Leagues. There was, Thurman added, a far greater threat to pure elections in the Republican North than in the Democratic South. An amendment of his empowered the committee to investigate frauds in the North, too.[22]

At the conclusion of the debate, the Blaine resolution and the Thurman amendment easily passed the Senate. The final tally was fifty-six to six, all negative votes being cast by Democrats.[23]

After an exhaustive study, the Senate investigators reported that the Redeemers had violated their pledge to protect the Negro. They revealed that tissue ballots had been used in every South Carolina county but one and that in Louisiana the Democrats had committed over forty political murders. Dozens of Southern Negroes had been whipped, beaten, mutilated, and driven from their homes because they were Republicans. The entire South was under the rule of a white oligarchy; freedom of speech was curtailed and Democrats often inspired Negro riots so that they would have an excuse for persecuting the colored men. The Senators urged their colleagues to correct the situation.[24]

In the face of facts like these, Congressman Horace F. Page of California decided to punish the South. He introduced a bill to enforce the second section of the Fourteenth Amendment, which empowered Congress to reduce the representation of any state permitting an abridgment of suffrage, in Louisiana, Mississippi, and South Carolina. Referred to the Judiciary Committee, the measure was buried there.[25]

Senator George F. Edmunds of Vermont acted next. He sponsored a resolution affirming that the Thirteenth, Fourteenth, and Fifteenth Amendments, which during the Civil War and Reconstruction had freed and enfranchised the Negro, had been legally enacted despite the fact that many Southern states had been out of the Union; that they were an integral part of the Constitution; that the people of each state of the Union had "a common interest in the enforcement of the whole Constitution in every State in the Union"; that it was the duty of Congress to protect the rights of every citizen; and that it was the responsibility of the executive branch of the government to enforce all laws. A second resolution instructed the Committee on the Judiciary to draw up a bill to safeguard the privileges of men of both races.[26]

Democrat John T. Morgan of Alabama struck back at the Republicans. He presented a substitute resolution which omitted all reference to the legal ratification of the Amendments and which declared that the government of the United States was "one of delegated powers alone." "Its authority is defined and limited by the Constitution," Morgan's proposals read. "All powers not granted to it by that instrument, nor prohibited by it to the States, are reserved to the States respectively or to the people." Further, Morgan argued, it was the states, not federal officials, who were responsible for enforcing the laws.[27]

The debate on these resolutions was spirited. Thomas F. Bayard, a Delaware Democrat, argued that the Republican proposals had "the odor rather of a partisan caucus than the labors of a committee room." He accused the opposition party of trying to usurp the powers of the states. The country needed peace and rest, not agitation, he concluded. Edmunds countered by denying that he intended to stir up sectional hatred and charged that Morgan's measures were part of a Bourbon scheme to defeat the entire purpose of his resolutions.[28]

The vote on both sets of proposals was strictly along party lines. Morgan's resolutions were defeated by a vote of thirteen to twenty-six, while the Republican measures were passed by twenty-three to sixteen and twenty-two to seventeen.[29]

In the long run the enactment of the resolutions did both the Republicans and the Southern Negro little good. A few weeks later, in accord with his second proposal, Edmunds, as chairman of the Judiciary Committee, reported a bill to protect the constitutional rights of all citizens, but Congress took no action on it.[30]

Despite the absence of concrete gains for the Negro, bloody shirt wavers were elated by their party's new show of determination. William Lloyd Garrison was sure that the Republicans would easily win the 1880 election if they followed the course charted by Blaine, Page, and Hayes. He happily noted

that a marked change for the better is taking place in public sentiment at the North in relation to the incalculably disastrous policy of President Hayes, and the practical disfranchisement of the entire colored population at the South, by shameless fraud, brutal intimidation and remorseless slaughter. . . . There is nothing which strikes terror or causes such foaming at the mouth in the ranks of the armed conspirators at the South, or elicits such responsible howlings from their servile minions at the North, as "waving the bloody shirt"—a term of their own devising in order to make jest of the most sanguinary outrages. . . . Yes, let "the bloody shirt" continue to be waved until an end be put to the shedding of blood by the organized assassins who are boldly and successfully setting the Federal Government at defiance, and trampling the Constitution and laws of the country under their feet. Let it be shown by "confirmation strong as proofs from Holy Writ" that the South . . . is still full of the habitations of cruelty; that her hands are stained and her garments saturated with blood; that her feet run to evil, and there is no judgment in her goings; that she is as disloyal in spirit as she was when she fired her first shot at Fort Sumter; . . . that in nothing does she so much glory as in her attempt to destroy the Republic, and in the successes of her Confederate leaders on the battle-field; that she has repented of nothing, and is ashamed of nothing that she has done, but exactly the reverse; that she despises the North (barbarism sneering at civilization) as she always has done, and counts as "mudsills" the Northern working-classes while endeavoring to use them for her own evil ends; that she is gloating over the prospect of soon having the reins of government over the whole country in her hands; that as for her leading men in Church and State, in Congress and out of it, "the best of them are sharper than a thorn-hedge," and the most deeply responsible for the numberless atrocities that have been perpetrated upon the loyal Southern population, white and black; and that nothing but perfect unity of spirit and action at the North, to the extent, at least, of out-voting "the Solid South" at the approaching Presidential election, can avert the most disastrous consequences to the country. "The bloody shirt!" *In hoc signo vinces!* [31]

William E. Chandler also warned the Bourbons that they were fighting a losing battle. The South could "as easily stop the stars in their course as prevent this inevitable ending of the slaveholders' rebellion and of all their bloody practices to avert its most important decreed political consequence: Human Equality." [32]

II

A short time later, during the first session of the Forty-sixth Congress, the Redeemers, as in the 1878 election, unwittingly played into Republican hands. In control of the new legislature as a result of the recent campaign, they stirred up opposition by trying to repeal the remaining election laws by attaching riders to the Army Appropriations Acts.

Both Half-Breeds, members of the Republican party faction led by Blaine, and Stalwarts, whose chieftain was Conkling, immediately objected. Blaine asserted that the maneuver was part of a plot to undo the Union victory in the Civil War. "All the war measures of Abraham Lincoln are to be wiped out . . . ," he warned his fellow Republicans. "The Bourbons of France busied themselves, I believe, after the restoration in removing every trace of Napoleon's power and grandeur, even chiseling the 'N' from public monuments raised to perpetrate his glory; but the dead man's hand from Saint Helena reached out and destroyed them in their pride and in their folly." Blaine admonished the Redeemers "that the slow, unmoving finger of scorn from the tomb of the martyred President on the prairies of Illinois" would "wither and destroy them. 'Though dead he speaketh.'" Declaring that by adding riders to essential legislation the former rebels were trying to force the President accept a measure he detested, Conkling argued that the Democratic maneuver would intensify, not relieve, the sectional issue. Logan classified the sponsors of the riders as "the ballot-box stuffers, the repeater, the white leaguer, the rifle-clubs, the men who go gunning for negroes to prevent their voting." [33]

Democratic leaders fought back. Bayard and Daniel Voorhees of Indiana said that truly fair and unimpeded elections could be guaranteed only by repealing all the acts passed during Reconstruction. They decried the use of troops at the polls.[34]

After Congress passed the riders, the problem became the President's responsibility. Bolstered by repeated visits from such Congressional leaders as Garfield,[35] Hayes rejected five appropriations measures containing riders. In his first veto message he declared that the election laws were needed to prevent the illegal disfranchisement of Negroes in the South and to end fraudulent voting in the large cities of the North. Promising to enforce the suffrage provisions of the Constitution, the President announced that the fight against the riders was, in part, a battle to preserve the independence and strength of the executive branch of the government. He would not be dictated to by Congress. While reserving the right to employ troops during emergencies, Hayes registered his opposition to the unwarranted use of force at the polls.[36]

After reading Hayes's words, many important Republicans congratulated him. Vice-President William Wheeler considered the President's answer to the Bourbons "a document impregnable in form and substance and which, alone, would secure you a place in the history of the country." Governor Shelby M. Cullom thanked Hayes for the people of Illinois and of the West.[37] State Republican conventions in Iowa, Massachusetts, New York, Maine, Ohio, Pennsylvania, and Wisconsin passed resolutions attacking the Bourbons and upholding the administration's position.[38]

The attempt to pass the riders was a costly mistake for the Democrats. While the move won nothing for them, it re-enforced the already strong Republican conviction that the Redeemers were not to be trusted.

III

Republicans demonstrated their newly found unity by running the campaign of 1879, which was largely for state offices, on a platform emphasizing sectional differences. Beginning the assault in Maine in July, Secretary of the Treasury John Sherman pointed to the riders as proof that the Democrats desired to nullify the laws of the land. He charged that the Bourbons, using "midnight murder and masquerade," had perpetrated in 1878 "election frauds more shameful than the ballot-box stuffing and repeating of Tweed and his infamous ring in 1868." To the Secretary financial questions were insignificant alongside these atrocities.[39]

Two months later Hayes joined in. In a fiery speech at Youngstown, Ohio, which again demonstrated the remarkable change that had taken place in his thinking, the former Major General reminded the members of his Civil War regiment that in 1872 and 1876 both Democrats and Republicans had recognized "the equality of all men before the law" and had sworn "to maintain emancipation and enfranchisement, and to oppose the reopening of the questions settled by the recent amendments to the Constitution." Despite these pledges, the President complained, the Bourbons still deprived colored men of their privileges. The 200,000 Negroes who had served in the Union army had won for their entire race the right to political and social equality. The nation would suffer unless the Southern problem was "speedily settled, and settled rightly." The chief executive urged Union veterans and good fellows of both sections to make it clear

that no public man in any party will be sustained unless he will undertake to carry out in good faith the pledges made in all our platforms in regard to the rights of colored citizens; unless he will support laws providing the means required to punish crimes against them; and unless he will oppose the admission of any man to either house of Congress whose seat has been obtained by the violation of the Fifteenth Amendment. The right of suffrage is the right of self-protection. Its free exercise is the vital air of republican institutions.

To establish now the states rights doctrine of the supremacy of the states, and an oligarchy of race, is deliberately to throw away an essential part of the fruits of the Union victory. The settlements of the war in favor of equal rights and the supremacy of the laws of the nation are just and wise, and necessary. Let them not be surrendered. Let them be faithfully and firmly enforced.[40]

Other Republicans followed the President's lead in Ohio. General Philip H. Sheridan informed a Fostoria audience that the Democrats could win only by coercing and intimidating Southern Negroes, while Blaine told a Bellaire gathering that "The question now before you is shall I vote in the interest of the Ku-Klux, and raise them to full control of the country?" At his home in Mansfield Sherman argued in a like spirit.[41]

After the Ohio election, which was won by the Republicans, the political scene shifted to the East. Conkling, Sherman, Evarts, Charles Foster, the newly selected Buckeye governor, Congressman Julius Caesar Burrows of Michigan, and Joseph H. Choate, the lawyer, delivered almost a dozen speeches attacking the South in New York, New Jersey, and neighboring states.[42]

The only prominent Republican to shun sectionalism was Ulysses S. Grant. Upon returning home from a twenty-six months' world tour in September, 1879,[43] he addressed a group of Confederate veterans in San Francisco with extreme politeness. Then in a Chicago speech Grant called the Southern Civil War generals men "who fought, and fought bravely," and stated that the former rebels had "equal claims with ourselves in the greatness of our great and common country." [44]

The former President's moderation even greatly impressed many previously unfriendly Northern newspaper editors. The New York *Evening Post* and the Chicago *Tribune* now dug up a long list of facts to show that Grant had always favored a mild Southern policy. They pointed out that in December, 1865, after visiting the recently defeated Confederate states, he had written to President Andrew Johnson, "I am satisfied that the mass of thinking men of the South accept the present situation in good faith." A year before his second term ended Grant had anticipated Hayes's policy by pulling the troops out of Mississippi and handing the state over to the Redeemers. Moreover, on March 1, 1877, the General's secretary had informed Republican Governor Stephen B. Packard that Grant favored withdrawing the army from Louisiana, too. And when in Edinburgh in September, 1877, Grant had remarked, "If I were home I would give Mr. Hayes and his policy all the support I could because the object aimed at is a noble one, and I hope he will succeed." [45]

Buoyed up by sentiments like these, Southerners became Grant worshipers. Influential papers like the Atlanta *Constitution,* the Vicksburg *Herald,* and the Augusta *Chronicle and Constitutionalist,* the voice of Alexander H. Stephens, endorsed the General for a third term. Desiring peaceful relations with the North, they felt that Grant, always a supporter of internal improvements projects, would also give the South its full share of the federal patronage and subsidies. The planters of Newberry, South Carolina, suggested a ticket of Grant for president and Bayard for vice-president.[46]

Many leading Georgians warmly praised Grant. Stephens complimented him "for his generous, magnanimous and patriotic sentiments," while General James Longstreet called him "the great American soldier-statesman." Even Robert Toombs, the old fire-eater, sent the General a congratulatory telegram when he arrived home.[47]

Observers noted that the boom was spreading rapidly. Postmaster General David M. Key of Tennessee said that Southerners favored Grant because they believed that he would end sectional agitation. John G. Schumaker, who had served three terms as a Democratic Congressman from Brooklyn, reported after a tour that "The people of the South are getting crazy about Grant. It's Grant! Grant! Grant everywhere!" The former

President, he explained, "takes just the opposite views of Blaine, Sherman and Hayes. His idea is peace, peace forever, and equal right to all, white as well as black. The Republicans have all the time been legislating for the black man over the white, and Grant is opposed to that and always has been. He always has thought the white man to be as good as the black." Schumaker predicted that the General would be a nonpartisan candidate for president in 1880.[48]

Hayes's annual message of December 1, 1879, contrasted sharply with Grant's recent utterances. Now the President was the Stalwart and the General the South's friend. Urging men of all sections to obey the election laws, Hayes asked that the defects in these measures be remedied and called upon state officials for aid. He was convinced that the peace and prosperity of the nation hinged upon the peaceful settlement of the race question.[49]

Undaunted by the administration's firm stand, Grant appealed to Southern Democrats for support. To bolster his strength in late 1879 and early 1880 he went on two tours of the South. During the first he made conciliatory speeches at Atlantic seaboard centers like Augusta, Beaufort, Savannah, and Jacksonville, while later he repeated the same tactics at Galveston, Little Rock, New Orleans, Mobile, Memphis, and Vicksburg.[50]

In spite of Grant's words the Stalwarts still believed that he was one of them. George S. Boutwell, Conkling, Logan, and J. Donald Cameron recalled that as President of the United States he had filled many Southern posts with carpetbaggers and had dispatched Federal troops to South Carolina just two weeks before the 1876 election. As Boutwell insisted, Grant was still the best person to help the "four millions of black fellow-citizens at the South who are utterly deprived of their political and civil liberty." [51]

Probably like a great many others, the Springfield *Daily*

Republican was puzzled. "It is one of the strangest anomalies in recent politics," the paper commented, "that northern stalwarts are for Grant as the strong man needed to stamp out a new rebellion, and ex-rebels are applauding his name to the echo as the one most certain to heal the remaining discords of war and bind us together as one people." [52]

The confusion was cleared away by the Republican national convention in June, 1880. The Stalwarts pushed Grant forward as the man to curb the Redeemers and to restore peace and order in the South. In nominating Grant for the presidency Conkling in verse reminded the delegates of the General's background:

> When asked what state he hails from
> Our sole reply shall be
> "He hails from Appomattox
> With its famous apple tree."

For thirty-six decisionless ballots the Stalwarts and Southern Republicans stuck by Grant. Finally the nation's Republicans broke the deadlock between the General and Blaine by compromising on Garfield.[53]

After that Grant, probably realizing that the machine politicians in both the North and the South, and not the reformers, were his true friends, once more adopted sectionalism. Speaking from the same platform as Conkling, he denounced the Solid South and the Redeemers.[54] The Grant boom was over and with it ended the only important opposition to the bloody shirt tactics of the two-year period of disillusionment and unity.

3

Exodus

DURING the 1870's and 1880's Republican interest in the Negro centered chiefly around the condition and status of the colored man in the South. Party members were principally concerned with such themes as suffrage, education, and civil rights. Occasionally, however, they were forced to deal with problems of a completely different nature. One of these was the first mass migration of Southern Negroes to the Northern states, which took place in 1879 and 1880. Throughout this movement, Republicans rallied to the aid of the colored man. They issued sympathetic statements, sponsored fund-raising campaigns, and opposed all attempts by the Redeemers to stifle or restrict the exodus.

Even before 1879 some important Republicans felt that Negro migration would permanently solve the Southern problem. In his last annual message to Congress, delivered on December 5, 1876, President Ulysses S. Grant justified his proposal to annex Santo Domingo by stressing that

the emancipated race of the South would have found there a con-
genial home where their civil rights would not be disputed, and
where their labor would be much sought after. The poorest among
them could have found the means to go. Thus, in cases of great
oppression and cruelty, such as has been practiced upon them in
many places within the last eleven years, whole communities would
have found refuge in Santo Domingo. I do not suppose the whole
race would have gone, nor is it desirable that they shall go. Their
labor is desirable—indispensable, almost—where they now are, but
the possession of this territory would have left the negro master of
the situation by enabling him to demand his rights at home on pain
of seeking them elsewhere.[1]

After he left office, Grant continued to press the scheme. In an
interview with the New York *Herald* in 1878 the General once
more argued that migration to Santo Domingo would solve the
race problem. His plan later received the endorsement of such
influential papers as the *Herald* and the Chicago *Tribune*.[2]

Rutherford B. Hayes, however, rejected his predecessor's pet
project. Early in 1878 he refused to help a band of Negroes
reach Santo Domingo because he considered the island's climate unsuitable for them. Still highly optimistic about the
permanent results of his Southern policy, Hayes argued that
the condition of the Negro was steadily improving and that
emigration was unnecessary.[3]

The next year Senator William Windom of Minnesota revived the discussion. On January 16, 1879, he introduced a
resolution setting up a committee of seven to assist the "partial
migration of colored persons from those States and congressional districts where they are not allowed to freely and peacefully exercise their constitutional rights as American citizens"
into areas where their privileges would be respected.[4]

Windom acted for a variety of reasons. Acknowledging that
Grant had "struck the right chord . . . in his message regarding the purchase of San Domingo," he felt that migration

"would lessen the power of the Southern employer and make the Negro practically master of the situation." [5] Equally as important was the encouragement the Senator received from officials of the Northern Pacific Railroad. These men hoped Windom could induce Negroes to purchase some of the federal land grants held by the road in Dakota and other Western territories. [6]

The Senate debate on the resolution was brief but bitter. Windom insisted that patriotism had inspired his proposal. All loyal Americans would surely support it. His measure would benefit both those colored men who migrated and those who remained in the South. Democratic Senator Eli Saulsbury of Delaware challenged Windom to prove that Negroes were abused. The expense involved in creating a commission would be far greater than the results would justify, he asserted. [7] Despite the harsh debate, the Senate took no action on the matter.

Soon after Windom introduced his resolution, groups of Louisiana and Mississippi Negroes began to migrate to Kansas. The Senator's proposal and the ensuing discussion had seemingly made many of them even more dissatisfied with conditions in the South. Since 1877, when the entire section fell into Democratic hands, a large number of colored men had been disfranchised. Some believed that they would eventually be reenslaved. Moreover, many freedmen were hopelessly in debt: they were often charged exorbitant fees for land, for animals, for seed, and for food. To make matters worse there had been a crop failure in Mississippi during 1878; drought, low prices, and a severe yellow fever epidemic plagued the state. Gullible colored men were only too anxious to believe a Negro named Dr. Collins, who traveled through the river counties of Mississippi preaching emigration, and agents of the Kansas Pacific and the Dallas and Wichita Railroads, who tried to induce sharecroppers to move to lands in Texas and the West. [8]

As the first waves of Negroes hit Kansas, Northern Republicans, anxious to strike a blow at Bourbonism, went into action. They formed a National Emigration Aid Society, elected Windom its president, and made Senators Hannibal Hamlin, Zachariah Chandler, and Henry M. Teller, Representatives James A. Garfield and Charles E. Williams, and William E. Chandler and George C. Gorham members of the executive committee. Both Stalwarts and Half-Breeds sponsored the organization.[9]

Zachariah Chandler wholeheartedly endorsed the new group. The Senator hoped "that our people will make an earnest effort to assist this downtrodden race." He was sure the exodus would "gain an irresistible headway in the course of the year, and be the means of eliminating from the South the question of caste." By depriving the Redeemers of their labor, the movement would "force these southern aristocrats and rebels . . . to be their own 'hewers of wood and drawers of water.'" When the planters were "compelled to earn their own bread by the sweat of their face, then will they become good citizens, and not till then." [10]

Other leading Republicans defended and encouraged the Negro. Windom denied that he had instigated the exodus and charged that it was an outgrowth of Bourbon abuses. He predicted that the number of refugees would increase sharply unless the rights of all men were respected. The two Republican Senators from Kansas, Preston B. Plumb and John J. Ingalls, scoffed at Democratic assertions that their party had planned the movement and had used propaganda to induce colored people to migrate. To them the exodus symbolized the spontaneous desire of an oppressed race to escape. Ingalls explained that Negroes had chosen Kansas because the state in the 1850's had been the home of John Brown and the center of a bitter fight for republican institutions. He reported that since the beginning of the movement the Bourbons had murdered at least twenty colored persons. In one instance a pregnant woman had been hanged by a mob when she indicated that she intended to join her husband in Kansas. Ingalls swore that as she was dying she gave birth to a child. Despite the fact that he had opposed migration to Santo Domingo, Hayes believed that the results of the exodus would be "altogether favorable. The tendency will be to force the better class of Southern people to suppress the violence of the ruffian class, and to protect colored people in their rights. Let the emigrants be scattered throughout the Northwest; let them be encouraged to get homes and settled employment." [11]

Only William Lloyd Garrison doubted the wisdom of the exodus. The veteran abolitionist admitted that the movement had been caused "by the poverty of the colored people and by the fact that they are ostracized and in some cases 'bulldozed' by the white men whose serfs they formerly were." But he was convinced that "The lot of the colored man is cast in the Southern States. There he must stay, and it will depend as much on his white neighbor as on himself whether his condition be prosperous or not." [12] Garrison naturally felt sorry for the few thousand migrants.

But what of the four millions of colored people in the entire South? Their exilement is a question not to be seriously entertained for a moment, either as a desirable or possible event. The American Government is but a mockery, and deserves to be overthrown, if they are to be left without protection, as sheep in the midst of wolves. If the nation, having decreed their emancipation, and invested them under the Constitution with all the rights of citizenship, can neither devise nor find a way to vindicate their manhood, then its acts have been farcical.[13]

As the exodus gained momentum, Republicans from all sections of the country aided the Negro in a variety of ways. Garfield introduced a resolution in the House authorizing the Secretary of War to issue rations and tents to colored refugees in Kansas, but it was bottled up in committee by the Democrats.[14]

Led by Governor John P. St. John, Kansas party members in
early May formed a Freedmen's Relief Association. The organization established a colony in Wabaunsee County, fifty miles
west of Topcka, and sold to Negroes land priced at $2.65 per
acre for only one-tenth down. It gave the freedmen the first
payment and provided barracks, food, and teams of animals
for them.[15] Murat Halstead's Cincinnati *Commercial* started
a colored emigrant fund, and Boston Republicans late in April
held a relief meeting at Faneuil Hall, at which Governor
Thomas Talbot presided and former Secretary of the Treasury
George S. Boutwell delivered the key address. Not content
simply with writing letters, Garrison collected large amounts
of clothing and money for the refugees, and after his death, in
May, 1879, his sons carried on his work.[16]

By far the most active and most important Republican in
1879 was General Thomas W. Conway of New Jersey, a former
Freedmen's Bureau officer. From March to November he devoted all of his energy to caring for colored persons, most of
the time traveling with them as they fled northward from
Louisiana and Mississippi.[17] Conway also solicited donations
for the emigrants: he persuaded Benjamin F. Butler to give
21,000 acres of Wisconsin farm land, Robert G. Ingersoll to
contribute $1,000 and half of his income for five years, and
Zachariah Chandler to settle and house one hundred colored
men on his Michigan estates.[18]

Conway especially resented Bourbon attempts to stifle the
exodus by force. To his dismay, by May, 1879, a group led by
General James R. Chalmers of Mississippi, whom bloody shirt
Republicans remembered as one of the Confederate heroes of
the Fort Pillow massacre,[19] had succeeded in closing the Mississippi River, which escaping Negroes used to take them to St.
Louis. By threatening to sink all boats carrying colored persons,
the Southerners frightened shipowners into stranding 1,500
Negroes along the banks of the Mississippi.[20]

Conway carried on a one-man campaign to correct this situation. When shipping line officials refused to listen to his pleas, he wrote direct appeals to Hayes, Windom, Blaine, Ingersoll, and Zachariah Chandler. "Every river landing is blockaded by white enemies of the colored exodus," he explained to the President, "some of whom are mounted and armed, as if we were at war, their object being to force the negroes back to the places they left. *This is* bondage." He reminded Hayes that "our colored brethren in the south have not yet been emancipated except on paper." Deputy sheriffs, armed with writs of attachment for debts sworn out by Southern planters, were seizing Negroes and forcing them to return home, "much as they used to do under the old fugitive slave law." To make matters worse, "horrid looking, evil disposed persons . . . acting in the interest of the bull-dozers of the south," were trailing Conway through the streets of the city and were threatening his life.[21]

Accompanied by the Rev. John Turner of St. Louis, Conway journeyed to Washington to enlist the President's aid. After listening to the protestants, Hayes told them that Negroes had a right to migrate and that this privilege would be maintained by the administration. He promised that if Conway chartered a private boat for the colored men, federal authorities would see to it that the vessel reached its destination safely. Any "resistance to lawful business carried on upon a National highway such as the Mississippi would be rebellion," Hayes insisted, "and there would be no doubt that the Government would afford its protection." [22]

After that, Conway, hoping to raise enough money to rent a ship for the fleeing Negroes, toured the East. With the aid of men like Wendell Phillips and Edward McPherson, editor of the Philadelphia *Press,* he sponsored meetings in New York, Philadelphia, and Boston, at which he raised over $10,000. But Conway never spent what he collected. Frightened by the

President's threat to intervene, the owners of the largest steamship line in St. Louis yielded to Republican demands and agreed to transport Negroes wherever they desired. Thereupon, Conway abandoned his Eastern trip and returned to the South.[23]

II

Although many Republicans encouraged and helped the Negro in 1879, Northern commercial interests, espousing views which they consistently advocated since 1877, strongly opposed the exodus. They argued that it would rob the South of needed labor, injure commercial relations between the sections, and seriously disturb the economy of the country, which only now was recovering from the depression of 1873.

Without exception business journals disliked the movement. The New York *Commercial Bulletin* advised its readers not to aid the fleeing Negroes. "Can the South or the North be benefited by encouraging the migration of that labor upon which our chief commercial crop is dependent?" it asked. "Can we afford to undermine the prosperity, nay the very existence of Southern trade by diverting from that section the population on which its industry is dependent? Could we select means better adapted for ruining that whole section and laying the basis for ineradicable sectional hostilities?" The Negro, used to a warm climate, would die off in the cold North, the publication predicted. The *Commercial and Financial Chronicle* felt that colored labor was needed where it was and advised Negroes to remain in the South. To it the northward drive was "plainly hasty, tumultuous, and unwise." According to *Railway Age*, the Negro, accustomed to toiling in gangs, could not successfully manage his own farm in Kansas.[24]

Commercial interests went out of their way to show their friendship for the cotton growers of Louisiana and Mississippi. When a convention of planters in Greenville, Mississippi, appealed to the "business men and benevolent societies of the North" to help arrest the exodus, the New York *Journal of Commerce* answered that "A great many generous hearted Northern merchants have probably refrained from contributing [to the Negroes] in fear that the South would misconstrue their action." The planters were "justly sensitive . . . to every word and deed in the North which bear the construction of interference between the late slave and the late master. We can assure the Southerners, once for all, that, excepting a few incurable fanatics who have little money or influence, the people of the North feel no desire to break up the present Southern labor system, and will contribute a hundred dollars to transport the refugees back to their homes from Kansas, to every dollar given by any rabid hater of the South toward depriving the capitalists of the only labor available for them." [25]

St. Louis businessmen also responded to Southern appeals. At the request of Mississippi valley planters with whom they did business, twenty-five leading merchants petitioned the city's steamship companies to make their rates so high that no colored persons could afford them. Often the shippers yielded to such pressure.[26] It was this attitude which prompted Wendell Phillips to scoff, "Are the numbers of fugitives insignificant? Why then do planters grow pale, and boards of trade protest and angry men rush together in noisy conventions?" [27]

III

During the second half of 1879 most Republicans continued to view the migration optimistically. Benjamin H. Bristow thought "great good will come of the Exodus. Perhaps it is the final settlement of the 'negro question.'" George W. Williams, the only colored member of the Ohio state legislature, wanted the movement to continue. "I was chairman of the Cincinnati Relief Committee which sent $3,800 and sixty or seventy boxes of clothing to the refugees; and I have given the subject thought," he explained. "I would rather that many should die on the way to other states than that they should settle down contented with their condition in their homes." John Sherman predicted that if Southerners did not allow "the colored people to freely enjoy their rights and privileges conferred by the Constitutional Amendments . . . the voluntary exodus of their labor is inevitable." [28]

Frederick Douglass was one of the few party leaders to disagree. He wrote:

I am opposed to this exodus because it is an untimely concession to the idea that white people and colored people cannot live together in peace and prosperity unless the whites are a majority and control the legislation and hold the offices of the State. I am opposed to this exodus because it will enable our political adversaries to make successful appeals to popular prejudice . . . on the ground that these people, so ignorant and helpless, have been imported for the purpose of making the North solid by outvoting intelligent white Northern citizens. I am opposed to this exodus because "rolling stones gather no moss," and I agree with Emerson that the men who made Rome or any other locality worth going to see stayed there. There is, in my opinion, no part of the United States where an industrious and intelligent man can serve his race more wisely and efficiently than upon the soil where he was born and reared and is known. I am opposed to this exodus because I see in it a tendency to convert laboring men into travelling tramps, first going North because they are persecuted, and then returning South because they have been deceived in their expectations, which will excite against themselves and against our whole race an increasing measure of popular contempt and scorn. I am opposed to this exodus because I believe that the conditions of existence in the Southern States are readily improving, and that the colored man there will undoubtedly realize the fullest measure of liberty, as in any section of our common country.[29]

Then late in 1879 the migration suddenly entered a new phase. Dissatisfied North Carolina Negroes began to move to

Indiana. There was much with which these people were disgusted. Many disliked the state road law, which required each man between eighteen and forty-five to pay a dollar fee or to work on the highways up to thirty days a year. They also resented the landlord and tenant act, under which a large share of all crops grown on rented lands was mortgaged to the landowner. Violators of these measures were subject to criminal prosecution. Some Negroes also complained that they were politically persecuted and that their labor supported large numbers of lazy whites.[30]

To Democratic and Mugwump editors the new exodus seemed part of a Republican plot to colonize Indiana, a state which in 1876 had gone for Tilden by only 5,515 votes out of a total of 431,070 cast.[31] The Louisville *Courier-Journal* accused the Republican state committee of importing Negroes for political purposes and urged Democrats "to organize promptly and thoroughly for a most formidable and aggressive campaign." The *Nation* reported that government clerks were helping colored men leave North Carolina "not on the score of humanity, but for party ends." The Cincinnati *Enquirer* charged that even Hayes was fostering the movement.[32]

Democrats in Congress reacted swiftly. Representative Charles M. Shelley of Alabama demanded that the House set up a special committee of five to study all aspects of the exodus, while Senator Daniel Voorhees of Indiana called for a thorough investigation of the migration to his state.[33]

Although the Shelley resolution was bottled up in committee, Voorhees's measure was debated at length. The Indiana Democrat asked Congress to determine whether "there is a conspiracy on the part of disreputable people, both white and black, to disturb the condition of the black race at the South and make them discontented and unhappy." Denying that he was motivated by partisanship, Voorhees asserted that his guiding principles were justice and equality.[34] Republican

Henry L. Dawes of Massachusetts derided the plot thesis. "What is the delusion, if they [Negroes] enjoy all their rights at home?" he asked.

Who makes a man believe he is deprived of his rights who knows he is enjoying them? Who deceived them? What is it that they are deceived in? Is it in fact that they do not enjoy political rights, or is it in fact that they do not enjoy the rights of every other citizen to acquire property and to the fulfillment of contracts and the protection of life and property like men? [35]

Windom announced that he would vote for the resolution but added that the committee should seek a remedy for the entire race problem and should designate a suitable place to which Southern Negroes could migrate. Disagreeing with Voorhees, Benjamin Hill, a Georgia Democrat, argued that colored men had every right to leave the South if they desired. He believed that Senate action was uncalled for. When it finally voted, the upper chamber passed the Voorhees resolution by a bipartisan vote of twenty-seven to twelve.[36]

During its investigation, the Senate committee waded through a mass of conflicting Republican testimony. Indiana party leaders, including William W. Dudley, United States marshal for the district of Indiana and a member of the executive board of the state committee, John C. New, chairman of the state committee, Colonel William R. Holloway, postmaster of Indianapolis and acting treasurer of the Republican state central committee, and E. B. Martindale, editor of the Indianapolis *Journal*, strenuously and repeatedly denied that they had fostered colonization. They swore that from the beginning they had frowned upon the idea of importing Negroes because it was too expensive and because it would undoubtedly provide the Democrats with campaign ammunition. They further swore that they had never raised a cent to aid the migration.[37]

But H. W. Mendenhall, an official of the National Emigration Aid Society, a Treasury department clerk, and a former

Indiana ward heeler, directly contradicted New, Dudley, Holloway, and Martindale. He testified that about October 1, 1879, he had suggested that two North Carolina Negroes, Samuel L. Perry and Peter C. Williams, take groups to Indiana, Illinois, or Ohio, rather than to Kansas. Mendenhall wrote Martindale of the idea, and the editor, through a friend, responded by inviting Perry and Williams to Greencastle, Indiana. There the two colored men were warmly greeted by several farmers who said they could use Negro laborers. As a result of this visit, fifty colored persons, the first to leave North Carolina, went to the Hoosier State.[38]

Conway's testimony was an even greater challenge to that of the Indiana leaders. He recalled that early in 1879 he had discussed colonizing Negroes in the state with Zachariah Chandler, Robert G. Ingersoll, and his brother, E. G. Ingersoll. With their approval Conway made a three-day trip to Indianapolis, where he spoke to Martindale, New, and Holloway. These three told him that they would be happy if they could get from five to ten thousand Negroes for Indiana. Conway testified that although his interest in the matter was solely humanitarian, New and Martindale were primarily concerned with political results. As Conway noted, they would have been fools to reject 10,000 Republican voters. No one in the Hoosier State, however, contributed money for any emigration project, although Robert Ingersoll did pay a portion of Conway's traveling expenses.[39]

Available evidence substantiates Conway's story. In a letter to Chandler, written almost a year before he testified, the General reviewed his Indiana visit:

In Indianapolis I saw several republicans who all agreed that we ought to send five or ten thousand [Negroes] into Indiana alone, and got their assurance that we could get employment for five thousand of them at once. I wrote the State Com. since I came [to St. Louis] that, as soon as the means were provided, I would forward as many as required. I talked with some of the freedmen themselves and they expressed a willingness to go as advised.[40]

Throughout 1879 Conway pressed the colonization scheme. In the fall he made a second trip to Indianapolis, this time for only a day, and again spoke to New and Martindale. Once more he received encouragement. Republican leaders promised to find homes for the Negroes. After that, Conway conferred with Chandler, who repeated his offer to build homes and provide land for one hundred good men upon his Michigan estates. He was corresponding with Chandler about the matter when the Senator died on November 1, 1879.[41]

Unknown to the committee, other prominent Republicans privately approved of and aided colonization. Sherman in November, 1879, felt that if the exodus "could be directed into Indiana it could still be better. The trouble is it is rather late now for political results next year, but it would be useful for the future." [42] Many Republicans contributed to the National Emigration Aid Society, which helped Negroes fleeing from North Carolina by securing homes and employment for them.[43]

At the conclusion of the long and detailed Senate inquiry, the majority and minority members of the Voorhees committee filed conflicting reports. The Democrats insisted that Indiana had been colonized, while the Republicans denied the charge.[44]

The Senate bitterly debated the reports. Voorhees charged that as early as the autumn of 1878 Indiana newspapers, "edited by republican Federal officials, were openly and systematically engaged in encouraging negroes to come and settle in that state, avowedly for political ends." He believed that Windom's resolution had caused the exodus. Pointing to the massive evidence accumulated by his group, he asked, "Who now will prate of the absence of proof that the emigration of negroes into Indiana was a political scheme known, planned, fostered, and carried on by the leaders of the republican party?" Windom denied Voorhees's assertions and asked a number of questions of his own. Why should Indiana Republicans import Negroes from closely contested North Carolina

where the party needed them? Would it not have been easier
and cheaper to take them from Kentucky? Why should 700 or
800 Negroes, only 200 of whom were voters, be sent to Democratic Indiana and 25,000 to solidly Republican Kansas? He
asserted that the colored people had really left North Carolina because they were murdered and outraged by the Bourbons, because they were denied adequate educational facilities,
and because the state courts discriminated against them.[45]

The truth lay somewhere between the Democratic charges
and the Republican counterassertions. Undoubtedly many Republican leaders welcomed the Negroes both as voters and laborers and found employment for them, but the state organization, according to all witnesses, contributed no money.

Almost as abruptly as it had begun, the exodus ended early
in 1880. A number of conditions discouraged other Negroes
from migrating northward. Word drifted back to the South
that the North was cold, that much of the land in Kansas and
Indiana was unfertile, and that in many areas there were more
colored people than could be cared for. A few disgruntled migrants even returned home. For the time being at least, most
Negroes agreed with Frederick Douglass that their destiny lay
in the South.[46]

4

Garfield: The Search for a Southern Policy

I

During the period in which he led the Republican party, James A. Garfield searched for a policy which would break up the Solid South. In succession he considered the bloody shirt, federal aid to education, and an alliance with the Virginia Readjusters as possible programs. Yet during his brief stay in the White House he did not adopt a definite course of action and left conditions in the South unchanged.

Only a year and a half before being nominated Garfield publicly deplored all efforts to exploit the Negro theme. "The man who attempts to get up a political excitement in this country on the old sectional basis will find himself without a party and without support," he said. "The man who wants to serve his country must put himself in the line of its leading thought and that is restoration of business, trade, commerce, industry, sound political economy, honest money and honest payment of all obligations. And the man who can add anything in the direction of the accomplishment of any of these purposes is a public benefactor." [1]

But in 1879 when Democrats tried to repeal the existing federal election laws by attaching riders to the Army Appropriation Act Garfield, chairman of the House Committee on Appropriations, became embittered toward the South.[2] By 1880 he had completely changed his old view and was willing to use the sectional theme during his campaign.

Disillusioned by the failure of Hayes's Southern policy, Republicans in 1880 adopted a platform which paved the way for the bloody shirt wavers. It denounced the Democrats for suppressing Negro suffrage and for attempting to repeal the election laws. Vowing to protect all voters "against terrorism, violence or fraud," the party stressed that the Constitution must be upheld.[3]

In his letter of acceptance Garfield argued in a like tone. He believed that "the wounds of the war" could not be completely healed until all men enjoyed the same civil and political privileges. If Southern atrocities continued, immigration to the section would cease, laborers would migrate, and property values would fall. The South would be prosperous only when "every voter can freely and safely support the party he pleases." [4]

Other Republican leaders agreed that the Negro question should be given special emphasis during the campaign. Disappointed by the results of his own program for the South, Hayes now felt that "The failure of the South to faithfully observe the Fifteenth Amendment is the cause of the failure of all efforts towards complete pacification. It is on this hook that the bloody shirt now hangs." [5] John A. Logan was sure that a strong Republican canvass could carry South Carolina and Florida. He recommended that the National Committee send to the South "several of our leading statesmen, men of national reputation whom the cutthroats would not dare molest." By arranging "to have a corps of tally-clerks at each voting precinct to take down the name of every Republican voter, and to have the voter openly announce 'I vote for Garfield,'" these visitors could easily prevent Bourbon frauds.[6]

As the campaign progressed the race issue was given increasing attention by Republicans, who used it to conceal a dispute between Garfield and Roscoe Conkling. Fearful that Garfield, if elected, would not give him the patronage and would follow Hayes's policies, the New York chief refused to endorse his party's nominee. In an attempt to iron out the matter, the Republican National Committee planned a party conference for the Fifth Avenue Hotel in New York on August 5 and 6.[7]

Although Conkling did not attend the meeting, his most trusted lieutenants, Richard Crowley, Levi P. Morton, and Thomas C. Platt, were there. After a series of talks, during which Garfield, in Platt's words, swore that "he had no sympathy whatever" with Hayes's Southern program, the New York faction agreed to support the candidate. A short time later, Conkling and Platt came out for the Republican ticket.[8]

The sectional theme was used to cover up the true story of the Fifth Avenue Hotel conference. The public was told nothing of the patronage disputes within the Republican organization; it learned only that a united political party had convened in New York and had pledged to protect fully the rights of the Negro.

The nation's most important Republicans devised the strategy decided upon at the Fifth Avenue Hotel. Garfield, Chester A. Arthur, the candidate for vice-president, James G. Blaine, William McKinley, Murat Halstead, Benjamin Harrison, John Sherman, William E. Chandler, Henry L. Dawes, J. Donald Cameron, Logan, Morton, and Platt were there. At a meeting held on the first day of the gathering George B. Loring of Massachusetts introduced a resolution pledging assistance to all Southern Republicans who desired it and certifying that no states would be abandoned to the Redeemers without a fight.

It was adopted by an overwhelming vote. In a fiery speech former Governor Pinckney B. S. Pinchback of Louisiana noted that in many areas colored men were lynched if they tried to vote. He urged nationally known and respected men like Blaine and Sherman to tour the South. Blaine answered that the party had no intention of abandoning the Negro and swore that not a single Northern Republican advocated such a policy. Sherman's "heart beat for all those who carried their banner through the southern states, be they white or black." He promised more aid for these men. Logan and Harrison joined in.[9]

After the Fifth Avenue Hotel conference broke up, Congressman Charles Williams of Wisconsin reviewed its work. "We have for the past forty-eight hours seen the leaders of the Republican party in session here to determine whether the South shall be abandoned to tissue ballots; to the bludgeon and bowie knife," he said. "Great God! Shall the blood of the 130,000 men who have been murdered for their Republicanism in the South be unavenged?" The party was determined to "break up the solid south and put an end to the right of a set of rebels to command the Union army from the floor of Congress when they could not defeat them upon the field." [10]

Garfield vigorously endorsed the sentiments of his fellow Republicans. He told a giant rally that during the Civil War he had "found that the hearts" of the 4,000,000 slaves

were God-inspired with the spirit of liberty, and that they were our friends. . . . We have seen white men betray the flag and fight to kill the Union, but in all that long, dreary war, we never saw a traitor in black skin. . . . Our prisoners escaping from the starvation of the prison, fleeing to our lines by the light of the north star, never feared to enter a black man's cabin and ask for bread. . . . And now that we have made them free, so long as we live, we will stand by the black citizens. . . . We will stand by them until the sun of liberty fixed in the firmament of our constitution shall shine with equal rays upon every man, white or black, throughout the Union.[11]

A large group of Republicans now began to canvass upon a bloody shirt platform. Sherman, William M. Evarts, Vice-President William A. Wheeler and others began refighting the Civil War. Jay A. Hubbell, chairman of the Republican Congressional Committee, optimistically wrote, "The party is harmonious and the fear of a solid South will draw thousands of voters to our ranks." [12]

Conkling cemented his alliance with Garfield by joining the campaigners. In a much heralded New York speech he harped upon the evils of Southern rule. "The general issue confronting us in this election is in itself and in its bearing sectional," he thundered. A Democratic victory, which could be achieved only if the Negro was illegally disfranchised, would enable the Redeemers, who constituted only one-seventh of the country's population, to control the economic policies of the entire nation. "I affirm that the broad issue," Conkling argued, "is whether our colossal fabric of commercial, industrial and financial interests shall be under the management and protection of those who chiefly created and own it, or shall be handed over to the sway of those whose share in it is small, and whose experience, antecedents, theories and practices do not fit them or entitle them to assume control." [13]

New York business newspapers, fearing that Southern trade would be adversely affected, strongly opposed Conkling's revival of the sectional theme. The *Journal of Commerce*, traditionally a Republican paper, said that New York merchants intensely longed for "a restoration of that peace and unity between the several sections of the country, and especially between the Northern and Southern States, which is essential to our prosperity, but which it seems impossible to obtain under the present organization." The paper noted that "Patriotism and property interests alike are naturally arrayed against sectionalism in every form. Conservative instincts are not confined to one party. Business men of both parties share in them for the same good reasons. Mr. Conkling's sectionalism can only make conservative Republicans anxious, and afraid to follow him." According to the New York *Commercial Bulletin,* also a Republican journal, merchants wanted peace, harmony, and quiet. They did not want to reopen the "lately-settled questions." After suffering through a seven-year depression, they hoped for a continuation of the recent economic revival. "Indeed," the *Bulletin* remarked, "it may be safely said that the controlling factor in the present campaign is the strong desire of the mercantile community to have, at least for the next four years, an era of political rest." Long after the canvass ended, the *Journal of Commerce* reviewed some of the Stalwart contributions to commercial prosperity: "What did Conkling and Platt care about the business interests of New York?" it asked. "What pride did they ever show in the true greatness of this State? What valuable idea did they ever contribute to the advancement or defense of her commerce and trade?" [14]

Cincinnati businessmen especially disapproved of the use of the Negro theme by the Republicans. The commercial interests of the Queen City of the West had recently completed construction of the Cincinnati Southern Railroad, which ran through Kentucky and Tennessee to Chattanooga, solely to attract trade. Facing southward and with no Northern back country to service, the city depended upon the South for its economic existence.

Despite this fact, Cincinnati's two most important Republican papers, Richard Smith's *Gazette* and Murat Halstead's *Commercial,* attacked the Redeemers almost daily. "The Democratic party belongs to the Solid South and has no will of its own," read a typical Halstead editorial. "The success of that party would make the war a failure, subordinate those who were victorious to the rule of the vanquished, and place the sword and the purse of the Nation in the hands of those against whom they were lately employed." Republicans would not "swallow all this for the sake of trade—actually turn the United States upside down—put the Solid South at the head of affairs —resume the old vulgar abuse of the Abolitionists and accept the Southern school books as history—declare ourselves the meanest of all God's creatures that the statesman of the shot-gun and the bullwhip may be so well pleased with us as to allow Southern merchants to buy in the best market!" The *Gazette* carried similar statements and wholeheartedly supported Conkling.[15]

The city's merchants resented these tactics. One hundred and fourteen of them, representing some of the largest businesses, drew up a strongly worded petition "protesting against the imputation by the partisan press of this city for political effect that we cherish any hostility to the people of the South." The complainers admitted that they wanted Southern trade but added that "our object is far higher than any mercenary end." They desired "to join our brethren of the Southern States in building up a more perfect Union, a Union of hearts as well as hands, believing that in peace and harmony with them, and throughout our country, will be found the pathway to a higher national life, and to increased prosperity for them and ourselves." [16]

This protest was primarily the work of members of Halstead's own party. Even the *Gazette* begrudgingly conceded that it "is signed largely by Republicans." [17] Among the scores of prominent and devoted Republicans objecting to the emphasis being placed on the Southern question were the officers of: Charles Jacob, Jr., and Company, a pork and beef packing firm owned by and named after the Republican mayor of Cincinnati; the Mosler Safe and Lock Company, one of the best-known organizations in the field; John and Alfred Simpkinson and Company, wholesale boot and shoe dealers; the Licking Rolling Mill Company, a huge iron and steel works; the Marsh and Harwood Company, manufacturing chemists; Sohn's

Brewery, owned by William S. Sohn, one of the city's most important Republicans; the Vine Street Brewery, owned by John Kauffman; and Isaac and Ezra Greenwald and Company, machinists and millwrights, manufacturers of steam engines, boilers, flour mill machinery, and mill furnishings.[18]

The commercial opposition to Smith and Halstead was so great that when Conkling campaigned in Cincinnati he was forced to devote a major portion of his speech to reassuring Republican businessmen that their Southern trade would not be destroyed if they remained faithful to the party of Lincoln and Grant. Among the Republicans seated in Conkling's audience, and to whom he obviously addressed his remarks, were such signers of the petition as Mayor Jacob, John Kauffman, William S. Sohn, Isaac G. Greenwald, and John Simpkinson. "Trade has been brought here; and now we are told that the pocket nerve is sensitive; that you must not consider and discuss the political questions of the day, because if you do, you will impair the Southern trade, which comes to this fair city," Conkling argued. "Fellow citizens, when you laid down the tracks to Chattanooga, you did not lay down your principles. When you all drove the spikes in those ties, you did not intend to drive nails into the coffin of free speech and free labor." Timid merchants, the Senator recalled, had used the Southern trade argument to defend the fugitive slave law in the 1850's, to oppose Lincoln's election in 1860, and to resist the active prosecution of the war by Union forces in 1861. "Let me say, as I need not say, for they know it, to all the business men of Cincinnati, there is no friendship in trade and no sympathy at a bank," Conkling went on.

Men go to the bank where they can borrow on the best terms. Men from the North and from the South go to the market where they can buy the best. The Southern trade comes to you over these iron tracks that the energy, the genius and the capital of Cincinnati have laid down, not because they [Southern customers] are fond

of you as Romeo was fond of Juliet . . . but because where a man's
treasure is there is his heart. . . . You show me a market where
the South can buy and sell more profitably than they can here, and
I will show you a market that they will go to, even if the whole of
Cincinnati prostitute itself in the dust and sing psalms to the Solid
South.[19]

Answering Conkling, the Democratic Cincinnati *Enquirer*
entreated Republican merchants to vote against Garfield. "Commerce is both friendly and selfish," the paper warned. "Cincinnati is really a Southern city, the largest city of the South. . . .
While partisan editors are asking men to vote as they shot . . .
is it not worth while for business men to vote as they ship, and
not to vote hate against their neighbors and customers as
though they were aliens and enemies?" [20]

Eventually, even Garfield came to the conclusion that too
much stress was being put on the Southern question. "The
argument of the 'Solid South' is well enough on its way and
ought not to be overlooked," he commented to John Sherman,
"but we should also press the questions which lie close to
the hopes and interests of our people." [21] But Sherman and
Conkling, along with such supporters of Hayes's policy as
George William Curtis of *Harper's Weekly*, rejected all pleas
and continued to emphasize sectionalism throughout the rest
of the canvass.[22]

The campaign strategy proved successful as the Republicans carried the election. Garfield's plurality, however, was less
than 10,000 votes out of over nine million cast.[23] Despite the
opposition of many important Republican merchants in cities
like Cincinnati, bloody shirt tactics in 1880 united the Conkling
and Garfield sections of the party and helped achieve victory.

II

Once elected, Garfield, was faced with the problem of find-
ing a permanent solution to the Southern question. A former

college president, a prominent and active member of the National Education Association, and a frequent and outspoken commentator on the methods and values of education, Garfield quite naturally considered schooling the national cure-all. He firmly believed that trained and intelligent men could solve the difficulties facing the country.

Garfield was not the first Republican who sought to improve education. In 1870 Representative George Frisbie Hoar of Massachusetts introduced a proposal for subsidizing common schools, and two years later Congressman Legrand W. Perce of Mississippi presented a bill appropriating revenues from public land sales for education. Senator Ambrose E. Burnside of Rhode Island, the famous Union general, sponsored a measure in 1879 which greatly resembled the Perce bill. It passed the Senate in December, 1880, by a vote of 41 to 6, all negative ballots being cast by Democrats, four of whom came from the South and two of whom were from Indiana. Twenty-two Republicans and nineteen Democrats endorsed the plan.[24]

The Republican platform of 1880 was the first in the country's history to recommend federal help for schools. It stated that it was "the duty of the National Government" to aid education and recommended that Congress act at once.[25]

Hayes strongly seconded these words. Each year in his annual message he asked Congress to assist common schools, and in official and unofficial statements during 1880 he was especially insistent. On August 11, 1880, the President told a Soldiers' Reunion at Columbus, Ohio: "To perpetuate the Union and to abolish slavery were the work of the war. To educate the uneducated is the appropriate work of peace." The central government should do its part whenever and wherever necessary; federal funds were especially needed in the South. The President repeated these sentiments on September 1 during a widely publicized speech at Canton, Ohio, and in his last message to Congress, delivered in December, 1880.[26]

Like Hayes, Garfield was optimistic about the effects of schooling. During the campaign of 1880 he publicly indicated that he believed federal aid to education could help solve the race problem in the South. The Republican candidate told a group of 250 Negroes that the Emancipation Proclamation had, in reality, settled nothing. The colored man required more than just a paper independence. "What is freedom without virtue and intelligence combined to make it not a curse, but a blessing? All that liberty can do for you," he told the Negroes, "is to give you a fair chance, within the limits of the Constitution, and by the exercise of its proper powers it is the purpose of the best men on this continent to give you this equal chance and nothing more." [27]

Soon after the election, Garfield felt it necessary to discuss education and the situation in the South with experts. He carried on a detailed correspondence with two Ohioans, Burke A. Hinsdale, his closest personal friend and president of Hiram College since 1870, and Albion W. Tourgee, a former carpetbagger and onetime justice of the North Carolina superior court, whose best selling novels, *A Fool's Errand,* written in 1879, and *Bricks Without Straw,* published the next year, were concerned with the problem of Reconstruction.

These three men had no intention of regimenting or strictly supervising schools, but they did hold certain definite views. They desired to help only public, not religious, schools. As Garfield wrote in his letter of acceptance, "it would be unjust to our people, and dangerous to our institutions, to apply any portion of the revenues of the nation, or of the States, to the support of sectarian schools. The separation of the Church and the State in every thing that relates to taxation should be absolute." Hoping to aid both whites and Negroes, the three Ohioans at no time stipulated that Southern schools be desegregated. They assumed, however, that the members of each race would be given similar educational opportunities. Concerned primarily with common schools which taught academic subjects, not with colleges or with vocational and manual arts institutions, the correspondents took it for granted that each school receiving government assistance would remain largely autonomous, although it would have to be in session a certain number of days each year and would, of course, have to meet any existing state requirements.[28]

Garfield began the exchange of ideas by asking Tourgee what the effects of the Republican victory would be upon the South. Tourgee answered that the Solid South, a political remnant of the slave system, was "an institution, a belief, a matter of growth and education and sentiment." To him Southern values were almost totally negative. The section was "solidly anti-reconstruction, anti-negro equality, anti-everything that the Republican party has done, but that is all." Tourgee recommended a two-pronged policy for breaking up Democratic control: education and civil service reform. Education could only be a long range solution to any problem; civil service reform and the appointment of Republicans of high intellectual caliber, not merely greedy carpetbaggers and ignorant Negroes whose only qualification was seniority in the party organization, were more immediate steps which Garfield could take. "Make the standard of integrity, capacity and character as high as you please—the higher the better," the judge advised. He told Garfield to abandon Hayes's policy of disqualifying Southern Republicans for office if the Democrats found them objectionable. Tourgee was sure that the Redeemers were momentarily stunned by the election of Garfield, but he believed they would soon re-embark upon their old course.[29]

Hinsdale found Tourgee's prescription inadequate. Education was the most vital part of any program for the South. It was far more important than "politics or politicians . . . but it takes education a good while to bring the desired result. It cannot accomplish much in the coming quadrenniate." Civil service reform alone could not build up the Southern branch of the party. Hinsdale argued that in addition the best and most prominent Northern Republicans must be encouraged to campaign in the South, and must try to attract outstanding whites to the party. Still, the Negro must not be abandoned. "The National government should do what it can under the laws, fairly to secure honest elections. It must not commit any foolishness." [30]

Garfield agreed. He had no doubt "that the final cure for the 'solid south' will be found in the education of its youth and in the development of its business interests, but both of these require time. We are likely therefore to have a southern question for many years to come," he told Hinsdale. "I do not believe a speedy cure is possible." Hayes's policy "has proved a dreary failure." Unfortunately for the country, the South "was rooted and grounded in feudalism based on slavery; and the destruction of slavery has not yet destroyed the feudalism which it caused. Nothing but time can complete its dissolution." Southerners must be told "that this is a modern free government, and that only men who believe in it, and not in feudalism, can be invited to aid in administering it; then give the south as rapidly as possible the blessings of general education and business enterprise; and leave the rest to time and these forces to work out the problem." [31] Thus Garfield, faced with the same problem that had confronted Hayes—how to strengthen the Southern wing of the party and guarantee Republican control of the national government—had come to a conclusion far different from that of his predecessor.

Near the end of December Tourgee sent Garfield an advance copy of his article on federal aid to Southern education, entitled "Aaron's Rod in Politics," which eventually appeared in the February, 1881, number of the *North American Review*. In it the judge noted that in the Republican platform of 1880 a political party for the first time pledged that it would help schools. Assistance was especially needed in the South. The sixteen Southern states, with one hundred and thirty-eight electoral votes, contained almost three-fourths of the nation's illiterates; forty-five per cent of the section's voters could not read their ballots. The former carpetbagger estimated that twenty-four per cent of the South's whites were illiterates, while about ninety per cent of the colored men, and over seventy per cent of the Republican party, could not read and write. The only solution of this appalling situation was national aid to common schools. The Congress, Tourgee then argued, was fully empowered to subsidize education. He recommended that it establish a national fund and distribute money to communities on the basis of illiteracy. All schools receiving aid would be required to meet certain general regulations, such as holding a specified number of class meetings each year, and would be inspected by local volunteer committees. Any allotment not used in a specific year would be kept in the general fund for the succeeding year. The government would in no case provide more than one-third to one-half of the money needed to operate a school. Limiting his demands to essentials, the judge did not require desegregation of Southern schools, nor did he specify the amount or the percentage of money which was to go to Negroes.

Tourgee felt that his plan had "the merit of putting the plaster directly on the sore." He believed that it would increase the intelligence of the voters; would "strike at the roots of the 'exodus' by enabling the laborer to guard himself from fraud by the terms of his contract"; would provide a basis for reorganizing the Republican party of the South; and would help eliminate both states' rights sentiment and the Solid South.[32]

By January Garfield, having thoroughly digested the views of both Tourgee and Hinsdale, was firmly convinced that the Negro was easily abused because he was uneducated. He indicated as much to a deputation of eleven prominent Southern colored men, led by ex-Congressman Robert Brown Elliot of South Carolina and D. Augustus Straker, professor of common law at Allen University, Columbia, South Carolina. Elliott protested to the President-elect that Negroes in the South were "but citizens in name and not in fact." In many regions they were deprived of the ballot "by means of armed violence, fraud, and intimidation." Even where colored men were in the majority, their rights were "illegally and wantonly subverted" by the whites. The Bourbon-controlled state courts offered them no redress. Worst of all, Southern state governments were unwilling to establish and unable to support proper educational facilities for Negro children. The former Congressman urged Garfield to recommend the establishment of a national system of education under strict federal supervision.

The President-elect's answer was emphatic. He stressed that white minorities were able to control Negro majorities "Because a trained man is two or three men in one in comparison with an untrained man, and outside of politics and outside of parties that suggestion is full, brimful of significance." Garfield insisted "that the way to make the majority always powerful over the minority is to make its members as trained and intelligent as the minority itself. That brings the equality of citizenship, and no law can confer and maintain in the long run a thing that is not upheld with a reasonable degree of culture and intelligence." The government should, of course, do all in its power to protect everyone. Yet, he believed, the race problem would be solved only when Negroes exhibited "the native hungering and thirsting for knowledge that the Creator has planted in every child to the last possible degree of their ability, so that the hands of the people shall reach out and grasp in the darkness the hand of the Government extended to help, and by that Union of effort the two will bring what mere legislation alone cannot immediately bring." [33]

Far from resenting such sharp words, the visitors strongly

endorsed them. Elliott could not "overestimate the importance of education for white and colored children alike. They must all be raised to a proper appreciation of the rights of others." Ignorant men were usually lawless men, while educated people invariably respected the privileges of all. Other members of the delegation agreed.[34]

In the meantime a man who preferred to remain anonymous but who was described by the New York *Times* as being as close to Garfield and as familiar with his thoughts as anyone alive—undoubtedly Hinsdale—guessed that the new President's Southern policy would revolve about aid to common schools. "He believed in education for himself and he believes in education for others," the mystery man commented. "One of his strongest grounds of faith in a Republic is that it must be an educated and educating Republic, and that the common school and the university work hand in hand for the preparation of citizens for the duties and the honors of citizenship." Garfield's associate was sure "that he will give serious and careful attention to the subject of education in the South, and thus aid the growing generation in better understanding the duties and demands of citizenship than their fathers have understood them. He will not urge any temporary expedients of settlement, but will insist on going to the root of the difficulty."[35]

In his inaugural address, delivered on March 4, 1881, Garfield did go to the root of the difficulty. He argued that only education could permanently solve the Southern problem. "The elevation of the negro race from slavery to the full rights of citizenship is the most important political change we have known since the adoption of the Constitution of 1787," Garfield told the nation. The President reminded Southerners that "there was no middle ground for the negro race between slavery and equal citizenship. There can be no permanent disfranchised peasantry in the United States." He promised to safeguard the rights of colored men, but the fact that they were uneducated greatly complicated the problem. Having given the Negroes the ballot, the government was "under special obligation to aid in removing the illiteracy which it has added to the voting population. . . . All the constitutional power of the nation and of the states and all the volunteer forces of the people should be surrendered to meet this danger by the savory influence of universal education," he went on. ". . . In this beneficent work sections and races should be forgotten and partisanship should be unknown. Let our people find a new meaning in the divine oracle which declares that 'a little child shall lead them,' for our own little children will soon control the destinies of the Republic." [36]

Garfield was determined to act. Two days after the inaugural he remarked to Hinsdale, "I am going to keep that subject before me all the time, and shall see that something is done in that if possible." Late in March, while speaking to a delegation of fifty colored Republicans from Louisiana, he renewed the assurances of his inaugural address and reaffirmed his intention to educate Negroes. He also expressed a desire to see the freedmen own the land on which they toiled. In June, 1881, Garfield and Tourgee held a long conference during which they discussed various aspects of and approaches to the problem. Soon after the death of the President, in September, 1881, Hinsdale wrote, "His plan was not worked out, probably, when he was stricken by the assassin's bullet; but his heart was fixed upon this as a prominent feature of his administration—national aid to public, and especially to Southern, education." [37]

III

Schooling was the long-range Southern policy which Garfield favored, but during the short period he was President he had to decide whether or not to support the Readjusters, or Independents, of Virginia. Led by William Mahone, a former

Confederate general, the Readjusters proposed to repudiate a portion of their state's debt. In 1879, after they won a sweeping victory, capturing fifty-six of the one hundred seats in the Virginia House of Delegates and twenty-four of the forty in the Senate, the Readjusters openly appealed to Negroes and suggested an alliance with Republicans. In the fall of 1879 they received strong support when Simon Cameron of Pennsylvania visited Mahone and agreed to throw his influence, and that of his followers in the Old Dominion, behind the Readjusters.

Many nationally prominent Republicans immediately objected to this projected union. Hayes, Blaine, Sherman, Grant, and William Henry Smith believed that an arrangement between their party and repudiators would prove disastrous. But by the end of the Hayes administration, former Democrats, encouraged by Mahone's success, had formed Independent movements in such Southern states as South Carolina, Georgia, and Arkansas.[38]

Garfield in 1879 had little sympathy with Mahone. "The negroes," he wrote, "have their fate in their own hands. . . . They have shown in the recent elections of Virginia the power they can wield in a division of opinion among white men; but they used it badly in electing a repudiator to the United States Senate. It was natural, however, that they should throw their votes against [the] old Bourbon Democracy, but in doing so they inflicted a serious if not fatal wound upon the honor and prosperity of Virginia." [39]

In March, 1881, the Republicans sorely needed Mahone. The Senate contained thirty-seven Democrats, thirty-seven Republicans, one self-styled independent, David Davis of Illinois, who promised to vote with the Democrats to organize the chamber, and Mahone. The Republicans could control the Senate only if the Readjuster and Vice-President Arthur voted with them.[40]

Even Republicans who hated repudiation now recognized that some arrangement with the Readjusters was a necessity. Conkling, Hoar, J. Donald Cameron, Preston Plumb, Marshall Jewell, chairman of the Republican National Committee, and George C. Gorham, editor of the Washington *National Republican* and Mahone's nominee for clerk of the Senate, urged the party to support the Virginia Senator. "Mahone is an iconoclast," Plumb wrote to Garfield, "and he will be bound to destroy the Bourbon power in the South." Carefully used, he would be of great value to the Republicans.[41]

Unconvinced, the President sought the advice of former governor Daniel H. Chamberlain of South Carolina, whose administration had been abandoned by Hayes in 1877. Chamberlain believed that "to countenance Mahone under any stress of so-called political advantage or necessity, as I believe Mr. Jewell and Mr. Gorham did in the last campaign, and as some prominent Republicans are now advising, is to betray and dishonor our party and the cause of good government, which is above all parties. Better by far aid the regular Democracy of Virginia, who on this issue are comparatively honorable," he advised the Ohioan. Mahone was in favor of giving the Republicans their rights, Chamberlain argued, only because this course would enhance the power of the Readjusters. The former governor felt that "we must be as ready to denounce and oppose repudiators who offer us political power or rights as those who deny them." Garfield answered that he agreed "fully with you in your views of Mahone and his party." [42]

After taking office Garfield was still plagued by doubts. Should he openly recognize the Readjusters and give their Senator control of the state's patronage? He consulted with his cabinet. "There was a strong feeling of distrust of the outcome of the Mahone alliance," the President noted, "and a desire to go very slowly." [43]

When a delegation of Virginia Negroes favorable to Mahone

visited the White House, Garfield straddled the issue. Emphasizing that he had closely followed events in their state, he told the colored men to take any steps which would help them secure their rights as citizens but advised them to remain within the Republican party. He reaffirmed his willingness to aid the Negro people at all times.[44]

The attacks of Gorham's Washington *National Republican,* which chided the President because he had not thrown the full support of the administration behind Mahone, stiffened Garfield. The editor was extremely bitter because a Democratic filibuster had prevented him from achieving the Senate office he desired. Garfield told Senator Henry L. Dawes that he would "cheerfully do anything I can to aid in securing a free vote and an honest count for voters of all colors in Virginia," but he was determined not to "aid any arrangement which includes in it advancement to a post of political honor a man who as editor in chief of a newspaper is daily assailing me and my administration." [45]

Despite the fact that Mahone helped the Republicans organize the Senate, the President finally concluded that he could not come to terms with a Readjuster. On May 29, 1881, he announced that any move "tainting our party with the flavor of repudiation . . . would be in every way calamitous." Although admitting that the Readjusters were bettering the Negroes' lot, Garfield stated that he would "not remove Republicans to appoint Mahone men. I shall do enough for Mahone to help him against the Bourbons but not abandon our organization." [46]

To a large degree Secretary of State James G. Blaine was responsible for the President's decision. Blaine, who had substantial investments in the industries of Virginia, told Garfield that the regular Republican party would soon be powerful enough to carry the state. He argued that if the administration supported Mahone it would alienate many Northern Republicans. Moreover, a bargain with the Readjusters would drive back into the Democratic fold many of the friendly and influential Southerners who desired to join the Republican organization on economic issues.[47]

When Garfield was assassinated, the Negro question was as much of a dilemma to Republicans as it had been a year earlier. The President had taken no positive action. The bloody shirt, so prominently used in the election of 1880, had not been adopted as Garfield's Southern policy; the administration's long-range plans for education had not been worked out in detail; and because of his dislike for repudiators the President had refused to recognize Mahone as the party chieftain in Virginia. Garfield, who died in September, 1881, thus bequeathed to his successor the best of intentions but little else of substance or value.

5

Politics as Usual

THE DEATH of Garfield spurred some men's dreams. Unlike his predecessor, Chester A. Arthur, the new President, could not command the respect of James G. Blaine, who realized that the race for the party's presidential nomination in 1884 would be wide open. As a result, warfare between these two key rivals marked the entire Arthur administration; during this struggle the plight of the Southern Negro became secondary to the quest for convention delegates.

Immediately after assuming office, Arthur demonstrated that he was not greatly concerned with affairs in the South. His initial message to Congress, delivered less than three months after he took office, was the first presidential address since the Civil War which did not mention the race question. To Arthur the subject was inconsequential.[1]

Some Republicans were elated by what seemed to them the most significant sign that the sectional issue was passing from the political scene. "Considering that President Arthur was identified with that wing of the Republican party which looked upon Southern outrages and the portentous dangers threatened by the 'solid South' as their most valuable stock in trade," commented the *Nation*, "this fact is very creditable to him." Rutherford B. Hayes found the President's silence "the most significant proof of the wisdom and success of my policy." [2]

A little while later, the administration made its only effort to aid the Negro, a short-lived and unsuccessful attempt to enforce the election laws in the South. Although the President had little interest in the matter, referring correspondence on frauds to his Attorney General, Benjamin H. Brewster of Pennsylvania, with no comments or instructions,[3] the latter, after reviewing the evidence in a contested election case for Congress, decided to act. He told federal authorities in Charleston: "The right of suffrage must be protected, no matter who suffers." Ordering his subordinates to prosecute "the most important persons who have been concerned in these attempts to defeat honest elections by fraudulent or forcible means," the Attorney General insisted: "There will be no example if merely insignificant persons are taken hold of." Once the Bourbon ringleaders were jailed, men of both races would "be encouraged to vote according to their convictions, and those who do vote will feel satisfied that their votes have been duly counted and surrender cheerfully to an honest result." He swore that he was "very much in earnest about this." [4]

Brewster's letter precipitated a bitter struggle in South Carolina. Samuel W. Melton, the United States district attorney, responded to it by indicting a group of influential and important men for stuffing ballot boxes,[5] but the Democratic governor of the state countered by instructing his attorney general to conduct the defense of the accused men.[6] As a result the government was unable to secure any convictions. After one man was finally found guilty, he was freed when two jurors complained

that administration appointees had intimidated them into voting against the defendant.[7]

Brewster hoped another approach would prove more successful. Commanding the United States marshal in Charleston
to carry out to the letter all regulations governing the registration of voters, he called for the immediate arrest of state or local
officers obstructing, hindering, or interfering with these rules.[8]
This strategy did not work either. Discouraged by his complete
failure to safeguard the ballot for South Carolina Republicans,
Brewster soon lost interest in the subject. After the summer
of 1882, Southern law enforcement officials received little aid
from the Justice Department.[9]

Melton was disgusted. Imploring Secretary of the Navy William E. Chandler to speak to the Attorney General about the
matter, he complained that the Southern wing of the party was
being deserted. "Of all the leaders in our party," he flattered
Chandler, "you alone . . . appreciate the 'true inwardness' of
affairs here, and the means by which the intimidation and fraud
employed for the suppression of a free ballot might be prevented." Brewster, by now totally indifferent to the struggle of
Southern Republicans, did "not invite . . . correspondence"
from them.[10] But the Attorney General could not be induced
to change his mind and perpetrators of election frauds went
unpunished.

II

Three times during his term in the White House Arthur refused to speak out in favor of civil rights for Southern Negroes.
The first instance occurred early in 1882, when the Right Reverend Daniel Alexander Payne, the senior bishop of the African
Methodist Episcopal Church, was expelled from a Florida train
because he refused to ride in a second-class car labeled "For
Colored People." Arguing in vain that he held a first-class ticket
and had a right to sit in a first-class car, the one-hundred-pound

senior bishop, seventy-one years old and the president of Wilberforce University, was forced off the train and had to carry fourteen pounds of baggage back to Jacksonville, five miles away, during the hottest part of the day. Negroes in Jacksonville and New York held indignation meetings and collected a fund to prosecute the case. When Florida officials did nothing, a deputation of church officers, accompanied by Frederick Douglass, personally protested to Brewster that the United States attorney for the northern district of Florida had failed to enforce the Civil Rights Act and that he had ignored all applications for legal redress. Although the Attorney General promised to investigate the matter,[11] neither he nor any member of his staff took further action. Brewster, in fact, did not even bother to ask his subordinates in Florida about the episode.[12]

The administration again showed that it was unwilling to help Negroes when it rejected the plea of John W. Niles, who had sponsored a plan to colonize his fellow colored men on a strip of Arkansas land. Arrested by state policemen for receiving money under false pretenses, Niles was tried and acquitted, but his funds, amounting to over $5,000, were confiscated. After unsuccessfully appealing through the Arkansas courts for the return of his money, he journeyed to Washington and laid his case before Congress. With the aid of John Sherman his protest was referred to the Senate Committee on Public Lands and the Judiciary, after which it was never heard of again.[13]

Niles's last resort was the President. In a letter to Arthur he charged that both private persons and state authorities willfully deprived Arkansas Negroes of their civil and political rights. As in the election cases, the President passed the matter on without comment to Brewster, who, in turn, rejected each of Niles's allegations. The Attorney General said that it was unfortunate the colored people of Arkansas could not reside on certain unclaimed public lands, but he argued that since these areas were under state control the national government could do nothing. The President and the Attorney General also could not help Negroes who were illegally imprisoned or arbitrarily fined. Brewster advised them to appeal erroneous judicial decisions to the federal courts and to adopt the same recourse when "cruel punishments are inflicted upon colored people at prison farms to which upon trifling pretexts they are condemned." He concluded by insisting that the states alone were empowered to stop mobs which violated Negro rights.[14]

Niles was furious. The "whole tenor of this answer," he said, "is simply to taffy the colored people of the South" who "have been misled by politicians and shysters in the South who have professed friendship to them." He advised Negroes seeking justice to leave the country.[15]

The matter dragged on, forgotten by almost everyone except Niles. Five years later, he told Sherman that he still had not gotten his $5,000 back. Truly, he believed, the colored man had been abandoned by the Republican party.[16]

The third civil rights incident of the Arthur administration flared into the open late in 1883. It stemmed from the decision of the Republican-dominated Supreme Court, speaking through Justice Joseph P. Bradley, to declare illegal the Civil Rights Act of 1875,[17] which guaranteed equal rights in inns, conveyances, and theatres to Negroes and forbade their exclusion from jury duty.*

An important segment of the Republican press applauded the court's ruling. The New York *Evening Post* observed that "The calm with which the country received the news . . .

---

* The five cases concerned complaints by Negroes that they had been refused equal accommodations or privileges. The court ruled that the first section of the Fourteenth Amendment, which guaranteed the rights of persons, prohibited only states and not individuals from restricting civil rights. It also stated that Congress was authorized by the Amendment to adopt only corrective and not general legislation. In dissent, Republican Justice John M. Harlan said that the Thirteenth Amendment, which ended slavery, clearly justified the Civil Rights Act. There is no evidence that Arthur or any member of his staff in any way influenced the decision.

shows how completely the extravagant expectations as well as the fierce passions of the war have died out." According to the Chicago *Tribune,* the verdict was "not likely to create surprise or disturbance." Expressing the merchant's point of view, the New York *Journal of Commerce* remarked that there were "places where the negro is welcome and his custom is desired; there are others where his presence at the tables and in the parlors will seriously interfere with the business of the house. . . . Why," it asked, "should the negro be forced upon the landlord to the injury of his business?" [18]

Many party leaders, however, disapproved of the decision. To Robert Ingersoll it was as "cruel as slavery's lash," while former Secretary of the Interior Samuel J. Kirkwood believed that the Republican members of the court had made a terrible mistake. Sherman said that the judges had undermined "the foundation stone of Republican principles. The Republican party could not endure for a day, but for the fidelity with which it has struggled for the equality of civil rights for all citizens, and against the intolerance of prejudice, color or caste." Louis T. Michener of Indiana noted the "considerable stir" created by the verdict. Sure that "Republicans still have the old feeling" for equal rights, he hoped that the President would recommend the adoption of a constitutional amendment embodying the concepts of the dead bill. "The discussion of the question in 1884," he went on, "will appeal strongly to the moral and liberty loving element of our party, which is so strong when aroused and so indifferent when not aroused." [19]

Negroes also objected to the court's action. "Our faith in the Republican party hangs by the frailest thread," commented T. Thomas Fortune of the New York *Globe.*[20] Colored men held protest meetings in Chicago, Pittsburgh, and San Francisco. At Indianapolis the reassuring statements of Senator Benjamin Harrison, who stated that the Republican party would amend the Constitution, if necessary, to safeguard the rights

of the Negro, had little effect as colored men formed a group
to lobby for the re-enactment of the law. In Washington, Frederick Douglass, scoffing at the statements of Ingersoll, who
urged Negroes not to blame the Republicans for what had hap-
pened, argued that the verdict had put seven million colored
people, "when on a steamboat or railroad or in a theatre, restaurant or other public place, at the mercy of any white ruffian
who may choose to insult them." [21]

After the initial reaction to Bradley's words died down, the
civil rights question became a matter with which the administration had to deal. Paying little heed to the urgings of men
like Harrison and Michener, the President, far from recom-
mending a constitutional amendment or even sponsoring a specific act, merely announced in his annual message that he would
approve any legislation which Congress saw fit to pass.[22] Republicans in Congress introduced five new bills to replace the
one declared illegal, but lacking the strong support of Arthur
they were unable to pass a measure.[23] As in the Niles and
Payne cases, the administration refused to take a strong stand
in defense of the Negro.

III

Little concerned with civil rights incidents and election acts,
Arthur had other plans for breaking the Solid South and for
reassuring his election in 1884. Disregarding the doubts which
had plagued Hayes and Garfield, the President abandoned the
old Republican organizations in the South and worked with
economic radicals such as General William Mahone of Virginia, Rufus K. Garland of Arkansas, George Washington Jones
of Texas, General James R. Chalmers of Mississippi, and General James B. Longstreet of Georgia. Once Democrats, these
men had become Independents after disagreements with party
leaders. Some of them were Greenbackers; others favored the
unlimited coinage of silver dollars; many attacked national

banks; Mahone wanted to readjust—his enemies jeeringly said repudiate—the Virginia state debt by transferring a portion of it to West Virginia and by reducing considerably the scale of payments. At the same time the Independents appealed to Negroes and Southern Republicans with a platform stressing free speech, a fair count, and the strict enforcement of all federal laws.[24]

Although at first glance there seems to be little similarity between Hayes's program in 1877 and Arthur's in 1882, the two schemes had the same objective. Both presidents attempted to foster Republicanism in the South by dropping the Negro-dominated factions and by appealing to discontented white Democrats. Hayes advocated a union with former Southern Whigs who desired internal improvements, while Arthur joined forces with the Independents, but here the differences between the plans end. Each man realized only too well that the Republican party, seriously challenged by the Democracy for control of the national government, needed strong Southern support if it was to remain in power, and each designed a program to do something about this situation.

By far the most important and most successful Independent was Mahone, who in 1880 was elected to the United States Senate. The next year, despite strong opposition, the Republicans of the Old Dominion formally recognized him as their leader by endorsing the entire Readjuster ticket for election.[25] Henceforth only a skeleton Republican party existed in Virginia.

Mahone received the full support of the administration. Soon after Garfield's death the Virginia Senator happily contrasted the Southern policies of the new and the old presidents. While Garfield had done very little to aid the Independents, and had to be pushed into doing anything at all, Arthur from the beginning had wholeheartedly thrown his weight behind all anti-Bourbons in the South.[26] To seal his alliance with Mahone, the

President gave him control of over 200 offices in the Treasury department, 1,700 in the Post Office, seventy in the federal courts, and many in the Norfolk navy yard.[27]

Arthur, moreover, publicly endorsed the Independents and criticized Negroes. He told a prominent Georgia Negro that the Republicans had placed the South in colored hands in 1868 only to find that the Democrats had regained control of the entire section a few years later. "You proved yourselves incapable of holding those States when they were placed bodily in your grasp," Arthur admonished. "Do you think you are capable of regaining what you so allowed to slip through your fingers? There is one thing you want to remember, and that is that men do not fight without hope of reward." If the Independents "are to conquer the Bourbons they will want the offices of their State, and they ought to have them." The President urged Negroes to "unite with the men who can give you success. I have made up my mind," he continued, "that a permanently defeated Republican party is of little value in any State, North or South, and that if any respectable body of men wages war on the Bourbon Democracy, with reasonable prospects of success, it should be sustained." [28]

Arthur frequently repeated these sentiments. During an interview with some white Republicans from Georgia he argued that it was foolish to appoint colored men to Southern posts "as Negro officials do not help the party as much as white officials." A few months later the President complained that he had "been constantly bored by these so-called Southern Republicans, who excel in office begging." [29]

Virginia Negroes received solace for the administration's abandonment of their organization when Mahone pledged to fight for their rights. The Senator wanted "every man to vote, white or black, and I want him to vote as he pleases, and to be neither threatened beforehand nor ostracized afterwards for expressing his free opinion." He was "tired of intolerance."

When men of both races lived harmoniously in the South, Northern capital and enterprise would "come on and develop our resources, and make Virginia as great as she ought to be." [30]

Many important Republican journals approved of Arthur's union with Mahone. Papers like the Washington *National Republican,* the Newark *Daily Advertiser,* the Hartford *Courant,* the Cincinnati *Commercial Gazette,* the *Independent,* and the Chicago *Tribune* stressed the many equalitarian reforms initiated by the Readjusters: they had eliminated punishment by whipping; had repealed the poll tax and enfranchised about 20,000 Negroes; had extended to men of both races the privilege of serving as jurors; had established the Virginia Normal and Industrial Institute for colored people; and had added $40,-000,000 to the state budget for education, most of which was used to establish new Negro schools.[31]

But to many Republican editors both Mahone and his policies were unpalatable. "If the Administration of President Arthur desires to maintain a fair degree of respectability and to avoid becoming an unbearable burden to the Republican party," noted the *Nation,* "it cannot too soon put an end to all political fellowship with Senator Mahone of Virginia." The St. Paul *Pioneer-Press* said that Mahone, since becoming senator, had done nothing but dispense offices. "A few who have watched and waited for the growth of political liberty in the South will more deeply regret the destruction of Virginia's fair hopes," it commented. *Bradstreet's* could not forget that the Readjusters were debt evaders. "It is to be hoped that the members of this corrupt combination will fail of their purpose to retain control of affairs in Virginia," the magazine preached. "The principles upon which they have acted are subversive of that morality which is after all the true life of the state." [32]

Arthur's endorsement of the Independents also split Republican leaders into two factions. To some Mahone was a champion of liberty. Grant, for example, claimed that Readjuster rule would result in freedom for all the voters of Virginia. With Mahone at the helm the Old Dominion would soon "be in a condition to invite immigration of people who will add greatly to the resources as well as to the population of the State. The interests of all citizens will then become so great that no fear need be entertained of bad government, no matter which political party may have the ascendency."[33] Senator John J. Ingalls agreed:

I believe in the universal diffusion of political rights, accompanied by efficient guarantees for the protection of life, the security of property, and the preservation of personal liberty. The Republican Party in the South has shown itself incapable of securing these ends. Were I a Virginian I should act with Mahone, believing that he represents the progressive elements, by whose supremacy race prejudice will be obliterated, the ballot made free and priceless, and the South regenerated through the beneficent energy of impartial justice and universal education.[34]

Even John Sherman, who as Hayes's Secretary of the Treasury had bitterly denounced all repudiators, now thought well of the Readjusters and endorsed Mahone.[35]

James G. Blaine led the opposition to Mahone. Long had he detested repudiators.[36] Moreover, as early as 1882 he and Arthur emerged as the leading contenders for the next Republican presidential nomination. Lack of Southern support had lost for Blaine the coveted prize in 1880, and he knew only too well that he would be defeated in 1884 unless he controlled the section. A Virginia delegation led by Mahone would go solidly for Arthur, but the regular Republican organization in the state almost unanimously favored the Plumed Knight. The contest between Blaine and the administration over Mahone, then, was to a large extent a prelude to the convention of 1884.[37]

Shortly before the campaign of 1882 began, Arthur at a cabinet meeting put Chandler and Brewster in charge of Southern affairs. Realizing that the two had far greater experience in such matters than he did, the President insisted that they employ every means possible to elect anti-Bourbons at the coming elections. Henceforth, the Secretary of the Navy and the Attorney General were to speak for the administration on the subject.[38]

At the very moment Arthur's official family was doing its utmost to help the Readjuster candidates, Blaine exploded a bombshell. In a long interview with the Chicago *Tribune* he bitterly attacked Mahone. Prefacing his remarks with a statement that he did not intend to interfere in any way with the Virginia canvass, Blaine proceeded to do just what he said he would not. "Frankness" forced him to express his "entire sympathy with the straight Republican movement in that State." He considered it "a great political blunder" for the administration to unite with the Readjusters. "The Republican party has been always devoted to upholding the public faith," Blaine said. For it "To turn around and join the repudiation wing of the Virginia Democracy" was "the last degree of folly." It was dishonorable for Republicans to associate with a man such as Mahone. Blaine suggested, however, that the federal government help Virginia settle its debt problem because the loss of West Virginia during the Civil War had "torn and dismembered" the state. "It is not, in my judgment, fair or right that Virginia alone should be made the victim for the sins of the dead Confederacy," he said. Not in the least concerned with the fate of the Negro, Blaine during his discussion completely ignored this aspect of the subject.[39]

Blaine was not content solely with giving interviews. He drew up plans, which were never used, for touring Virginia with Frederick Douglass, who was to tell colored Republicans that if they supported Mahone they would cease to be recognized by Blaine's friends and would not be in line for future benefits.[40]

Arthur and his followers fought back. The President now announced that he intended to support the Independents in

North Carolina.[41] George C. Gorham, editor of the Washington
National Republican, the administration's semi-official journal,
viciously denounced Blaine and accused him of allying with
the Redeemers.[42]

Even Chandler, until recently a vigorous supporter of Blaine,
scolded his onetime idol. To him, as to almost every prominent Republican since 1877, the issue was largely political. The
terms of the constitutions recently adopted by Pennsylvania and
New York had seriously crippled the party in the North, the
Secretary told Blaine. If the Republicans were to win the next
House of Representatives, they must cooperate with the Independents. The party needed twenty Southern seats.

It is our imperative duty to get them if they can be obtained by
honest and honorable means. The real question cannot be evaded
by cavilling about Mahone and the readjustment of the Virginia
debt, which has now ceased to be an issue or a practical question;
nor about Chalmers and his Fort Pillow record. Those are only
incidents of a great popular revolt at the South against Bourbon
democratic rule and practices. Every independent democrat or
coalition candidate at the South fully and sincerely pledges himself
in favor of a free vote, an honest count, the obliteration of race dis-
tinctions and popular education by a common school system; while
in every case the Bourbon democratic candidate is in fact against
all these principles and depends for his success upon their suppression.

Chandler advised Blaine to endorse the Independents "immediately and emphatically." [43]

Soon thereafter, Gorham initiated a new line of attack against
Blaine. He claimed that, by abusing Mahone, Blaine was de-
parting from the policy of Garfield, who had personally told
Gorham, J. Donald Cameron, and Charles Emory Smith of the
Philadelphia *Press* that Mahone's memorandum on the debt
question was an "honest document." Garfield allegedly had
pledged to treat Mahone as an administration senator and

had favored an arrangement between the Republicans and the Readjusters.[44]

The great pro-Blaine editors of the East, Charles Emory Smith of the *Press* and Whitelaw Reid of the New York *Tribune*, defended their hero. Although Smith refused to comment upon the validity of the Garfield interview, to which he had supposedly been a witness, he vigorously attacked the administration's plans for the South. Mahone's war on Bourbonism was admirable, but "his arbitrary assessments and his open proclamation of the spoils system" were the very antitheses of good government. Moreover, Arthur's endorsement of Chalmers was detestable. It was too much to expect Republicans to endorse a man who "so conspicuously and offensively supported the Bourbon policy of fraud, terrorism and atrocity. We do not want to revive the unhappy memories of the war, but we cannot forget that Chalmers was the butcher of Fort Pillow." [45]

Unlike Smith, Reid took direct issue with Gorham. His paper recalled that only two weeks before being shot Garfield had told a delegation of Virginians that, as a lifelong Republican, he was "positively and emphatically opposed to any party or people *whose belief would militate against the public faith or credit*. Virginia Republicans must decide," Garfield had continued, *"whether the Readjuster movement was tainted with repudiation. If it was, they ought not to support it."* The *Tribune* commented on the obvious: "Somehow there is a strange discrepancy between the authentic public words of the President and the private assurances which he gave to Mr. Gorham." [46]

A few days later, Reid published a devastating editorial on the administration's Southern policy. Throughout Virginia, he asserted, Readjusters were replacing loyal Republicans in office. In the Lynchwood post office an ex-Confederate soldier had recently displaced a one-legged Union veteran. At Manassas a lady whose family had been loyal to the Union was turned out of the post office because her brother opposed

Mahone. In South Carolina the administration was supporting Colonel E. B. C. Cash, a rebel "guilty of murders so atrocious that they shocked a community accustomed to scenes of blood." Chalmers, too, was despicable. Arthur's policy of placing

the negro vote under the control of the desperadoes of the South is ominous of evil. There is no moral strength to such a movement. It is inherently and inevitably bad—bad for the Republican party in the South, bad for it in the North, bad for the negro, bad for the country. . . . To take a new departure and accept for Republican leaders in the South men so bad that they were forced out of the Democratic party is a blunder so deplorable and withal so stupid that no previous Republican Administration would ever possibly commit it. Should not a halt be called? [47]

As the public champion of the administration's program, Chandler did not let these remarks go unanswered. Only an alliance between the Independents and the Republicans, he told Reid, could end atrocities such as that recently perpetrated in Lancaster County, South Carolina, where Democrats had shot four colored men in broad daylight during a meeting addressed by Cash. The white butchers of these Negroes had been allowed to go free. If the anti-Bourbon vote of the county was "not entirely suppressed," Chandler went on, "it will not be for lack of political murders." The Lancaster victims must be avenged. "Their blood cries from the ground to Northern Republicans." [48]

The editor and the Secretary, representing respectively the views of Blaine and Arthur, continued their argument throughout the next year. Late in 1883 the *Tribune* again denounced the Independents. A bargain with the Readjusters, the paper said, would cost the party more votes in the North than it could possibly gain in the South. When Mahone was "ready to advocate Republican principles, openly and without reservation, honorable and advantageous alliance is possible. Until then," Reid believed, "the Republicans had better look to the intelligence and the convictions of Northern voters for success, as they have done hitherto." [49]

Chandler read the editorial "with regret." To him the debt question was dead. "It was but an incident of a great struggle against Bourbon Democracy in favor of free speech, free education, free suffrage, and an honest counting of ballots." He pleaded with Reid to change his paper's policy.[50]

After Reid made a few favorable comments about Mahone, the Secretary thanked him. "In the fight that is before us," Chandler wrote, "the southern question is important and we must encourage every anti-Bourbon who takes his position without regard to his past." He urged Reid to give as much space as possible to the recent butcherings of Negroes by the Redeemers.[51]

Some anti-Readjuster members of the regular Republican organization of Virginia, which strongly supported Blaine, also troubled the administration. In open letters to the President, to the Secretaries of the Navy and the Treasury, to the Postmaster General, and to the head of the Civil Service Commission, John F. Dezendorf, a former member of Congress from the Norfolk district, accused Mahone of violating the civil service act by levying assessments against officeholders and by making federal offices rewards for services to the Readjuster party. According to Dezendorf, some friends of the Senator who received pay checks from the Norfolk navy yard had never seen the place and could not tell a battleship from a torpedo. Worst of all, Mahone's policies had seriously demoralized the colored voters of Virginia, who now believed that they would never obtain political, social, and economic equality.[52]

Dezendorf got little sympathy from the administration. Postmaster General Walter Q. Gresham told him that if he had any further complaints about Virginia officeholders he should inform the authorities at Washington directly, not through the newspapers.[53] Chandler charged that Dezendorf, "a constant

candidate for Congress since 1878," was "seeking special support from the voters" employed at the Norfolk yard.[54]

Dezendorf's rejoinder was just as scornful. He accused
Chandler and the President of "turning a deaf ear" to "the many
wrongs being perpetrated on Republicans in Virginia . . .
being as I am bound to believe, committed to the support of
Senator Mahone by an arrangement which could not be violated." Having failed to obtain aid from the administration,
the Republicans of the Old Dominion would now appeal to
the people of the North.[55]

A board of naval officers, after investigating, decided that
the accusations against the commandant of the navy yard were
unjustified. Chandler warned him to be more orderly and economical but dismissed the charge that political assessments
had been levied against workers. The Secretary also denied
that naval officers were unduly subservient to Mahone.[56] So
far, the Virginia Senator's friends in the administration had
defended him against all comers.

IV

In supporting the Independents, Arthur and Chandler, concerned principally with building up their party in the South,
were aiding some of the colored man's worst enemies. Chalmers,
Cash, and Longstreet were pronounced Negro baiters of long
standing; in Georgia the President gave the patronage to Emory
Speer and deserted William Pledger, the colored state Republican chairman; and even to Mahone, the darling of the movement, the welfare of the Negro was certainly a secondary
consideration.[57]

Despite this fact, Southern Republicans followed the administration's advice and between 1880 and 1882 shifted their support to Independent candidates. In the Congressional elections
of 1882 the South sent eight Independents, four more than in
1880, and eight Republicans to the House. Six of the Inde-

pendents came from Virginia, one was from North Carolina, and Chalmers represented Mississippi. Although in 1880 the Republicans had taken twenty-nine of the forty-three Virginia counties with Negro majorities, the party carried none in 1882. The Readjusters, however, triumphed in thirty-three. The story in North Carolina was similar. The Republicans in 1880 won seventeen of the state's twenty-two Negro-dominated counties, but two years later they lost all of them, while the Independents carried nineteen of them.[58]

Most Negro leaders accepted Arthur's schemes because of their long association with Republicanism and because they depended upon patronage for their livelihoods. Frederick Douglass, by now a party wheel horse, in 1882 refused to accompany Blaine on an anti-Readjuster tour of Virginia because he was "just as heartily in favor of the Mahone movement in Virginia as any man now on the stump assisting that movement." He approved "of any decent movement looking to the abolition of the color line in American politics." John Mercer Langston, the Old Dominion's most prominent Negro, who was serving as Arthur's minister to Haiti, agreed. "The success of the Mahone movement in Virginia means education, liberty, a free ballot, and a fair count for the colored man and the abolition of the whipping-post," he stressed, "and I am for it heart and soul, and not against it." [59]

Like Douglass and Langston, almost every Negro paper endorsed the administration. T. Thomas Fortune's New York *Globe* alone accused the President of deserting the colored man. Like the rest the Washington *Bee* believed that "The sure road to progress for the colored people in Virginia is their adherence to the liberal policy" advocated by Senator Mahone. Before "this revolution under General Mahone was made a fact, a black man stood as much chance to get justice as a cat would to get out of perdition without claws." [60]

Although a few Negroes suggested that members of their

race form their own party, William Calvin Chase, owner of the *Bee*, discounted such talk. The instigators of the idea, he said, were relatively obscure figures, like the editor of the Savannah *Echo*, Fortune, Peter H. Clark of Ohio, who recently had become a Democrat, William Still of Pennsylvania, and George T. Downing of Rhode Island. The great colored leaders— Douglass, Langston, Robert Brown Elliott of South Carolina, ex-Senator Blanche K. Bruce of Mississippi, and John R. Lynch, Republican national committeeman from Mississippi—were all loyal to Arthur. Of the 120 Negro newspapers in the country only two, the *Globe* and the *Echo*, criticized the administration, "and the *Echo* only so far as relates to local politics. On national issues," Chase went on, "that newspaper is reliably Republican." Fortune was "an able writer, but his influence is confined to his readers. He does not affect public opinion at large among our people to any great extent." The Washington home of Bruce, the Register of the Treasury, was a meeting place for prominent colored men, Chase related. The tenor of the discussions carried on there conclusively showed "that the negro has not weakened and will not weaken in his allegiance to the Republican party, and that desertions are mainly due to spite or to the desire and hope of office." [61]

Almost immediately, Fortune declared war upon Chase. He called the editor of the *Bee* a partisan who spoke only because the Republicans had bribed him with printing jobs paying a few hundred dollars a year. "Mr. Bruce and Mr. Lynch have each rebelled against party dictation in refusing to indorse Fort Pillow Chalmers," Fortune argued, "although commanded to do so by Mr. Chandler, who furnishes Mr. Arthur's Administration with what I might call organizing brains—and a pretty mess he has made of it so far." The Republican record since 1876 had been disgraceful. To elect Hayes and Wheeler the party had abandoned the Negroes of South Carolina, Louisiana, and Florida to the Bourbons. Once in the White House, Hayes had capped a "whining, vacillating, temporizing policy" by appointing dozens of Southern Democrats to office. Garfield had done little better. Having received a delegation of South Carolina Negroes, headed by ex-Congressman Robert Brown Elliott, a graduate of Eton College in England, with a "haughty and indifferent manner," he callously advised them that if they went home and studied Webster's speller they would be on the road to success. Garfield had also revoked Douglass's appointment as marshal of the District of Columbia and had given him instead an inferior post, Recorder of Deeds. The present administration was just as bad. It was supporting such chronic Negro haters as Chalmers, Cash, Speer, and Longstreet and had completely ignored the services rendered to the party by colored men like Lynch, ex-Governor Pinckney B. S. Pinchback of Louisiana, and D. Augustus Straker, professor of common law at Allen University, Columbia, South Carolina.[62]

So closely allied were most Negroes with the Republican party that Arthur's opponents could accomplish little. A national colored convention held in Louisville in September, 1883, took a neutral position: the administration was neither censured nor endorsed.[63]

Eventually, even Fortune came out for Mahone. He finally admitted that because of the Independents the Negroes of Virginia were happier and freer than ever before. Mahone had "revolutionized the State, so that it is no longer a heaven for whites and hell for the blacks." [64] The Negro revolt, extremely limited to begin with, thus quickly died out.

v

The Independents prepared carefully for the 1883 elections, which were mainly for state offices. During the summer of that year, Mahone, Longstreet, Cash, Chalmers and other leaders met in Washington to define campaign strategy. They also discussed the best means of obtaining the nomination and election of Arthur, their protector and abettor, in 1884.[65]

The Independents' plans for 1883 collapsed when two incidents paved the way for a smashing Bourbon victory in the South. The first one occurred on the Saturday before election day in Danville, Virginia. In that city Negroes constituted a majority of the town council, over which a carpetbagger presided, four of the town's nine policemen, all the justices of the peace, the clerk of the market, and twenty of the twenty-four renters of stalls in the market. During a brawl between men of both races, two whites and seven Negroes, four of whom later died, were shot.[66]

The whole state was ablaze. The Democrats conjured up visions of Black Reconstruction. The governor called out the state militia. In Lynchburg a mass meeting, presided over by General Jubal A. Early, unanimously approved a resolution urging whites to keep Negroes "in their proper places." The Redeemers now carefully and systematically suppressed the Republican vote of the Danville area. The citizens of Danville, who in 1882 had cast 841 Readjuster and 663 Democratic ballots in an election for Congressman-at-large, in 1883 gave the Bourbon candidates for the state legislature 905 votes and the Readjusters only twenty-eight. Of the 235 colored registrants in North Danville only three, all Democrats, dared to vote in 1883; the Readjusters, who in 1882 had secured 115 votes, did not receive any the next year. In the nearby town of New Design only one of the 465 registered Negroes showed up at the polls. The Bourbons were equally as successful in other areas. The Readjuster tally in Charles City County, whose colored population was almost two and one-half times as great as its white, shrank from 481 in 1882 to sixty-one in 1883, while the Democratic score leaped from 214 to 405. In Charlotte County, Negro by two to one, the Redeemer vote tripled.

Sweeping the state, the Democrats captured two-thirds of both branches of the legislature. The defeat broke the back of the Readjuster movement. Congratulations poured into Democratic state headquarters from all over the South.[67]

The second atrocity took place at Hazelhurst, Mississippi. On the evening before the election Congressman Ethelbert Barksdale told a mob that the Democrats would win even if it required the use of shotguns. The next day, a group of vigilantes murdered J. P. Matthews, the white chairman of the Republican Executive Committee of Copiah County, who had defied a warning to stay away from the polls. As a result of the election Mississippi fell more deeply than ever under Bourbon control.[68]

The Independent defeats in 1883 had the same effect upon Arthur as the Republican failures in Louisiana and South Carolina in 1878 had had upon Hayes. Arthur now became convinced that his Southern program had failed. Clearly, the Independents could not be expected to beat the Redeemers in 1884. The President, therefore, informed a White House conference of party leaders that the Danville and Copiah County incidents were to be kept constantly before the public. He hoped that by election time a Solid Republican North could be arrayed against the Solid Democratic South. The Danville murders were regarded as ample proof that the Readjusters were not fairly treated by the Democrats. Mahone would still be supported by the administration, but Arthur and Chandler no longer expected him to carry Virginia. All Republicans were encouraged to wave the bloody shirt.[69]

The President angrily blamed Blaine and the New York *Tribune* for the collapse of the Independent movements. He told a New York *Times* reporter that the Virginia defeat was the result of the insidious tactics of those Republican politicians and editors who had continually and openly complained about Mahone's principles and methods. By denouncing the Readjusters, they had paved the way for the Bourbon triumph. Since the election the courts of Virginia had been purged of Independents by the Redeemer-controlled state legislature; not one Mahone man had been left on the bench. Honest elections were now a thing of the past in the Old Dominion. Because of Blaine the Democrats were as solidly entrenched in Virginia as they were in South Carolina, Mississippi, and Alabama; Independents throughout the South, who had looked to Mahone for leadership and inspiration, were in a state of despondency and despair.[70]

The administration's new plans for the South were speedily put into effect. With the aid and support of Mahone, John Sherman introduced, and the Senate passed by a party vote, a resolution to investigate the "Alleged Election Outrages in Virginia and Mississippi." [71] Chandler's newspaper, the Washington *National Republican,* issued long denunciations of the Redeemers. To it the Danville and Copiah County murders clearly revealed the brutal nature of Bourbonism. Proudly the journal announced that Grant believed Southern atrocities should be an important issue in the coming election.[72]

The reports of the Danville and Copiah County committees followed political lines. The Republican majority investigating the Mississippi murder recommended that each House of Congress refuse to seat members elected by frauds. It concluded that Matthews had been "slain solely because he was an eminent and influential Republican, that his death might strike terror into opponents of the Democratic party and enable that party, being in a minority of legal votes, to take possession of Copiah County." The Democrats countered by affirming that the Republicans, being in need of ammunition for the coming presidential campaign, were using the incident for political purposes.[73]

The Danville committee reached similar conclusions. The Republicans complained that the slaughter of the four Negroes had been premeditated and that the killers had gone free. They suggested a reduction in the Congressional representation of any state which allowed suffrage to be abridged. The Democratic minority viewed the affair as an encounter which, like the Copiah County case, was being blown up out of all proportion by ambitious Republican politicians.[74]

A short while after the completion of the investigations, the Republican national convention met at Chicago. Virginians sent two delegations. The regular Republican group was solidly for Blaine, while the Readjusters favored the President. After a controversy the convention seated the Mahone faction, whose banner read "We are for Arthur because Arthur is for us." On the fourth ballot Blaine was nominated for president. Although he now professed friendship for the Readjusters,[75] the candidate actually had little use for them. In August Blaine's friends told Mahone that the Independents would no longer be aided. As Mahone later lamented, "we were absolutely abandoned by the National Committee [in 1884], though we came within three thousand votes of giving our electoral vote to Blaine and Logan." With the Republican organization tightly in Blaine's hands during the next four years, the Independent movements in the South disappeared completely.[76]

All of Arthur's schemes had little permanent effect upon the life of the Negro. In 1884 Southern Republicans were no better off than they had been in 1881. Frederick Douglass, whose loyalty to the party never wavered, later had the last word on Arthur's policies: "there is nothing in his career as President of the U. S. that proves him to have had any sympathy with the oppressed colored people of the South." [77]

6

Manufacturers, Mugwumps, and Merchants

I

DURING 1884 and 1885 three important groups of Northerners opposed agitation of the sectional question. The first one consisted of those Republican politicians and Eastern manufacturers who believed that if the race issue was dropped Southern whites interested in a high tariff would undoubtedly join the Republican party and would break up the Solid South. Mugwumps * also disliked the war themes. They argued that the Negro, ignorant and easily controlled by machine politicians, was not worth worrying about. Only the forces of time and education, they felt, could permanently solve the race problem.

* Although the Mugwumps, or Northern Independents, in some ways escape definition, they generally advocated tariff reductions, sound currency, and civil service reform, and were not bound by party loyalties. With a few exceptions they were Anglo-Saxon Protestants, lived along the Eastern seaboard, and were linked to the culture and habitat of New England. They are not to be confused with the Southern Independents discussed in the previous chapter.

The last group contained merchants who feared that their Southern customers would be offended if sectional themes were stressed. They too demanded that the war questions be taken out of politics.

Early in 1884 James G. Blaine, the Republican presidential nominee, adopted the argument of the Eastern manufacturers. Like Hayes in 1877 and Arthur in 1882, he decided to ignore the plight of the Negro and to try to win over to Republicanism a special body of Southern whites. Shunning the bloody shirt, the candidate in his letter of acceptance wooed Southern protectionists. He happily noted that differences between the North and South were being quickly rubbed out. The two sections were friendlier now than at any other time since the founding of the Republic. According to Blaine, the South needed "capital and occupation, not controversy." Its prosperity depended upon the continuance of the Republican tariff and currency programs. Southern industrialists who voted Democratic were actually lending "their Electoral votes to destroy their own future." [1]

Important Republican papers applauded the letter. "Those who hope for a new unfurling of 'the bloody shirt' will find no encouragement in Mr. Blaine's generous and manly utterance concerning the South and its relation to the whole Union," commented the Newark *Daily Advertiser*. The Chicago *Tribune* called Blaine's words "conciliatory and patriotic." [2]

Blaine believed a series of high tariff speeches would put West Virginia in the Republican column in October. "Appealing to a new South," he urged a Grafton audience "to look to the front, to the future." West Virginia, Virginia, North Carolina, Georgia, Alabama, Louisiana, and Tennessee were "all interested in a protective tariff, and the question is, which do they prefer to gratify prejudice, or to promote general prosperity!" West Virginia could "lead the way, she can break this seemingly impregnable barrier of the Solid South; . . . solid on what?

Solid on a prejudice, solid on a tradition, solid upon doctrines that separate the different portions of the Union." He implored residents of the state "to join in a union not merely in form, but a union in fact, and to take part in the solution of the industrial and financial problems of the time." [3]

The National Committee, led by Benjamin Franklin Jones, president of Jones and Laughlin steel corporation, did its part. In "An Appeal to the South" it requested "the sympathy and cooperation of all the citizens of all sections who recognize the supremacy of the great and living economic questions that rise above all old issues." Jones urged former Southern Whigs interested in a high tariff to "take up—under the leadership of [Henry] Clay's successor and with the tremendous advantage of 23 years of republican protection vindicating the beneficence of Clay's statesmanship—the American policies for which [Andrew] Jackson and Clay fought, and were ready to die if need came." Under the "'American system' of protection" the South had industrialized at a phenomenal rate. North Carolina already had ninety-two cotton mills; Tennessee had eighty-three; Georgia, sixty-two; South Carolina, thirty-one; Maryland, twenty-four; Alabama, twenty-three; Virginia, fourteen; Mississippi, eleven; Louisiana, seven; Texas, six; Kentucky, five; Arkansas, four; and Florida, two. Since 1880 the South had doubled its annual output of plows, had added 900,000 new spindles and 8,000 miles of rails, and had increased its assessable property by $640,000,000. Moreover, coal production in Georgia had risen from nothing in 1870 to 154,000 tons in 1880; during the same period Alabama had gone from 11,000 tons to 322,000 tons. This great progress would be jeopardized if the South yielded to prejudice and voted for Grover Cleveland.[4]

Despite their active campaign, Blaine and Jones failed in West Virginia. The Republican party went down to defeat, although it registered sizable gains in many areas. Of the state's fifty-five counties, all of which had white majorities, nineteen, five more than in 1880, went Republican in 1884. While Garfield had captured only two of the seven biggest coal mining and industrial counties, Blaine took six of them. The Republicans won two of the three largest iron producing counties in both elections.[5]

Disillusioned, Blaine altered his tactics. The bloody shirt was once more unfurled. At Fort Wayne a short time after the West Virginia debacle, the candidate insisted that frauds in the October election "have put a new phase on the National contest, or rather they have reproduced an old phase." He charged that the Democrats controlled the 153 electoral votes of the sixteen Southern states by illegal methods. If Cleveland was elected in November, rebels would dictate the nation's economic policies. "It would be as if the dead Stuarts were recalled to the throne of England, as if the Bourbons should be invited to administer the government of the French Republic, as though the Florentine Dukes should be called back and empowered to govern the great Kingdom of Italy." [6] In a series of stump speeches throughout Indiana, Blaine repeatedly stressed this theme.[7] In spite of his original intentions he had adopted the argument used, in one form or another, by every Republican presidential candidate since the war.

II

The Mugwumps were ready for Blaine and his sectionalism. Although many of them had once championed the Negro, they were by now disillusioned and wanted the Republican party to drop the race question.[8]

One of the first of the group to change his mind about the freedmen was Carl Schurz. In 1865, after a Southern tour, he had recommended that the Negro be enfranchised, disregarding the fact that "the [white] masses are strongly opposed to colored suffrage." [9] But in 1870, when he realized that uneducated Negroes were an easy prey for spoilsmen, Schurz admitted that he had erred. As his autobiography relates, "There was discernible in Mr. Schurz's attitude on the Southern question profound discontent with the practical working of negro suffrage and of the Republican party machinery in general as well in the reconstructed States." To his disgust the machine politicians in Missouri, his home state, dominated the scene by manipulating ignorant, but enfranchised, Negroes. Henceforth, Schurz steadfastly opposed all legislation designed to aid the colored man. And he assumed that anyone who tried to stir up sectional passions had yielded to the worst elements in the Republican organization.[10]

Although the transition in the thinking of George William Curtis, the editor of *Harper's Weekly*, was far different, he eventually reached the same conclusion. Like Schurz, Curtis after the war had favored Negro suffrage. He argued that the freedmen had proven their loyalty and deserved the ballot. Admittedly, many of them were ignorant, but so were "great masses of the Northern voters. Education," he wrote, "is a good thing; but it appears that some of the staunchest patriots in the land can not read, and that some of the basest traitors are highly educated." [11] In 1872 his magazine attacked Horace Greeley, the Democratic and Liberal Republican presidential candidate, because he supposedly had allied with the enemies of the freedmen. Curtis supported Hayes's course in 1877, but by the next year he once more concluded that the Bourbons were not to be trusted. During the 1880 campaign *Harper's Weekly* vigorously denounced the Solid South. The permanent change in Curtis's thinking occurred in 1882. He then said that the Southern question was dead. The federal government could do nothing more to help the Negro.[12] After that, Curtis joined Schurz in resisting all attempts to stir up the race issue.

A third distinct case was Edwin L. Godkin of the *Nation*. Although he begrudgingly advocated the enfranchisement of the Negro after the Civil War, he never abandoned the convic-

tion that white Anglo-Saxons were inherently superior to "ignorant foreigners" and atavistic colored men. "I do not oppose
the admission [to suffrage] of such Negroes as shall prove their
fitness," Godkin wrote in 1865. ". . . What I ask, and meant to
ask was not that the blacks shall be excluded *as blacks,* but
simply that they shall not be admitted to the franchise simply
because they are blacks and have been badly treated." The
former slaves should be put to "a moral as well as an educational
test, such, for instance, as proof of disposition to earn a liveli-
hood, or support a family by honest labor." [13] The next year
Godkin recommended the disfranchisement of all Negroes who
could not learn to read within two years. Only by developing
his intelligence could the colored man distinguish between
"statesman and demagogue; between honest public men and
knavish public men; between his own real friends and his real
enemies." Although Godkin originally supported the Radical
plan of Reconstruction, which provided for military enforcement of Negro suffrage, he was convinced by 1871 that this
venture had failed. "We owe it to human nature to say that
worse governments have seldom been seen in a civilized country," the editor admitted. "They have been composed of trashy
whites and ignorant blacks." Control of Southern affairs should
be returned to those "who have most influence and knowledge." [14] Godkin hereafter believed that "The real independence of the voter at the South will come, as elsewhere, slowly
through education, the acquisition of property, and the mutual
respect which results from long-continued order, prosperity,
and general intelligence." The simple truth was that the freedmen were unfit for the role the Republicans desired them to
play: "Any party in which the negro is in the majority, cannot
help having its policy, if not shaped, greatly influenced by
their political ignorance and incapacity." [15]

The full force of the unsystematic but powerful Mugwump
opposition to sectionalism was first felt in 1884, when members

of the group bolted the Republican party and supported the Democratic candidate for president, Grover Cleveland. James Freeman Clarke, the Unitarian minister, early in the campaign decried the "republican bourbonism" which deemed it necessary to rehash the war issues. He denied that Blaine could solve a problem which had completely baffled Grant.[16] A few weeks later, at a national meeting of Mugwumps, chairman Charles R. Codman of Massachusetts asserted that he detested Southern outrages against the Negro as much as any man, but he refused to believe that the Democrats were responsible for them or that the Republicans could stop them. "No, gentlemen," he stated, "the truth is that time and education and enlightened self-interest and the influence of civilization and Christianity are the agencies that must be relied upon to prevent these crimes." [17] Similarly, Henry C. Lea, the Philadelphia reformer, argued "that to-day long-headed Pennsylvania ironmasters are more afraid of Southern pig than Southern votes." [18]

The most vociferous of all the Mugwumps was Thomas Wentworth Higginson. A former abolitionist and wartime commander of a Negro regiment, he had favored sectional reconciliation since being mustered out.[19] At a Vermont rally for Cleveland he announced that he "was sick and tired of having the colored people of the South, whom I know so well, used merely as pawns or dice in a game played by political tricksters." Higginson hoped that all younger men would reject outdated themes and make honest government the question of the day. The next month, in a widely publicized address entitled "The Young Men's Party," he pointed out that the Republicans endlessly glorified a "single Copiah massacre," but they said nothing about the hundreds of Southern counties in which integrated schools were open to children of both races on equal terms. It was ridiculous to believe that ignorant Negroes could control intelligent whites. "Sooner or later," he said, "in the most unlimited form of popular government, education and property will assert their inevitable influence for good or for evil." [20]

Senator George Frisbie Hoar fought back. He told the Massachusetts Republican convention that the Independents were intentionally ignoring Bourbon atrocities in the South. Cleveland could be elected only if the Democratic minority controlled the South "by murder and fraud." It was "idle" and "wicked" of men like Higginson to tell "us, when we call the attention of the American people to these facts, that we are waving the bloody shirt." [21]

Other issues, some of which proved to be more vital than the race question, played roles in the campaign of 1884. Of prime importance were the "Mulligan letters," which showed that Blaine, while a Congressman, had been bribed to help obtain a land grant for an Arkansas railroad. Curtis reprinted them in *Harper's Weekly* throughout the canvass. Blaine's chances for the presidency were also hurt when, shortly before election day, he failed to rebuke a clergyman for referring to the Democrats as the party of "Rum, Romanism, and Rebellion." Many of the Irish Catholic voters in New York undoubtedly turned against Blaine because of this incident. All of these factors were felt on election day when Cleveland beat Blaine, although nationally the Democratic plurality was only 62,000 votes.[22]

To Thomas Nast, the foremost Mugwump cartoonist, the results marked the end of the Southern question. His cover illustration for the *Harper's Weekly* number of November 22, 1884, entitled "One of the First-Fruits of the Victory," showed a Negro clasping hands with a Southern planter under an American flag as the newly elected President approvingly remarked, "Shake heartily boys!" Nast reserved a special reward for Blaine. In "Spontaneous Combustion" the Republican candidate was blasted into the stratosphere by the exploding gases in his carpetbag, labeled "20 Years of Bloody Shirt—And More (?)." [23]

By now Hoar was completely disgusted. "Whether our mug-wumps will ever be of any value to any good cause, I am not prepared to say . . . ," he wrote Henry Cabot Lodge. "They are totally indifferent to the fate of the negro and the establishment of honest suffrage at the South, and indeed have not much belief in the capacity of mankind in general for suffrage anywhere." [24]

Blaine now resorted to bloody shirt tactics. In a bitter speech delivered at Augusta, Maine, he charged that the Bourbons had cheated him out of the presidency. Over 1,100,000 Negro voters, representing forty-two electoral votes, had been illegally disfranchised in the South. Blaine noted that Louisiana, Mississippi, Alabama, Georgia, and South Carolina had forty-eight electoral votes and 5,800,000 people, three million of whom were disfranchised Negroes. Yet Wisconsin, Iowa, Minnesota, Kansas, and California, with 5,600,000 people, none of whom were robbed of their constitutional rights, also had forty-eight electoral votes. Thus, reasoned Blaine, 2,800,000 Southerners had as much political power as 5,600,000 Northerners; the vote of one rebel was equal to that of two Union men.[25]

The Mugwump press mercilessly condemned Blaine's logic. The *Nation, Harper's Weekly,* and the Springfield *Daily Republican* agreed that the "utterances of this remarkable demagogue" proved that the country had been remarkably fortunate "in escaping four years of him with his varied powers of mischief and his relentless activity in the Presidential chair." [26] Clearly, the Independents hated sectionalists.

III

With the opposition controlling the national government Republicans throughout the North in 1885 followed the course charted in Blaine's Augusta speech. They repeatedly protested against Southern outrages. Early in the year William M. Evarts, the new Senator from New York, insisted that the Redeemers "remained in heart, substance, and purpose" as rebellious as they had been in 1861.[27] Significantly, Murat Halstead entitled his anti-Southern article in the *North American Review* for March, 1885, "The Revival of Sectionalism."[28] At Woodstock, Connecticut, John A. Logan delivered an Independence Day speech in support of equal rights for all citizens.[29] Iowa and Pennsylvania Republicans framed strong planks on the free ballot, while papers like the Syracuse *Journal*, the Hartford *Courant*, and the *Iowa State Register*, formerly silent on the race question, began hammering away at the Bourbons.[30]

The sentiments of William E. Chandler were typical of those Republicans who resented Cleveland's victory. "Every dog may have his day," he revealed, "but that of the treasonable northern democracy allied with southern suppressers of free suffrage by fraud and murder will be a short one." All true Republicans would "fight against the democratic party, led by the confederacy again in the saddle. It will not this time take four years to unhorse it."[31]

During the Massachusetts campaign Republicans frequently denounced the Bourbons. Hoar stressed that his party was the true friend of the South. Republicans had sponsored bills to educate the section's illiterates, had passed tariffs to protect its infant industries, and had adopted the war amendments to free all Southerners from the shackles of slavery. To the Senator the election of 1884 was a disgrace which could have been easily avoided if the federal government had enacted the legislation necessary to protect all voters. In a like tone Henry Cabot Lodge argued that the highest Republican duty was to preserve "the freedom and purity of the ballot box."[32]

Mugwumps again opposed this kind of talk. In an open letter on "The 'Suppressed' Negro Vote," Higginson explained that he and other abolitionists, including James Freeman Clarke and Francis W. Bird, had studied "the southern question apart from the bias of politics" and had come to the conclusion that colored men neither needed nor desired Northern aid. After having corresponded with and talked to many of the South Carolina, Georgia, and Florida Negroes who had served in his Civil War regiment, Higginson was certain that few of them were illegally disfranchised; most of them admitted that they did not vote simply because they were uninformed and not interested in politics.[33] Higginson even condoned the enactment of complicated Southern election laws designed to confuse illiterate Negroes, such as the Eight-Box act requiring separate ballots and receptacles for each office being voted upon. Since only educated men could comprehend involved methods, these measures amounted to a literacy test and achieved indirectly what many Northern states decreed directly. "The Massachusetts way," Higginson went on, "is more honorable, no doubt; but suppose an attempt were made to import our system into South Carolina, it would at once be denounced in every Republican convention as an outrage almost worthy of Mississippi."[34]

To Republicans this reasoning was detestable. Former Governor John D. Long of Massachusetts had little use for "Col. Higginson and the [Boston] Advertiser [who] say 'education should be on top.'"[35] And Hoar denounced "my mugwump friends" who called any discussion of Southern frauds

waving the bloody shirt. They tell us that, if we will hold our tongues about these things, they will come back to us perhaps, and give us a majority again where we have lost it. For one, it is not with me a question of majority or minority. It is a question of God's truth. . . . If the Lord be God, we will serve him. Whoever else may desert, the republicans of Massachusetts will serve this standard and will keep it flying. This is a contest between good and evil.[36]

The battle between the Republicans and the Mugwumps was not limited to Massachusetts. New York Independents disliked the sectional tactics of Joseph B. Foraker of Ohio, Senator George F. Edmunds of Vermont, and John Sherman, all of whom were canvassing the state for the Republican gubernatorial candidate. Asked why it so vigorously opposed the use of the war issues, the New York *Evening Post* answered it was because Northern politicians had "never discoursed upon the suppression of the suffrage at the South, except as an argument for keeping themselves in power, and as a reason why the country should not be disgusted or enraged by the gross abuses in administration which the Republican party practiced, permitted, or connived at." In the 1870's Stalwarts had employed the theme "to reconcile us to the whiskey thieves and the knavish Cabinet officers of the earlier Grant administration, and to the general corruption of the party in power." Under Hayes, they had invoked it "to reconcile us next . . . to the abandonment by that statesman of even the slightest attempt to reform the civil service with which he began his Administration." Garfield had adopted the Negro question "to reconcile us to . . . use during his canvass of the spoilsman's tools to secure his election and to his delivery of the foreign service of the Government to be sunk by Blaine in trading ventures for the building up of his own political fortunes. Though last not least," Blaine had stressed sectionalism during the 1884 campaign. "In short," the *Post* announced, "during a period of fully fifteen years, whenever the Republican party was called to account for any shortcoming," its sole answer was the bloody shirt.[37]

As election time drew near the Mugwumps stepped up their assault. Led by Curtis and Schurz, thirteen of their leaders issued a public letter in which they condemned the Republicans for creating a false issue. According to the signers, Cleveland since taking office had made remarkable progress in solving the Southern problem.[38] Schurz also published a separate denunciation of the men who were trying to stir up prejudice. He argued that in recent years conditions in the South had improved immensely. The colored people were now more prosperous and happier than ever before. Moreover, Southern Negroes themselves protested against the use of the race question by Northern agitators. Republican bloody shirt speeches were nothing more than "vicious and unpatriotic clap-trap." [39]

After the Democrats swept the New York election, Foraker acknowledged the important role played by the Mugwumps. He complained that Empire State Republicans had been "afraid to speak for the enforcement of the Fifteenth Amendment, for fear some Mugwump would be offended—in short, the canvass appeared to me to be conducted as though the party was afraid to be the Republican party." [40] Curtis and Schurz had done their work well.

IV

Mugwumps were not the only ones who felt that the Republicans should drop the war issues. During 1884 and 1885 strong opposition to sectionalism developed among Cincinnati businessmen. When, after the defeat of Blaine, Murat Halstead, editor of the Cincinnati *Commercial Gazette*, endlessly denounced Bourbon frauds and intimidations in the South,[41] dozens of important merchants of both parties objected. To increase their trade with the South they had recently built, at a cost of $20,000,000, the Cincinnati Southern Railroad. Now to their dismay Halstead was insulting the city's best customers almost daily.

Firms engaged in almost every branch of trade complained. One of the partners of the large dry goods house of Specker, Buddeke and Company, which occupied a five-story building in the center of town, announced that "The action of the Commercial Gazette in its wanton abuse of the South is suicidal and ruinous to this city. I might say it is outrageous." The merchants of the Queen City had worked hard to win the commerce which the Republicans were driving away. "I can not understand what is to be gained by it," he said. The Millcreek Distilling Company, whose plant covered practically one side of a city block, cancelled its subscription to the *Commercial Gazette* because of Halstead's editorials. At the spacious Gibson House, which accommodated seven hundred guests, officials reported that the city's salesmen were furious at Halstead. According to James B. Schuyler, the hotel's chief clerk, "New York and other Eastern drummers laugh because the St. Louis, Chicago and Louisville salesmen supply themselves with copies of the C. G. and show them to the Southern trade in order to get their business themselves, and take it away from Cincinnati." The South, he pointed out, was the Queen City's natural market. Indianapolis, Dayton, Springfield, and Columbus were all rivals for Northern commerce, while St. Louis cut Cincinnati off from the Southwest. In these circumstances, the Republican tirade was pure folly.

Many of Cincinnati's most prominent Republicans were among the disgruntled businessmen. John and Alfred Simpkinson, boot and shoe wholesalers, were loyal party members of long standing and often served on committees welcoming nationally known Republicans to town. But now Alfred Simpkinson said:

The Commercial Gazette is certainly doing Cincinnati a great wrong. It may be helping the Republican party, but it is hurting the business interests of Cincinnati terribly. I am sure if the editors of that paper could understand how we have striven for Southern trade they would not keep up this fomentation and strife. Business men more than any other class have been trying to cement the North and the South together in closer relations, and nothing can accomplish that great object more rapidly than the amenities of commerce and the ties of business honor . . . . nothing should be done that will prevent the South from trading with Cincinnati.

George G. N. Newton, a partner in the groceries and fine candies firm of Reihart and Newton, agreed:

Though the C. G. is my favorite paper I am free to say that I don't think it is right for it to carry on the way it does. We all want the Southern trade, and it is our natural field. It should be coaxed to come here instead of being scared off. There should be no division of the country. Business is one thing and politics another, and now that the election is over we should all accept the result manfully and cheerfully and help the vast commercial interests in every way possible.

Alpheus Cutter, of the wholesale drug firm of Runkle, Cutter, and Company, was sure that Halstead would "drive away what Southern trade we have. We will surely be undermined by other cities only too anxious to step in and take our business off our hands. We are Republicans here, but we regret the action of the Commercial Gazette exceedingly." George Ward, of M. Bare and Company, dealers in cordage and shot, also disapproved of Halstead's course: "We want all the Southern trade we can get and are naturally indignant when an attempt is made to drive it away. If there was any reason for this snarl, this showing of the teeth, it would be different." But, he concluded, there was none; the *Commercial Gazette's* methods were inexcusable.[42]

Southern businessmen were quick to anger. A drummer for a prominent Cincinnati clothing house reported that one Tennessee merchant displayed the *Commercial Gazette's* articles and asked salesmen from the Queen City, "Can you expect us to buy goods of you when your people allude to us as murderers, ku-klux, intimidators and ballot-box corruptors and say we are driving the negroes from the country? What support had we ought to give a city that does not rank us above common criminals?" Some Southern dealers, the commercial traveler continued, displayed signs reading "No Cincinnati drummers need apply." Similarly, a representative of Knost Brothers and Company, importers and traders in toys, fancy goods, and druggists' sundries, reported that in Kentucky he "found general kicking. 'We like your goods, we like your houses, but we can't continue to do business with you if your city treats us as if we were a lot of pick-pockets and outlaws,'" he was told. Captain H. C. Hines, the mayor and most important merchant of Bowling Green, Kentucky, said he bought most of his goods in Cincinnati and deeply resented the Republican assaults. Moreover, a group of prominent Montgomery, Alabama, citizens appealed to the Board of Trade and to the mayor of Cincinnati to stop Halstead.[43]

V

Considerable commercial pressure was also put on Ohio Republicans during 1885. To a large extent Joseph B. Foraker, the Republican gubernatorial candidate in that year, was forced to adopt a sectional platform. When he had run for governor in 1883, clever Democrats had turned most of Ohio's Negroes against him. They had insisted that Foraker had proven that he was an anti-Negro when, years before, he had defended an old school chum in a civil rights suit brought by a colored girl. Further, the Democrats had claimed that Foraker had transferred to Cornell University in 1869 because Ohio Wesleyan University had admitted a colored student. These telling arguments had persuaded every Negro editor in the state that Foraker hated members of their race.[44]

When the stories were revived in 1885, Foraker believed that he would once more be defeated unless he could refute them. "The negro vote was so large that it was not only an important but essential factor in our consideration," he later wrote. "It would be impossible for the Republican Party to carry the state if that vote should be arraigned against us." [45]

The Republican solution to this problem was sectionalism. Their party platform demanded a free ballot and a fair count. Throughout the campaign Sherman, Foraker, William McKinley, and Halstead developed a limitless number of variations on the same theme. They talked endlessly about the million disfranchised Southern Negroes and about Bourbon violations of the Constitution and the war amendments. To them states' rights sentiment was as strong as ever in the South. The Democracy stood for fraud and violence, while Republicanism meant freedom and human equality. And, adopting Blaine's favorite argument, they reminded Ohioans that it required three times as many votes to elect a Buckeye to Congress as it did to elect a Mississippian.[46]

Foraker's plight was of little concern to Cincinnati businessmen. Spurred on by the Democratic Cincinnati *Enquirer*, they protested against the Republican tactics. Smith, Myers, and Schnier, a manufacturer of shaftings and pulleys, revealed that a Southern boycott had already forced them to fire forty-three of their 125 workers. Henry Rikhoff and Company, parlor furniture producers, blamed the Republicans because they were now using only fifty men. D. K. Norton and Sons, makers of saw mills, engines, and boilers, admitted that they had cut their usual force of twenty-five in half:

Our trade is largely with the South. The Southern merchants always pay the largest prices and are always easy to sell to. There can be no doubt in the minds of the business men that the present course of the Commercial Gazette is hurting the trade of Cincinnati. . . . Our agents report a dissatisfaction all over the Southern States with the treatment the Southern people are receiving at the hands of the Commercial Gazette.

Several businessmen suggested that a protest meeting be held.

Well-known Republicans joined the chorus. William H. Alms of Alms and Doepke, a wholesale and retail clothing establishment covering half a block and fronting on three streets, stressed that because of Halstead and Foraker the store's drummers were being shunned by their regular Southern customers. Arthur P. Harmer, secretary and treasurer of the Greendale Furniture Company of Lawrenceburg, remarked, "I'm a Republican, but I don't believe in this bloody shirt business. It's hurting trade." He was sure that "if the Commercial Gazette keeps up this racket much longer Halstead will have to be squelched, or this part of the country won't have any Southern trade to speak of." [47]

Southern merchants, such as those of Pulaski, Tennessee, boycotted Cincinnati establishments. The editor and publisher of the Pulaski *Citizen,* who annually spent from $1,800 to $2,000 for paper at each of three dealers, now bought elsewhere. Captain T. F. Arrowsmith, who owned a dry goods store and purchased thousands of dollars worth of goods each year from Cincinnati merchants, said that many of his customers refused to buy merchandise made in the Queen City. The hardware firm of Buford and Carter, which previously had done business mainly with Cincinnati houses, was changing. A partner believed that in a half hour he could show a visitor at least one hundred persons who refused to buy Queen City products. Moore and Daily, general merchants, said they formerly bought from $8,000 to $10,000 worth of goods annually from McAlpin and Company, Louis Stix and Company, W. S. Dickinson and Company, and John Shillito. They now boycotted all Republicans. Ezell and Davis formerly stocked a complete line of Cincinnati stoves. Because their customers refused to purchase these products, they now carried only a model made by Resor and Company. [48]

Despite these complaints, the over-all pattern of the Ohio campaign favored the Republicans. Foraker was elected governor by 359,281 votes to 341,830, and Sherman was later reelected to the Senate by the state legislature. The Republicans, however, lost Hamilton County, in which Cincinnati and almost all the patrons of the Cincinnati Southern Railroad were located, by 34,696 to 34,050, although Blaine had carried it in 1884 by 38,744 to 33,248. [49]

To bloody shirt Republicans, Cincinnati henceforth was a city without a soul. "Cincinnati," wrote William E. Chandler in 1890, "sells her honor and her humanity for southern commerce." [50]

Attacks by sectionalists upon businessmen, such as those in Cincinnati, soon became common. Chandler asked New Hampshire Republicans whether they meant to desert the Southern Negro:

Or do you demand that agitation shall continue until fraud and murder used as ordinary political agencies shall cease to elect congresses and presidents of the United States? The commercial spirit of the North before 1861 deprecated the agitation of the slavery question as injurious to trade. It is the same commercial spirit, I fear, which now creates a seeming indifference to the vital question of a free ballot. But a nation which puts money and its uses before man and his liberty cannot long endure as a republic. Where I have stood on this question, I shall remain, as long as life shall last. [51]

Senator John C. Spooner of Wisconsin believed that the attitude of the Republican party upon the suffrage issue "should not be a cowardly one. We should not allow ourselves to be deterred from a fearless and persistent discharge of duty in this respect, either by the commercial spirit of some of our own people, or by the senseless cry of 'bloody shirt' which the Democrats hurl at us." [52] A prominent Southern Negro, John R. Lynch, former Republican Congressman and onetime speaker of the Mississippi House of Representatives, issued a similar complaint: "Too many of our leading men, I fear, are indifferent to the vital question of a free ballot at the South, in obedience to the commercial spirit of the North, which seeks to avoid the issue on account of an apprehension that its agitation will prove injurious to trade." [53]

Unmoved by the arguments of Spooner and Chandler, many major Republicans by the end of 1885 realized that the war questions were not powerful enough to carry an election. The party that year had barely won in Ohio and had lost in New York despite an unusually active campaign. The prominent and persistent opposition of Mugwumps and merchants in important cities like Cincinnati, Boston, and New York to sectionalism forced Republican leaders to consider other ways of breaking the Solid South.

7

Protection for the Negro or for Industry?

BY THE middle 1880's many powerful Republicans had become converted to the plan unsuccessfully used by Blaine in 1884. In an effort to build up Republicanism in the South and to win for their party control of the national government, they decided to play down the Negro question and to emphasize the tariff issue. Realizing that Southern industrialists and planters increasingly favored protection, they came to the conclusion that if the race problem was out of the way a high tariff platform would induce a large number of Redeemers to desert the Democracy.

Advocates of this new departure reacted unfavorably to the sectional tactics of Blaine and John Sherman during the canvass of 1886. At Sebago Lake, Maine, in August, Blaine, still smarting from his defeat in 1884, argued that the Democratic party was the worker's greatest enemy. By giving the Southern Negro "inadequate compensation for his . . . toil," the Bourbons were "steadily crowding down" the standard of living of the white Northerners who did the same kind of work as the colored men. Moreover, free trade Democrats wanted to reduce the tariff and subject citizens of the United States to the rivalry of "the highly skilled and miserably paid labor of Europe." With the Redeemers in control of the government, "the wages of the American laborer will fall as certainly as effect follows cause." [1]

While campaigning in Pennsylvania a few months later, Blaine repeated this theme. He told Philadelphians that the Democratic party desired "to break down the tariff and throw the laboring men of the north into competition with foreign labor and with the two millions of southern laborers who are underpaid." A Pittsburgh audience learned from him that colored iron workers in Birmingham, Chattanooga, and sections of Virginia made between fifty and seventy cents a day for doing a job which earned Pennsylvanians a dollar and a half. Northerners would soon be dragged down to the Southern level unless Negroes received more pay "for what they earn in the sweat of their faces." At Shamokin, Blaine once more insisted that the political organization "whose policy raises up a rivalry of two million colored workmen in the south at sixty and seventy cents a day is not the party to which the interests of white labor can be entrusted." The enactment of the Democratic platform, "with its free trade and its grinding of the poor throughout the south," would bring chaos. [2]

Although using a vastly different approach, Sherman helped Blaine wave the bloody shirt. In a Philadelphia speech he claimed that the Bourbons illegally disfranchised six million Negroes. Like czarist Russia, the South tolerated only one party; voters were forced to accept Redeemer candidates. The Senator urged Southern high tariff men and Northern Democrats to help stop political outrages. [3]

Despite the fact that these tactics won the Pennsylvania

election for the Republicans, the campaign was far from agreeable to the American Iron and Steel Association, the leading spokesman of this important industry. As attested to by its motto, the group was interested primarily in "Protection to Home Industry," not in the Negro. In existence since 1864 the Association employed three principal weapons: its *Bulletin*, money, and tariff tracts. The first, issued weekly, was edited by James M. Swank, secretary of the organization. The second was frequently used; just before the election of 1886, for example, when things looked gloomy in Ohio for the Republicans, Swank flooded the state with campaign donations. Prominent Republicans, such as William McKinley, Justin Morrill, and William D. Kelley, wrote the Association's pamphlets, which were generously distributed throughout the country. In the mid-eighties, the fortunes of the group were intimately connected with those of the Republican party. Senators Nelson W. Aldrich, William B. Allison, Sherman, and Morrill were in almost constant contact with Swank, and the Association's president, Benjamin Franklin Jones, a close friend of Blaine and a partner in the steel firm of Jones and Laughlin, Limited, was chairman of the Republican National Committee from 1884 to 1888.[4]

Swank was very upset by the tone of the Pennsylvania campaign. During the canvass he talked privately with both Blaine and Sherman "about the Southern situation." He assured them "that Virginia and West Virginia could be detached from the Solid South in 1888 upon the tariff issue" and noted that in recent years the Republican party had made huge gains in both states. Free trade Democrats like John Carlisle, Speaker of the House since 1883, and Henry Watterson, editor of the Louisville *Courier-Journal,* were no longer universally admired in the former Confederate states. Southern rice, sugar, tobacco, pig iron, iron, and lumber interests required and demanded protection. "The right of the black men of the South to vote and have their votes counted should be strenuously insisted on, of course," Swank advised, "but besides this we need not longer I think wave the 'bloody shirt,' but rather, as vastly more politic, press the tariff issue upon our Southern brethren." [5]

In line with Swank's thinking were the conciliatory statements of his close friend and fellow protectionist, Representative William D. (Pig Iron) Kelley of Philadelphia. During a Southern tour late in 1886 the Congressman made a number of speeches which took issue with those of Blaine. Colored laborers in mining and manufacturing areas were fairly well paid, he reported; in fact they often received as much money as their white counterparts in Pennsylvania. Back home once more, Kelley again insisted that the Negroes he had seen were relatively prosperous. Tenant cotton growers of both races had a hard time of it, but factory workers were certainly not as mistreated as Blaine had said. The neat white rows of houses in Southern industrial centers proved that.[6]

II

Swank was not alone in believing that the Republicans could break the Solid South in 1888 by drawing protectionists away from the Democratic party. The Portland *Oregonian* noted that free traders like Carlisle and Watterson, on the one hand, and Samuel J. Randall, the protectionist former Speaker of the House from Pennsylvania, and such voices of the New South as Senator Joseph E. Brown of Georgia and the Atlanta *Constitution,* on the other, were engaged in an "irrepressible conflict" which would "soon divide the south as it does both parties in the north." Agreeing that economic issues were replacing racial animosities as the deciding factors in Southern politics, the New York *Commercial Advertiser* predicted that if the Republicans emphasized a high tariff they could "hopefully enter the south . . . and contest elections upon equal terms with the democrats." The Washington

National Republican urged Southern protectionists to "let intelligence lead them instead of prejudice . . . by uniting with the Republican party [to] secure the triumph of the old Whig principles which Henry Clay advocated and their fathers voted for." The New York *Tribune* was certain that Swank's program would carry Virginia, North Carolina, and South Carolina for the Republicans in 1888.[7]

Important Democratic and Mugwump journals urged the Republicans to adopt the new Southern policy. The Macon (Georgia) *Telegraph* said: "If the Republican party should drop the sectional torch, the bayonet and the bloody shirt, and with olive branches for banners and business principles and measures for weapons come into the Southern States; if their lines were of steel rails and their forts factories, nothing could stand before them." The Augusta (Georgia) *Chronicle* agreed: "If the Republican party would drop all efforts to excite sectional prejudice, it could enter the South with reasonable hopes of gaining the ascendency in several of the Southern States. . . . the sectional talk of politicians . . . keeps up sectional party lines and makes the 'solid South' a formidable factor in every national election." According to the Mugwump Boston *Herald,* "It would be for the interest of the people there and for the interest of the nation generally" if the South split on the tariff.[8]

Men of both parties and from both sections frequently said the same thing. One prominent Republican, Andrew D. White, former president of Cornell University and onetime United States minister to Germany, argued that several Southern states could be "brought away from the solid South" on the question of protection to American industry. Judge William A. Burwell of New Orleans, an officer of the American Shipping League, pointed to the enthusiastic receptions given men like Randall and Kelley during Southern trips in 1886 as proof of the popularity of high tariff principles. "If the race and sectional issues are not agitated in the campaign of 1888," he prophesied, "education and Protection would walk safely if not triumphantly through the South." After a three-week visit in the South, Edward H. Ammidown, president of the Protective Tariff League, reported that economic themes were of great importance in that section, although, he added, in some areas it was still political and social suicide for a white man to be a Republican.[9]

During March, 1887, Sherman, in speeches delivered while touring the Gulf and Atlantic states, played up the South's tariff requirements. Shortly before commencing his trip, the Senator remarked to the Cincinnati *Enquirer* that Republican prospects were excellent in Virginia, Alabama, Tennessee, and Georgia. Eventually, he predicted, "the white vote in the South will divide, and when it does the negro vote will then be counted. . . . In fact, the negro vote will then be not only counted, but likewise courted." [10]

Early in his journey Sherman became involved in a civil rights squabble. When a Birmingham hotel proprietor refused to let five prominent colored men visit his rooms, the Senator immediately packed his bags and left. He then received the delegation at his new residence. This incident, Sherman recalled a few days later, "was the only disagreeable thing on the trip. I wish it hadn't occurred." The hotel owner "was one of the few left of the old type of Southern 'nigger' haters, and I suppose that and the temptation to gain a little notoriety for himself and an advertisement for his hotel impelled him to act as he did." [11]

In a Birmingham speech the visitor appealed directly to the industrialists of Alabama. "You have stored in the surrounding hills elements of a wealth greater than all the banks of New York," he told them, insisting that the path of Southern progress led straight to the Republican door.[12]

Sherman's next and most publicized stop was Nashville.

"Tennessee and Kentucky," he explained in his memoirs, "had been Whig states strongly in favor of protection, and before the war were represented by John Bell and Henry Clay. I claimed my fellowship with the people of Tennessee in the old Whig times, and, aside from the questions that grew out of the war, assumed that they were still in favor of the policy of protection of American industry by tariff laws." [13]

In the most important address of his tour Sherman mentioned to a Nashville audience that the rights of all citizens should be safeguarded, but he stressed the Southern need for Republican policies. "You are as deeply interested in the tariff question as Pennsylvania," he said to citizens of Tennessee. If the state adopted protectionism it would become "rich and prosperous beyond all former experience." [14]

Democratic and Mugwump journals quickly recognized Sherman's motives. "It is through the tariff that Sherman calculates to break into the Solid South," commented the Kansas City *Times*. The Nashville speech "was a bold bid for Southern support on a tariff platform." The New York *Times* happily noted that Sherman was no longer emphasizing sectionalism. The fiery, old Republican approach was being discarded and an attempt was being made to build up the Southern wing of the party by using economic themes. [15]

Even a free trader like Watterson admitted that Sherman was using a powerful argument. "I am looking every year for a break-up of the Solid South," the editor revealed to the Chicago *Tribune*, "and it will be a good thing for the country when it comes." But, he insisted, "it will never come until the Republican party of the North drops its sectionalism, ceases its attempts to array race against race, and buries the bloody shirt. That garment should be burned and its ashes scattered." As long as the Republicans "keep alive the memories of the war, keep aloft the banner of sectionalism, seek to aid and maintain negro dominance under the sentimental guise of equal rights, and all that, just so long will the white people of the South maintain a solid front." Still, he recognized, "the old Whig leaven is there in all the States"; many Southerners "love the memory of Henry Clay and the idea of Protection, internal improvements, centralization." Virginia, North Carolina, Tennessee, and Alabama, Watterson believed, were "ripe for a break-up." The Republicans had a grand opportunity. The question was whether they were clever enough to take advantage of it. So pleased was Swank with Watterson's words that he reprinted them in full in the *Bulletin of the American Iron and Steel Association*.[16]

As a result of his tour Sherman became the most publicized man in America. During April, 1887, interviews with him became common, and in all of them he spoke of a new, dynamic South. To a Pittsburgh journal he commented that Republicanism was "growing just as fast as the South grows. . . . The Southern people are as anxious to subserve their interests as we are to subserve ours, and they are not slow in falling to the fact in manufacturing districts that the defeat of the free-trade party is their salvation." [17] Squelching rumors that whites and Negroes would never work together, the Senator informed the Cincinnati *Enquirer* that Southern industrialists were not racial bigots. He found that only the poor whites hated Negroes. Both the Philadelphia *Press* and the New York *Herald* learned from him that six Southern states—North Carolina, Florida, Louisiana, Mississippi, Alabama, and Tennessee—were "naturally Republican." Only race prejudice prevented them from bolting the Democracy.[18]

The Senator's followers were sure that the trip had done political wonders for him. Richard Smith, co-owner of the Cincinnati *Commercial Gazette* and one of the country's most ardent Sherman-for-President men, now felt that the Senator, if nominated, would easily carry Tennessee, Virginia, and West

Virginia on the tariff issue. Sherman could "do it beyond question." [19]

Then just when Sherman seemed most popular he changed his approach to the Southern question. In a speech before the Illinois state legislature on June 1, 1887, he once more became the bloody shirt waver of old. Negroes in the South, he declared, were robbed of their ballots and intimidated. Cleveland was a usurper, having been elected president by fraud and in violation of the Constitution. Worst of all, he appointed ten former rebels to office for every Union man. [20]

The Senator's new strategy was widely denounced. Comparing the Sherman of Nashville with the Sherman of Springfield, the *Nation* declared, "Unless the testimony were overwhelming that the same man made the same two speeches, it would be impossible to resist the conviction that there was a mistaken identity." To Watterson, the Ohioan was once more a "red republican." "The South, having had its bellyful of blood, has gotten a taste of money, and it is too busy trying to make money to quarrel with anybody," he said. "But as long as the red republicans insist on keeping this black issue alive at the front the South will vote solidly." [21]

Perhaps the *Nation* and Watterson could see differences in Sherman's two addresses, but until the day he died the Senator said he could not. "Any one that will read them will see that they are in no sense inconsistent," he told the *Enquirer* shortly after his visit to Springfield.

One was devoted to the history of the two parties, their achievements, their objectives and aims and their standing before mankind in the light of recorded history; it was a presentation of what each party had wrought in the past, and what each promised and was able to give in the future. The other was devoted to a condition of affairs that commands the attention of thoughtful men, and the existence of which can not be successfully disputed. The subject of each has a distinct and separate existence, and to discuss them both on separate occasions involves neither inconsistency nor contradictions.[22]

In later newspaper interviews, in public letters, and in his memoirs, Sherman repeatedly took this position.[23]

The Senator's wavering did not end here. Three months after the Springfield speech, Sherman once again altered his course. He repeated the sentiments previously expressed at Nashville to a Wilmington, Ohio, audience. The Redeemers would be greatly aided by a high tariff, he argued. "We ask of the South nothing but obedience to the Constitution, respect for the rights of the freedmen among them, and an impartial study of republican policy." [24]

Although seemingly inexplicable, Sherman's changes of tactics can be readily understood when viewed in the light of events since 1877. Like Hayes in that year and Chandler in 1883, his chief concern was in building up Republicanism in the South. Willing to try all methods to strengthen the Southern branch of his party, Sherman quite naturally could not see any differences in his talks because to him the similarities were far greater than the inconsistencies. Although the techniques employed in each varied greatly, the objective of each—the creation of a truly national Republican party—remained the same. The Ohio Senator was merely trying to see whether the bloody shirt or an appeal to high tariff men in the South would prove more effective.

III

Unlike Sherman, some Republicans still unwaveringly believed that the Negro, not former Whigs, must be the center of any Republican organization in the ex-Confederate states. William E. Chandler of New Hampshire, for example, found the growing desire for a Southern policy emphasizing protection distasteful. Early in 1887 he asked important Republicans in Louisiana, Florida, Mississippi, and South Carolina the best means of strengthening the federal election laws. "I think when we get ready," he advised Edward McPherson of Philadelphia, "we can open the southern question with good effect on a new line." [25]

When the first session of the Fiftieth Congress met in December, 1887, Chandler, who had been elected to fill a vacancy in the Senate, vigorously denounced the South. First, he introduced a bill to regulate the election of Congressmen in the four states about which he had inquired a few months before. The measure never reached the floor of Congress. Then he sponsored a resolution directing the Committee on the Judiciary to determine whether the colored vote had been suppressed during the recent municipal election at Jackson, Mississippi. Working on the assumption that any debate would merely glorify sectionalism, the Democrats allowed it to pass with practically no discussion. The vote, 29 to 23, was almost entirely along party lines. [26]

The majority and minority reports filed during the summer by members of the investigating committee settled little. According to the majority, the colored voters of Jackson for the past fourteen years had been strong enough to elect a Republican mayor. Eager to redeem the city, some Democrats had organized a White League, which warned Negroes not to run for office or to vote during the coming canvass. So forceful were these threats that no colored persons showed up at the polls. One of the guiding spirits behind the Bourbon plan was a United States district attorney who had been forced to resign by Cleveland. But, complained the Republicans, two other federal officials who had been leaders of the White League had not been disciplined by the administration. The minority report, signed by four Democrats, denied that any government men had taken part in the episode and disagreed in details with the majority. [27]

The bloody shirt tactics of Chandler and his cohorts did not end with the Jackson affair. Of even more concern to them was Cleveland's nomination of Lucius Q. C. Lamar, the Secretary of the Interior from Mississippi, as a Supreme Court justice.

Lamar had little stomach for a sectional fight. Sensing that he would be attacked by Republicans, he said he would rather have his name withdrawn than foment discord. Claiming that he had devoted the last twenty years of his life to Union causes, he insisted that the South was as patriotic as any section of the country.[28]

Republicans disliked Lamar primarily because of his attitude on the race question. Senator John C. Spooner of Wisconsin complained that the nominee had been instrumental in evolving the "'Mississippi plan,' which drove the Negroes into the swamps and, by assassination and threats, suppressed the Republican vote." Governor Joseph B. Foraker of Ohio was "sick and tired of the conservatism that asks for the confirmation of Lamar in the name of unity and fraternity" while outrages such as the Jackson affair were perpetrated in Mississippi. To him Republicanism consisted of more than just a high tariff; it also meant hostility to crimes against the Negro.[29]

Sectionalists also found fault with Lamar's Senate record. They pointed out that in 1879 he had denounced the resolutions of George F. Edmunds of Vermont reaffirming the legality of the Thirteenth, Fourteenth, and Fifteenth Amendments. Instead Lamar had supported the substitute of John T. Morgan, an Alabama Democrat, who believed that these measures had been forced upon the South. This allegation was thoroughly distasteful to those whose party had been responsible for the Civil War and Reconstruction acts.[30]

The revelations of Charles Foster, former governor of Ohio, who once had a private talk with Lamar on the South, the Negro, and white rule, intensified Republican hostility to the nomination. According to Foster, Lamar had said that "'Negro government was necessarily ignorant, and ignorant government was necessarily vicious and bad; that the white people of the South would continue to govern their states.'" Any attempt to enforce the election laws was impractical. While the Mississippian "deprecated murder and Ku-Klux methods," he felt that Southern whites were destined to dominate the section and would do so by one means or another. Telling Republican friends in confidence of the interview, Foster declared that neither Lamar "nor any one else entertaining the sentiments he does, should become a United States Judge."[31]

Chandler tried to organize the resistance to Lamar. Encouraging Whitelaw Reid of the New York *Tribune* to oppose the Mississippian, he termed the nomination a "calamity." "That Lamar was a rebel is not the argument," the Senator wrote; "that he still advocates the doctrine of secession as right; and is a bull dozer is a potent argument." Chandler hoped the *Tribune* could persuade William M. Evarts of New York to denounce Lamar and could keep Don Cameron of Pennsylvania, Dwight M. Sabin of Minnesota, John H. Mitchell of Oregon, and Philetus Sawyer of Wisconsin, all of whom reportedly approved of the nominee, in line. With the party holding a precarious majority of two in the Senate, Chandler insisted that every Republican vote was a valuable one.[32]

Reid adopted these suggestions. In a series of editorials his paper pleaded with Evarts, a distinguished attorney, to reject the appointment of this supposedly incompetent and inexperienced lawyer. A few days later the *Tribune* happily noted that Evarts had come out against Lamar. Other editorials urged the Senators named by Chandler to vote with the bloody shirters.[33]

Only a few Republicans openly supported the nomination. One of them, William M. Stewart of Nevada, wanted all men to forget old passions and to stick to the tariff, currency, and other "living issues of the day." Another, Sawyer, stressed that Lamar was capable and had earned a seat on the Supreme Court.[34]

Eventually, the Senate approved the appointment, 32 to 28. Three Republicans, Leland Stanford of California, Harrison H. Riddleberger of Virginia, and Stewart, voted with the Democrats.[35]

To Republicans interested in penetrating the South on a high tariff platform, the furor over Lamar was a major blunder. As the New York *Commercial Advertiser* dejectedly reported, the party had succeeded only in stirring up partisanship. If the Senate had approved the nomination without rancor, many Southerners would have become convinced that sectionalism was dying. Protectionists would have edged even closer to the Republican camp. As it turned out, Lamar was confirmed and Southern high tariff men were needlessly antagonized. "The republican party cannot afford to make such mistakes as these," the journal warned, "at such a time as this, merely to gratify the antediluvian spite of a few senatorial fossils and one uneasy little picayune politician from New Hampshire." [36]

IV

As the presidential campaign of 1888 approached, the tariff issue grew larger and larger. President Grover Cleveland's annual message of December 6, 1887, made the problem even more acute. Without consulting the leaders of his own party, the President spoke of nothing but the need for tariff reform, pointing out that protection fathered trusts and mothered high prices. Protectionist Democrats found little to like in the statement. They drifted closer than ever to the Republican party.[37]

While Democrats were arguing the merits of protection and free trade, Republican leaders were debating whether to emphasize the free ballot or the tariff. In this dispute Chandler represented the bloody shirt element, while Grenville Dodge, the New York railroad executive and former Congressman from Iowa, and James S. Clarkson, the Republican National Committeeman from Iowa, presented the views of the protectionists.

The immediate cause of the discussion was a series of editorials carried during January and February of 1888 by Clarkson's paper, the Des Moines *Iowa State Register*. One article, entitled "The Party Platform for 1888," recalled that "In 1884 the platform in some way failed to draw to it the support of the great business interests of the seaboard cities." Republican industrialists who had bolted and voted for Cleveland had been responsible for the loss of states like New York, New Jersey, and Connecticut. These men believed that the Republican "party and its platform were not mindful enough of the business and commercial interests of the country in several important directions." Clarkson was convinced that "the seaboard cities are determined to have good relations re-established with the South, and are as determined in this respect as they were in the days before the war. It is also clear that there is no longer a majority in the North to respond to the nobler issues on which the Republican party has so long stood." By championing fair and honest elections in the South and the Union soldier in the North, the Republican organization had virtually defeated itself. If it emphasized these antiquated arguments in the coming canvass, it would again lose.

According to Clarkson, new questions were replacing the old. The commercial elements of the North had accepted the war issues as settled "and as no longer needing defence at least until they are attacked. This is what the business men of New York and all the seaboard cities anxious for the Southern trade are saying, and what the majorities of the North are beginning to say also." The next Republican platform should "be nationalized and made so broad as to cover every state in the Union, and so broad as that the hundreds of thousands of men in the South who believe with it on the business interests may be able to stand on it and vote for it." Clarkson predicted that Kentucky, North Carolina, Tennessee, West Virginia, and Virginia would go Republican in 1888 if the tariff, not the war issues, were stressed by the party.[38]

This editorial was widely circulated in the East. So significant did Edwin L. Godkin consider it that he printed an endorsement of it in the New York *Evening Post* and its weekly edition, the *Nation*. Stephen B. Elkins, the Republican National Committeeman from New Mexico, was so moved by the *Post's* account that he wrote Clarkson a congratulatory note.[39]

Almost daily during the first two months of 1888 the *Register* urged the Republican party to adopt the fresh course. Southern Negroes would be greatly aided by the new approach, reasoned Clarkson upon another occasion. When parties were based upon economics, not race, all political organizations would actively seek colored support and fully accept every voter.[40]

Greatly influenced by these articles and by meetings with Clarkson, Dodge urged Chandler to abandon sectionalism. Believing that the Senator's policy of "making faces" was ruinous, he insisted that the party would lose twenty-five per cent of its regular vote should it adopt a pro-Negro platform in the coming election. "We have got to appeal to new interests; to the business interests of the country, and if we can't carry this country on a protective tariff I don't see upon what we can carry it," Dodge preached to Chandler.[41]

Clarkson applauded the railroad man's letter. If the Senator could "see anything in the gradual and remorseless diminution of the Republican vote, under the constant platform of the 'bloody shirt' and old war issues to justify him in any hope to make gains in the future on the same line, he is a more sanguine man that I can be," the editor wrote Dodge. Voters in the Northern cities were no longer moved by the old sectional cry. On the other hand, although the Republican stand on the tariff had lost much of its potency in the East, it was remarkably young and vigorous in the South. Moreover, "Southern Republicans oppose Chandler's election bills, which, with a Democratic House and a Democratic President, stand no more chance of passing then they do of being added by popular consent to the golden rule." Should they be approved by Congress, the Senator's measures "would only make the Solid South still more solid." And they would set a horrible precedent which the Democrats, when in power, might use to interfere with elections in New England or even in Iowa.[42]

After reading these criticisms, Chandler defended his course. Clarkson's argument about the loss of Northern votes "proves nothing," he answered. Historically, the Senator believed, the Republican party had existed for a number of basic reasons: to resist the extension of slavery; to win the Civil War; to free the slaves; to institute Negro suffrage; and to secure the war amendments. "The tariff has been only an incident of these great labors." To make it now the main question would shatter the party. Republicanism would go "to pieces like a dissolving cloud." The party must rigidly control Congressional elections. If it did not it was doomed, he warned.[43]

Unconvinced, Clarkson publicized his views at every available opportunity. To a Chicago *Tribune* reporter early in February he predicted that the coming Republican convention would approve a platform accepting "the war issues as settled" and leaving the way "open for all men who are with it in the South on present issues to join with it for the future." Such an approach, the editor felt, would enable the party to carry two or three border states in November. Louisiana might even be won this April if the tariff on sugar was played up and if the Democrats fought among themselves. One important Republican who pondered over Clarkson's words was former Senator Benjamin Harrison of Indiana, who had recently been defeated for re-election. Impressed by them, he called them to Elkins's attention. The New York *Times* also recognized the significance of Clarkson's remarks and reprinted them in full for Eastern readers.[44]

The next month in the *North American Review* Clarkson continued his campaign. He pointed out that to the two million young people who were enfranchised every four years the Civil War was history, not a personal experience. These men did not care about sentimental issues. They could be converted to Republicanism only by "live," not "nobler," themes.[45]

v

The struggle between high tariff and bloody shirt Republicans continued through the election of 1888. At an Indiana Republican convention early in the year a feud broke out when Albert J. Beveridge of Indianapolis demanded that the platform stress the Southern question, rather than the tariff. He was positive that Blaine's disregard for the Negro had caused the defeat of 1884. Disagreeing, the Hartford *Courant* noted that "There are a good many whigs left over in the southern states; many of them are uneasy in their present political associations; they ought to be in the republican party, where they belong by heredity and by natural affinity; and no honorable effort should be spared to get them there." The Portland *Oregonian* said that nearly every Southern state had a large high tariff element: in Texas it was the wool growers; in Louisiana the sugar producers; in Alabama and Tennessee the iron and coal miners; in South Carolina the rice planters; and in Kentucky the hemp and bagging industries. Many important Southern newspapers, including the Atlanta *Constitution,* the Richmond *Dispatch,* the Nashville *American,* the Mobile *Register,* and the Birmingham *Age,* also disliked free trade. "A common interest unites the advocates of protection in all parts of the country," the *Oregonian* observed.[46]

Leading men of both sections continued to talk about Southern tariff needs. Russell Alger, the former Governor of Michigan, was sure that North Carolina, Virginia, Kentucky, West Virginia, Tennessee, and possibly Alabama could be carried in 1888 on Clarkson's platform. The Democrats would certainly divide on economic issues, predicted Major J. F. Hanson of Macon, Georgia, the largest cotton manufacturer in the South. Still, he added, "The fear of negro supremacy is ever present with a Southern man. . . . But for its existence the Solid South would dissolve like a rope of sand." [47]

As convention time approached a few Republicans still demanded that the freedmen be protected. Writing in the preconvention issue of the *North American Review,* Senator John J. Ingalls of Kansas reminded his fellow party members that the Redeemers, by preventing Negro suffrage, actually stole the thirty-eight seats in Congress allotted to the South because of its colored population. Under the Fourteenth Amendment, these representatives should be taken away unless Negroes were allowed to vote. In the coming canvass, he argued, there would be but one "paramount issue, surpassing every other; before which tariffs, taxes, currency and surplus shrink and dwindle with nothingness; impartial justice and equality of all men before the law." Joining in, Chandler wrote that "The Republican party can never abandon its efforts to enforce the 15th Amendment. . . . There is an eclipse of faith just now in the minds of some Republicans," he lamented. "Our business men are indifferent to the sentiment of devotion to human rights, at least where the persons concerned are black." But there would soon be a "revival of fidelity and courage." He advised Southern Republicans to "look for the coming of the morning." [48]

The morning of which Chandler dreamed was not ushered

in by the Republican national convention of 1888. Dominated by men who believed that the race issue should be played down, the gathering approved a platform which slighted the Southern question. Employing unusually weak and vague terms, the party recognized the "supreme and sovereign right of every citizen, rich or poor, native or foreign born, white or black, to cast one free ballot in public elections and to have that ballot duly counted." It held the "equal representation of all people to be the foundation of our Republican government" and denounced the Democratic victory of 1884 as the triumph of fraud and intimidation.[49]

In 1888 Benjamin Harrison was the Republican presidential nominee, but the National Committee controlled the campaign. Led by Chairman Matthew S. Quay, a Pennsylvania Senator, Vice-Chairman Clarkson, and Secretary Jacob Sloat Fassett of New York, the group decided to ignore completely the race issue.

This verdict greatly disturbed Spooner. "You are right, that the [Southern] question is not receiving due attention in the campaign," he confided to a correspondent. Afraid that the bloody shirt would "deter Democrats who are likely to come to us on the tariff," the National Committee had committed a "damn outrage" by ordering that the Negro problem be forgotten.[50]

Undaunted by any rules which Quay and Clarkson might devise, Chandler doggedly carried on his own little sectional war during the summer of 1888. Early in June he called for an investigation of the credentials of Randall L. Gibson, who in April had been re-elected Senator from Louisiana, on the ground that the colored vote had been suppressed. At intervals during the session the upper chamber debated the subject and gave the race theme new, if temporary, life, but it took no action.[51]

Foraker was just as firmly convinced of the National Committee's folly. The party, he wrote, was making a serious error in ignoring the "nullification of the Constitution." Particularly galling to the Ohio Governor was the fact that Blaine, upon returning to the United States from a long European stay, had said that the campaign should be fought entirely on the tariff. Economic questions, disagreed Foraker, were "infinitesimally small alongside the Solid South business." The Ohioan intended to give a future audience at Richmond, Indiana, "a full dose of the ballot." He was sure that the followers of the state's Civil War governor, Oliver P. Morton, would listen with delight to his words.[52]

To Foraker's dismay, the National Committee used every possible means to stop him from employing sectionalism. When the Governor proposed to canvass the South itself, Clarkson told him that the Committee was against the scheme because "it would arouse the old Southern spirit and cause them [the Democrats] to poll a great many thousand votes who would otherwise remain at home."[53]

Foraker sulked throughout the remainder of the campaign. "I have no patience with the cry that everything should be ignored in this contest, except the tariff," the Governor told a Texas Republican. He wholeheartedly believed "in a free ballot and a fair count, and my conscience will not allow me to be still about so grave a matter." He had "more hope of breaking the Solid South through the building up of the Republican party there by guaranteeing protection to such men as yourself, than by hammering away at it from the outside, upon some cold question of business."[54]

The National Committee's relations with Anna Dickinson, the lyceum queen, showed how it handled deviationists. After agreeing to make thirty campaign speeches for a $3,750 fee plus a $1,250 bonus if Benjamin Harrison won, Anna tried to outdo Foraker. She stirred Midwestern voters with tales of "the brave, splendid, heroic, martyred souls that went down to the

battlefield and the prison pen from 1861 to 1865." To her the
Redeemers were little more than Negro-hating rebels who now
"brazenly come before you and claim your suffrages and your
support as your friends." [55]

Anna's speeches appalled Clarkson and his associates. Even
she realized that the Republican leaders were "not rejoiced
over my non-tariff talk," but she insisted that "the people and
the old soldiers, especially," were "well content." Without
warning Anna's bookings were cancelled and her tour was
completely disrupted. At Clarkson's suggestion she returned
home. Finally, in a move obviously designed to put her where
she could do the least harm, the campaign strategists sent her
to some small and relatively insignificant New York towns. In
all, Anna delivered only about half the number of talks she was
supposed to, and, despite a long, drawn-out lawsuit, she never
collected all the money promised her.[56]

The National Committee also tried to keep Republican newspapers quiet. When Whitelaw Reid asked whether it was ad-
visable to dramatize Southern atrocities, Fassett replied that
he was "very emphatically of the opinion that it would be a
mistake to give any particular emphasis" to these incidents.
"This," he concluded, "is also the general opinion of the Committee as I understand it." [57]

Meanwhile, Harrison released his letter of acceptance. The
"colored people do not ask special legislation in their interest,"
he opined. Negroes only desired "the common rights of American citizenship." But they would instinctively mistrust the Republican party if it asked for their support in those sections
where free elections prevailed and ignored their plight where
they were obviously disfranchised. The letter was, Harrison
told Russell Alger, designed not to place "any impediment in
the way of those who are managing the campaign," and he was
glad to have Alger's assurance that he had not.[58]

Once a firebrand on the race issue, Harrison by election day had become completely converted to the views of Swank and Clarkson. The transformation in the candidate's thinking constituted a mild revolution. His Washington's Birthday speech of 1888, delivered in Detroit, would have satisfied even Chandler. In it he demanded that the Southern Negro be protected. During June and July, 1888, he frequently spoke cordially of the South, but he stressed that the right of all citizens to vote must be upheld.[59]

After that, Harrison abandoned sectionalism. On October 5, he told a group of Negroes that the race problem would be solved if Southern protectionists voted Republican. He was convinced that the party of free trade would soon lose the South.[60]

One evening just before the election Harrison forcefully expressed his new sentiments to a close friend, Harvey M. La Follette, the Indiana Superintendent of Public Instruction. The candidate said he opposed sending Northern carpetbaggers southward and was against appointing ignorant Negroes and ignorant whites to office simply because they were Republicans. Harrison revealed that, if elected, he would recognize those Southerners who favored a high tariff and were really Republicans on the "live issues of the day" but who voted Democratic "for historical reasons." He was hopeful of thus winning the support of thousands of influential white men and was confident that his policy would completely solve the Southern social problem.[61]

Other major Republicans thoroughly approved of Harrison's words and of the National Committee's tactics. Sherman told the New York *World* that West Virginia and Virginia would be Republican if the tariff question dominated politics. He added that these states were kept Democratic by the threat of Negro rule. Sherman believed that the South should be allowed to solve the race problem for itself, decried bloody shirt speeches such as he himself had made only fourteen

months earlier, and deplored attempts by men like Spooner
to play up the Negro theme. Vice-Presidential candidate Levi
P. Morton's letter of acceptance, issued only a few weeks before
election day, ignored the situation in the South entirely and
dealt solely with economic problems.[62]

The West Virginia campaign was the type Republican
leaders hoped would break up the Solid South. There, as the
New York *World* reported, "the race question appears to have
been eliminated from politics." Republicans preached the high
tariff gospel in every area of the state. The American Iron
and Steel Association did its part; West Virginia received
56,000 tariff tracts.[63]

Election day was November 6. By the next day the nation
knew that Harrison had won, but the decision in the border
states was uncertain. On November 9, a bold, black New York
Tribune headline spread the glorious news: "The Solid South
Broken: West Virginia Republican." "It is the beginning of
the break in the Solid South," Blaine informed Harrison.[64]
Chauncey Depew, president of the New York Central Railroad, reported to a jubilant gathering at the Union Club in
New York that the victory would mark the disappearance of
the sectional issue from the national scene. Tennessee, Alabama, Florida, North Carolina, and West Virginia would be
Republican and protectionist by 1892.[65]

The count in West Virginia proved to be extremely close.
The state tottered back and forth, first seeming to go for
one candidate and then for the other. The final tabulation
revealed that the Democrats had captured it by 1,873 votes
out of a total of 159,188.[66]

In other Southern states the results were almost as close.
Cleveland took Virginia by a plurality of 1,539 out of 304,093
votes cast; North Carolina by 13,118 out of 285,473; and Tennessee by 19,791 out of 303,736.[67] Thanks to the National Committee's strategy, Harrison received more Southern ballots than

any other Republican presidential candidate since the end of Reconstruction.

For the first time in twelve years the Solid South appeared to be cracking. The Republican party at last had a policy which attracted substantial and important white Southerners. Complete success seemed to require but one additional ingredient: time.

8

The End of a Dream

I

THE CAMPAIGN tactics of Benjamin Harrison and the National
Committee in 1888 indicated that the new administration
would abandon the Negro and try to induce white high tariff
Southerners to join the Republican party. Between the election
and the inauguration there were important signs that the
President-elect intended to pursue such a policy.

The Indianapolis *Journal*, the paper closest to Harrison,
hinted that he would. Owned by the President-elect's warm
friend, John C. New, and edited by Elijah W. Halford, who
later spent four years in the White House as Harrison's personal
secretary, the daily soon after the election carried two significant editorials on the Southern question. Although denying
that they spoke for the new administration, the newspapermen
undoubtedly echoed their master's voice.

Entitled "Harrison and the South," the first article contained
a strong appeal to Southern industrialists. Happily noting that
Harrison's vote in the ex-Confederate states had been larger

than that of any Republican presidential candidate since Grant, the paper speculated that many of these ballots had been cast by protectionists displeased with "democratic bourbonism." "The really progressive men of the South, though perhaps calling themselves Democrats, have no sympathy with free trade," the *Journal* insisted. "They regard it as a menace to the prosperity of the South and they are right." The high tariff men of the South would not regret Harrison's victory. The President-elect was "in all respects a patriotic American statesman, large enough and broad enough to take the entire country in the scope of his vision and his efforts for its welfare." His election would mark "the dawn of a new era of good feeling between the North and the South, and the development of a new national sentiment, based on a better understanding of our common interests." According to the New York *Times,* these words clearly indicated that Harrison would "seek to organize a Southern Republican Party on the basis of protection." [1]

The second editorial, "The South and the New Administration," was similar. It emphasized that the President-elect wanted the South to receive "its full share in the blessings and benefits of a truly national policy and administration." The development of industry in such states as Tennessee, Georgia, and Alabama, the *Journal* went on, illustrated that sectionalism was dying. The Republican party had made its recent "fight for protection more largely for the South than for the North," since the "infant industries" of the former Confederate states required "the nursing mother of protection." Harrison would have but one policy for the entire country: prosperity. He would seek the support of all high tariff advocates. "We feel certain," concluded New and Halford, "there are men strong enough and able enough in the South, devoted to the future of their States and homes, to break down the inane prejudice that has so long kept them out of their share of the good things of the Nation." [2]

James S. Clarkson, one of Harrison's closest advisers, supported this stand. In a Chicago *Tribune* interview he estimated that during the recent election "nearly 100,000 ex-Confederates voted the Republican ticket—27,000 in Virginia, 24,000 in North Carolina." In the latter state all of the Republican candidates for office and all of the members of the state committee were former Confederates who now favored a high tariff. "The border States," Clarkson revealed, "practically came to us, led by the protection issue, and broke the Solid South. We had an honest majority in Virginia and West Virginia. We stand today half and half in Tennessee and North Carolina." He predicted that the final solution of the Southern problem was at hand. "It will," he said, "be a settlement recognizing and preserving all the fruits of the war—one that will recognize in the South as much as in the North what the Nation owes to the Union soldier, yet a settlement that will leave the future to deal with the questions of the future." The Harrison administration would "go South with a healing hand and with a desire to develop every interest and protect every right of all the citizens in those States." It would educate Negroes and prepare them adequately for their roles as citizens. Clarkson was sure that the color line in Southern politics would soon be broken and that men of both races would shortly join parties based upon economic issues. A former colonel, he insisted that Union veterans were more deeply interested than any other group in developing peaceful relations between the sections. They desired to see the country fully at peace before they died.[3]

Other influential Republicans encouraged Harrison to ally with Southern high tariff men. Commodore Arthur E. Bateman, the rich Wall Street broker and part owner of the Atlantic and Danville and other Virginia railroads, told the President-elect that the "whole business element in the South is naturally attracted to Republican doctrine." Southern factory owners and planters, he believed, had "nothing in common with the old

Bourbon Democracy except prejudice, but that is disappearing before the industrial progress of the South in recent years, and all that is necessary to attach the business and manufacturing interests permanently to the Republican party is a liberal and conciliatory policy in the distribution of Federal patronage." James G. Blaine also favored the appointment of conservative Southerners who had put aside the hatred and bitterness of the war and were interested in the material development of their section and in the welfare and happiness of all the people.[4]

Congressman Leonidas C. Houk of Tennessee was enthusiastic about Republican chances in the South. He bragged that in his state "the Republican party is the party of wealth, respectability, and brains. . . . Three out of five Democrats are with us on the tariff. . . . With all the questions growing out of the war removed Tennessee is Republican by a big majority." To him, as to Clarkson, the brightest sign was "that the ex-Confederate soldiers, men of character and intelligence, are coming into the Republican party. Mahone's wonderful leadership in Virginia has brought 60,000 Confederate soldiers into the Republican ranks in that State, which is sure to become Republican in 1892." If Harrison adopted the policy advocated by so many party members, "thousands of Democrats of the best, most progressive sort" would "cast their lot with the dominant party." [5]

The President-elect indicated that he was in full accord with these views. He told Congressman Jacob H. Gallinger of New Hampshire "that the best manner in which to break the solid South will be to interest democrats and republicans in an economic way. This, should the republican party remain in power for eight or twelve years, will cause a split in the South on economical questions, probably the only way in which such a split could occur." [6]

Harrison further revealed his ideas on the South during his dealings with Colonel Charles W. Woolley of Cincinnati. Born about 1831 Woolley, a Democrat, was a member of a prominent and wealthy Kentucky family. Long a powerful figure in both Ohio and national politics, he received national notoriety when the New York *Tribune* uncovered a series of cipher dispatches which proved he had tried to bribe members of the Florida canvassing board during the disputed election of 1876.[7] As the years passed, Woolley's political attitude changed. By 1886 he was willing to switch allegiance to the Republicans. He confidentially wrote Sherman that he would accept an appointment from Governor Foraker of Ohio if one were tendered. A high tariff Democrat, Woolley completely endorsed the Republican tactics of 1888. He advised Sherman that should the party drop sectionalism and stress economic issues it would break up the Solid South and would "have the support of tens of thousands of tariff democrats in the north who are holding away from [the Republicans] . . . for fear" that the party would "follow Senator Chandler's lead in race matters." [8]

From 1887 on, Woolley followed the tariff struggle in Congress with interest. Since Cleveland's message of December, 1887, House Democrats had passed the Mills bill, which drastically lowered duties. In the Senate the Republican majority in September, 1888, countered with the Allison bill, which maintained high rates on all items except rice and sugar. Congress reconvened in December, 1888, to reconsider the muddled tariff question.[9]

In close touch with events in Washington, Woolley was sure that many of the Redeemers would vote for a Republican tariff bill if Harrison assured them that he did not intend to uphold Negro supremacy. When the President-elect gave the Colonel a private letter explaining his position, the Ohioan began contacting Southern protectionists.[10]

First on Woolley's list was Colonel R. E. Rivers, the owner of three large sugar plantations in Louisiana, who had previously complained about the ruinous rates of both the Mills

and Allison bills. To Woolley the key issue was whether the
Southern planter would "actively favor protection and so save
his state," or whether he would "continue to favor the principles
of the Mills Bill, contrary to his judgment as a protectionist,
because he favors opposing the negro right or wrong." If
the Southern high tariff man would "step to the front—fight for
the economic interests of the whole country, his brother here
will see that he is not unduly troubled under President Harrison
about the claims of the gentlemen of African descent," he
told Rivers. "In fact it is becoming well understood in the
West that General Harrison is not himself maliciously inclined
—should your planters see the situation as we do!" Advising
the sugar producers to campaign actively for protection,
Woolley enclosed a copy of the reassuring note from the
President-elect.[11]

Woolley reinforced his arguments with newspaper clippings.
He sent Rivers a recently published letter from Harrison to a
Southern journalist and an editorial from the New York *Herald*.
In the first the President-elect strongly hinted that he would
drop the race question and appeal to Southern high tariff men.
"The policies in legislation advised by the Republican party I
believe are wholesome for the whole country," he wrote, "and
if those who in their hearts believe with us upon these questions would act with us, some other questions that give you
local concern would settle themselves." The *Herald* editorial,
entitled "Sound Advice to the South," called Harrison's letter
"right and wise and true statesmanship. If the Southern protectionists refuse to respond," it concluded, "on them will be
the responsibility." [12]

Continuing his correspondence, Woolley wrote next to John
Sherman. He enclosed copies of letters from protectionist
Senator Joseph E. Brown of Georgia and from Harrison, advising Sherman that they were being sent without the consent
or knowledge of the authors and asking that each be destroyed

after being read. Like Woolley, Brown was greatly disturbed by both the tariff struggle and the race problem. He feared that the proposed Senate reductions would destroy the rice industry in Georgia, while a strong Republican policy might well result in Negro domination of the South. "There are a great many old line Whigs who supported his [Harrison's] grand-father, who if the race question were eliminated from politics, are very much inclined to rally to him," the Senator advised Woolley. "Still that question is upon us and how we are to manage it peacefully and harmoniously, is the great problem of the age." [13] During the Senate debate on the Allison bill, a few weeks later, Brown repeated his protectionist argument. He demanded protection for the rice planters of Georgia, who paid fourteen times as much for their labor as their competitors in China, and for Southern industries, which were younger and more brittle than those of other sections.[14]

After exchanging views with Brown, Woolley conferred with Congressman Samuel J. Randall, a Philadelphia Democrat, and then went to Washington to be closer to the scene of action. In frequent letters to Sherman he expressed the fear that harsh talk by bloody shirt Republicans would ruin any interparty alliance. "Buy a muzzle for Senator Chandler and send me the bill," he advised Sherman, adding that it should be strong enough to keep the New Hampshire senator permanently quiet.[15]

In the long run Woolley's political machinations accomplished little. The confused tariff situation ended with each branch of Congress refusing to accept the measure of the other. During the struggle, however, Harrison, through Woolley, had once more indicated that he would forsake the Negro and foster a white, high tariff movement in the South.[16]

II

Meanwhile, Southern protectionists were begging Harrison to adopt the new Southern policy. In December a deputation of Alabama industrialists journeyed to Indianapolis to see the President-elect. Led by Thomas I. Seddon, president of the Sloss Iron and Steel Company and son of the Confederate Secretary of War, and W. H. Woodward, president of the Bessemer Iron and Steel Company, the group consisted of ten prominent iron, steel, and coal men, who controlled over $30,000,000 in invested capital. Each of the delegates was an ardent protectionist. Six were Democrats and four were Republicans. They advised Harrison to stop pampering the Negro, to appoint able men of both races to Southern offices, and, above all, to institute a high tariff policy. The visitors were certain that their program would lead to the creation of two Southern political parties based upon economics, not color. They presented a petition signed by two hundred industrialists, representing another $30,000,000 in capital, imploring Harrison to follow the suggestions outlined. Twenty of the sponsors were Republicans and one hundred and eighty were Democrats. After the meeting the Alabamians reported that the President-elect was most receptive and cordial as he listened and spoke to each member of the group. "Our only regret," remarked Seddon, "was that the whole South could not have heard him." [17]

Corresponding in scope and tone was the less publicized visit of a delegation of Atlanta industrialists. Georgians like Rufus B. Bullock, a former Republican governor but an associate of such business-minded Democrats as Governor John B. Gordon, decried all attempts to stir up the race issue and recommended a program identical to that proposed by Seddon. They also urged Harrison to establish a white, high tariff organization in the South.[18]

Other protectionists also moved. High tariff men of both parties in Tennessee planned a meeting. In Pickens, South Carolina, "independents and old line Union men" held a convention on February 4, 1889, and formed a white Republican party. The leaders included former Greenbackers and Democrats and claimed the support of over 125,000 voters.[19] A group of one hundred and thirty-two men from Grenville County, South Carolina, asked Harrison, his prospective cabinet, and all Republican senators to create an official white, high tariff party.[20]

III

In spite of these significant movements in the South, Republican sectionalists continued to demand that the Redeemers be punished. After the election both Foraker and Chandler advised Harrison to enforce the war amendments. "My views are not extreme or unreasonable," Chandler insisted. He argued that in states like Mississippi and South Carolina the Bourbons purposely kept alive the race issue in order to frighten voters away from the Republican party and suggested that Harrison appoint a fearless, aggressive Attorney General to prosecute violations of the election laws.[21]

Senator John J. Ingalls of Kansas went just as far. He believed that the Southern question would remain the most important in American politics for at least another generation and feared that the problem would intensify as Negroes became more educated and acquired more property. He too urged Harrison to adopt a strong Southern policy.[22]

During the second session of the Fiftieth Congress, which convened in December, 1888, the bloody shirt men made an unsuccessful attempt to instill life into the race issue. Chandler reintroduced his resolution to investigate the Louisiana canvass of April, 1888, the aim of which was to unseat Democratic Senator Randall L. Gibson because Negroes had supposedly been intimidated at his election, but his efforts proved unsuccessful. Hoar demanded that the Senate look into Southern frauds in general and the Louisiana case in particular, but he, too, was ignored. Sherman, by request, introduced a bill to regulate federal elections. It died in committee.[23]

To round out the short session the Senate disposed of another

matter. Almost two years before the upper chamber had ordered a committee to determine whether three white Republicans had been driven from Washington County, Texas,
because of their political beliefs. The matter dragged on until
February 13, 1889, when the investigators finally read their
report into the *Congressional Record* with a recommendation
that Congress take steps to safeguard the rights of all men.
Again the Senate did nothing.[24] As the Cleveland administration drew to a close, the defenders of the Negro in the Republican party seemed powerless.

IV

Harrison's inaugural, delivered on March 4, 1889, clearly
showed that he planned a new departure in the South. The President tied the race and tariff problems together. No longer, he
stated, were some states "necessarily only planting states" and
others industrial. Almost every area of the country contained
important manufacturing interests. Unfortunately, despite
their common problems and similar needs the sections still
mistrusted and feared one another. "Shall the prejudices and
paralysis of slavery continue to hang upon the skirts of progress?" he asked. Speaking directly to old Whigs, Harrison
argued "that if those men in the South who now accept the
tariff views of Clay and the constitutional expositions of Webster would courageously avow and defend their real convictions they would not find it difficult by friendly instruction
and cooperation to make the black man their efficient and
safe ally, not only in establishing correct principles in our
own national administration, but in preserving for their local
communities the benefits of social order and economic and
honest government." He believed that "At least until the good
offices of kindness and education have been fairly tried the
contrary conclusion can not be plausibly urged." The new
President then announced that he had "rejected the suggestion

of a special Executive policy for any section of the country."
Uniform enforcement of the laws would take place throughout
the country.[25]

Even Democrats recognized the significance of Harrison's
remarks. In a long chat with the New York *Herald*, Roger A.
Pryor, a New York City lawyer who had lived in the South
for thirty-seven years and in the North for twenty-three, said
the address showed that Harrison would abandon the Negro
and would emphasize a high tariff program in the South. A
free trader, a former Confederate officer, and onetime editor
of the Richmond *Examiner*, he predicted that such a policy,
coupled with the appointment of capable men to office, would
undoubtedly break up the Solid South. The President, however,
would be forced to fight two important influences: the tradi-
tional association of most Southerners with the Democratic
party and scared Bourbon politicians who would play up all
the myths connected with Black Republican misrule when
they believed they were losing power. He prophesied that
as soon as the fear of Negro domination wore off the tariff
would become the dominant theme of Southern politics. Former
Whigs, who favored protection, liberal federal expenditures,
and internal improvements, would happily support Harrison.
The President had cleverly appealed to these men by invoking
the spirits of Clay and Webster in his speech. If Harrison's
scheme worked out, Pryor said, his administration would be
one of the most notable in American history.[26]

This incisive interview created a furor. Democratic journals
like the Augusta (Georgia) *Chronicle* and the Charleston
News and Chronicle joined with Republican papers like the
Portland *Oregonian*, the Hartford *Courant*, and the New York
Tribune in heartily approving both Pryor's analysis and Harri-
son's plans.[27]

Southern high tariff men also responded to the President's
message. Democratic Representative Alfred A. Taylor of Ten-

nessee pointed out that the coal and iron producers would surely make his state Republican in the near future. Congressman William C. Oates of Alabama, long a defender of white supremacy, remarked, "Sometimes I feel I am more of a Republican than Democrat, and there are many people in my state who are beginning to feel the same way. On all things but the race question I believe we are Republicans. If the Republican party can eliminate the race question from its politics, remove from our people the danger of local negro domination, it can have several Southern states for the asking." [28]

The new idea in Southern Republicanism was represented by Hamilton Dudley Coleman. Recently elected to the House by the second congressional district of Louisiana, he opposed the gang led by ex-Governor Pinckney B. S. Pinchback, a Negro. Coleman, a prominent manufacturer, was president of the New Orleans Board of Trade; his district included the nine richest wards of the state. Repeatedly advising Harrison to ignore the old spoilsmen in Louisiana and to appoint only qualified whites of both parties, he predicted that in a short time over one-half of the Democrats in Louisiana would join the Republican party. Nine-tenths of the Negroes in the state, he estimated, admitted that their co-racists were ignorant and unfit for office.[29]

Spurred on by the inaugural, Alabama protectionists acted. On April 10, 1889, three hundred Republicans, independents, and Democrats from all parts of the state met at Birmingham and formed a high tariff party from which colored men were excluded. Former Republican governor William H. Smith, one of Alabama's most prominent scalawags during Reconstruction, was elected president of the association. Lewis E. Parsons of Birmingham was chosen vice-president, and Charles P. Love, editor of the Huntsville *Independent,* was made treasurer. Chairman of the convention was General James H. Sloss of Huntsville, a member of a leading industrial family. The iron and steel manufacturers of Alabama almost unanimously supported the movement, and Thomas I. Seddon, the lifelong Democrat who had led the delegation to Indianapolis the previous December, was a key backer.[30]

Negroes and the state Republican committee immediately objected. Barred from the white gathering, one hundred and thirty colored men formed their own and passed resolutions denouncing the protectionists. Similarly, a group led by Chairman R. A. Mosely of the state Republican organization also held a protest meeting.[31] Later, the Negroes sent a delegation to Washington to find out how the administration stood. Upon leaving a conference with the President on April 20, the colored men expressed great disappointment, being thoroughly convinced that members of their race would not be appointed to important offices in the South.[32]

The situation in Louisiana closely resembled that in Alabama. Late in April white Republicans met at Jeanerette, formed a high tariff league, appealed to Southern protectionists everywhere for support, and asked Harrison for official recognition. Soon after, former governors William Pitt Kellogg and Henry Clay Warmouth, two prominent pro-Negro white Republicans, visited Washington and urged Secretary of the Treasury William Windom to select a superintendent of the New Orleans mint who opposed the new organization. Windom informed them that no appointments favorable to them would be made for some time to come. Later, Kellogg, reviewing the situation, said he was firmly convinced that Harrison had engineered the Jeanerette movement.[33]

Events in the South disgusted Stalwarts. In May the New York *Age* commented that the administration had as yet given "no indication that the colored Republicans are to have the square deal, such as they are entitled to." [34] Although stressing that he had complete faith in the President, Chandler said that apparently Harrison intended to do strange things in the

South; "to ignore the colored people; to put Southern Republicans in the background, and to give the Southern offices to Cleveland Democrats who advocated protection." The administration undoubtedly desired to build up the Southern wing of the party by winning the friendship of high tariff men, but, Chandler warned, if Southern protectionists "shake hands only for office they will get few, if any." [35]

Chandler tried to rally Eastern Republicans. In a long letter to the New York *Tribune* he demanded action to end Southern outrages. The Senator argued that Iberia Parish, Louisiana, where according to the 1884 registration there were 2,491 whites and 2,795 Negroes, was a typical case. In the 1884 gubernatorial election the Republican candidate received 1,400 votes, while his Democratic opponent got only 830. Then in August, 1888, a widely publicized outrage occurred: eleven Negroes were murdered by a white mob "for no crime whatever." When the ballots for president were counted three months later Cleveland got 1,594 votes and Harrison but nine. Chandler argued "that the motive in all these brutal and always unpunished murders of negroes is political." Colored men were "intimidated, tortured and slaughtered" because they wanted to vote Republican. "How can the young men of the South grow up peaceful, well-behaved and refined members of society, when in order to carry on political Government they are incited to brutal assaults upon a helpless and defenceless race?" the Senator asked. "The people of the South should look to themselves as the ultimate sufferers from that treatment of the negroes which they are encouraging." [36]

Despite these protests, the President in June officially recognized the white man's movement in Alabama. He made Lewis E. Parsons, who had sent out the invitations for the Birmingham conference in April, the United States district attorney for middle and northern Alabama. No longer was there any doubt about the administration's position.[37]

Soon after, Harrison told a group of Southern whites that
he sympathized with them and knew intimately the problems
they faced. His family had deep roots in the South, having
resided in Virginia for two centuries. He promised to appoint
Negroes only to those minor positions which did not involve
that "personal contact with and official authority over white
citizens . . . which you and your people find so offensive." [38]

In the same month the country learned the details of the
administration's Southern policy, which had been worked out
after a series of conferences with important senators and Southern Republicans of both races. A white, high tariff party would
be formed in the South. The Negro was to be kept in the
background and given only minor posts and an attempt would
be made to detach states like West Virginia, North Carolina,
and Louisiana, where there were large numbers of protectionists and former Whigs, from the Democratic fold. The administration was sure that colored men would remain loyal Republicans when they realized that the party intended to restore
tranquillity in the South.[39]

The Republican reaction to the program was mixed. The
New York *Press* called the plan "an intelligent one, and, in
spite of all that carping Democrats can say against it, [it]
will prove a winning one." Chandler and prominent Northern
colored men disagreed. William Calvin Chase, editor of the
Negro Washington *Bee*, felt that a high tariff party could
only result in evil. Colored men had expected more than this
from a Republican administration. Chandler noted that "while
we want to enlarge the Republican party in the south by the
introduction of more white men, the way to enlarge it is not
by forming white Republican clubs but by enforcing the
fifteenth amendment." [40]

v

At two Southern elections scheduled for the last half of
1889, the Congressional canvass in Louisiana's third district

and the gubernatorial race in Virginia, the new policy was to be tested. Administration leaders hoped that here the Solid South would be split and a new, protectionist Republican organization would be created.

The Louisiana campaign provided the Republicans with their initial opportunity. To the dismay of William Pitt Kellogg, who favored a strong policy,[41] Louisiana Republicans nominated a rich sugar planter, Henry C. Minor, for Congressman. A Republican only since 1884, Minor had been a delegate to the national convention of 1888.[42] Emulating the scheme which had brought his close friend Hamilton Dudley Coleman victory the year before, the candidate appealed to white protectionists. He opposed identifying himself with men like Warmouth, fearing that he would surely be defeated if he were.[43]

The Republicans were determined to win. Although only a seat in the lower house of Congress was involved, the National Committee spared no effort. First, it saturated the district with pamphlets, such as one by Senator William P. Frye of Maine on protection and another by Harrison on labor.[44] Then, going to lengths unheard of since the end of Reconstruction, the Committee sent three Northern Republican Congressmen to the area to discuss the tariff.

Arriving in Louisiana on successive days, each of the Representatives gave a long interview to the New Orleans *Times-Democrat*. The first was Julius Caesar Burrows of Michigan, an ardent protectionist. The sole issue in this canvass, he said, was the tariff, by which "alone the South can hope to build and establish her industries." Asked whether he intended to deal at all with the status of the Negro, Burrows replied that he was surprised to learn that the race question "was playing a part in the present election." Next to arrive was Jonathan H. Rowell of Illinois, an important member of the House Elections Committee. He frankly acknowledged that he came "at the request of the National Committee," and not at the insistence of Minor or of the state Republican organization. His purpose, too, was to discuss the tariff exclusively. The third member of the triumvirate was Samuel R. Peters of Kansas. Like the others, he was sent to expound on protectionism. Peters was especially well liked in Louisiana because he had once helped the New Orleans Sugar Exchange protest to the Senate Finance Committee the fifty per cent reductions in the Allison bill.[45]

During his campaign, Minor stressed a completely Whiggish program. In speeches and in his letter of acceptance he advocated a high tariff on sugar, the production of which in the United States, he correctly said, was largely confined to his district, and federal appropriations for levees and dikes. He strongly emphasized his opposition to Kellogg and to the regular Republican state organization.[46]

In spite of the spirited Republican canvass Democrat Andrew Price thrashed Minor, 18,761 votes to 11,405.[47] Clearly something had gone wrong, but what? Burrows, who left the district a day before the ballots were cast, gave a reason. "From what I have seen elections are a travesty in Louisiana," he said. The Congressman suggested that to save time and money the governor of the state might just as well dispense with all formalities, make out the necessary forms, and automatically hand certificates of election to the Bourbon candidates, who were certain to win by fraud anyway. Similarly, Minor attributed his defeat to the Democratic suppression of the Republican vote.[48]

In reality the Republicans fared poorly in all sections of the third district. Intimidation undoubtedly took place in St. Martin Parish, which in 1880 had 6,876 Negroes and 5,783 whites, for Price received 966 votes to only ten for Minor. Yet Minor, running little better than Harrison had in 1888, was able to carry only two of the state's four largest sugar-producing parishes, all of which were overwhelmingly colored. And he lost all six of the white-dominated parishes by substantial margins.[49]

A split within the Republican ranks badly hurt Minor. Completely disregarded by the administration's plans, Kellogg threw the colored vote of the district against the Republican candidate. In many towns Negroes formed Democratic clubs and cast large blocs of votes for Price. The Republicans were also injured by the fact that the Allison bill had cut the sugar tariff by fifty per cent.[50]

The final tabulations did not surprise the Springfield *Daily Republican*. "This is the exact result predicted by the *Republican* when the plan to build up a white Republican party in the South was first given out," it commented.[51]

VI

By the summer and fall of 1889 there were other signs that the Southern Negro thoroughly disliked the new Republican policy and would not fall into line. In late July the colored people of Newberry, South Carolina, objected because Postmaster General John Wanamaker refused to appoint a Negro postmaster. The revolt, however, centered in North Carolina. When Negroes in Mecklenburg County did not receive federal patronage, they burned Harrison and his cabinet in effigy. Thousands of angry Negroes attended a protest meeting and accused the President of discriminating against their race. They decided to send a committee to Washington when Congress assembled in December to protest.[52]

After the Louisiana debacle, Republican eyes turned to Virginia. In the Old Dominion two white factions, one led by ex-Senator William Mahone, a former Confederate general, and the other by James D. Brady, claimed to represent the Republican party. Administration leaders realized that unless the dispute was peacefully settled Virginia would go Democratic in November.[53] Quay and Clarkson, therefore, met with the heads of the rival groups in Washington and ironed out all their differences. Both sides agreed to support Mahone's call for a convention on August 22 at Norfolk, and they regarded the former Senator as the logical and most powerful candidate for governor. This decision showed a complete disregard of the Virginia Negro, since in 1888 Mahone had opposed the election to Congress of the state's most prominent colored man, John Mercer Langston, on the grounds that the Old Dominion was not yet ready to be represented by a Negro.[54]

A few weeks later, the Norfolk convention nominated Mahone for governor. Its platform emphasized the tariff issue and practically ignored the race question. No Negro candidates were put on the ticket, two ex-Confederate officers being selected to run for lieutenant governor and attorney general.[55]

Virginia Democrats made no secret of the fact that they intended to play up the threat of Negro domination. No matter what tactics Mahone used, they were sure that Bourbonism would once more be vindicated by the people of the state.[56] Wade Hampton, now a United States Senator from South Carolina, urged the Democrats to stress this theme. The Republicans, he said, were "trying to win by introducing the Economic question in the South. But as long as the matter of local self-government demands our attention our people cannot divide on this issue. Whether a man is a Protectionist or a Tariff Reformer, the safety or welfare of his home is paramount to the tariff." [57]

Mahone delivered his major campaign address at Abingdon on September 23. After briefly defending the free ballot, he ridiculed the Democratic emphasis on the race issue. "This pretended concern for the safety of our civilization," he said, "is merely to mislead and turn away the more thoughtless and gullible of our population from the exercise of their political rights in the direction of their own convictions and interests." The Negro problem was "employed as a mere scarecrow to excite prejudice and fear, in the hope of diverting the white working-man from casting his ballot for the candidate he honestly prefers." Devoting a major portion of his speech to Republican tariff policy, Mahone claimed that it was responsible for the growth and prosperity of the country from 1861 to 1880.[58]

Mugwump and Democratic papers ridiculed both the speech and the Republican campaign tactics. "As was expected, Mahone devoted much of his [Abingdon] tirade to protection," commented the Richmond *State*, "that being his favorite method to obscure the real issue from the people of Virginia." The barrels being shipped from Washington to Virginia lately, the journal insisted on another occasion, were filled with money which Quay and the National Committee were using to bribe voters. The New York *Times*, now Mugwump, noted that the character of the Republican party was indeed changing. To this paper it was "now plain beyond dispute, that the President, through Mahone, is engaged in organizing a white protectionist Republican party in the South, in which the share of the negro shall be confined to casting his vote." This new attitude was "inconsistent . . . with the principles and professions of the Republican party for the past quarter century." [59]

These attacks did not shake Mahone's confidence. He predicted that any Republican losses suffered in the Negro areas of the state would be more than offset by gains from the "protected industries" in the southwestern counties of Virginia.[60]

Important Republicans helped Mahone. Thomas B. Reed, J. Donald Cameron, William McKinley, John Sherman, Quay, Burrows, and Clarkson, all of whom shared Mahone's political faith, also shared his home for days at a time. Reasoning that the Negro would remain a Republican even if deprived of political patronage, these men reported that their purpose was to build up, as far as possible, a white man's party in the state.[61] In October Clarkson toured the Old Dominion for the National Committee. The electoral votes of Virginia were sorely needed by the party, he wrote the President. The state must be carried at all costs. "I have told M[ahone] we will supply all the M[oney] needed" to win, he confided.[62] Clarkson met with anti-Mahone Republicans and threatened all those who refused to support the Republican ticket with political ostracism. By the second week of October, Mahone, who in other years had not received a cent in campaign funds, had been given over $25,000 by the National Committee.[63]

Shortly before the election Burrows was optimistic. He had "no great hope" of strengthening the Republican organization in the South "except by encouraging and building a white Republican party . . . which can be done on the issue of protection to American industry better than any I know of." He believed that in time free elections would take place in the South.[64]

Election day was November 5. When it was over, Philip W. McKinney, the Democratic nominee for governor, had 162,654 votes and Mahone but 120,477. The Bourbons captured sixty-nine of the one hundred seats in the lower chamber of the state legislature and twenty-six of the forty in the upper.[65] It was an amazingly poor showing for the Republicans considering that Harrison, without even campaigning in the state, in 1888 had lost by only two thousand votes.

Like Minor, Mahone was soundly beaten in all areas of his state. He captured only seven of the fifty-six white counties, five fewer than the party had taken in the 1885 gubernatorial election, which was also a Democratic landslide. The story in the colored belt was just as bad. Mahone was victorious in only nineteen of the forty-three counties with Negro majorities, although in 1885 the Republicans had won thirty-three of them. In Charlotte County, with 10,949 Negroes and 5,704 whites, the Democrats amassed 1,709 votes to 785 for Mahone, and in Halifax County, which had 20,295 Negroes and 13,293 whites, the Bourbons received 4,097 votes and the Republicans only 1,920. Mahone did even worse in industrial regions. The three largest iron and steel producing counties, Allegheny, Henrico, and Page, all of which were Republican in 1885, now went Democratic. Other counties with substantial manufacturing interests, including Campbell, Frederick, Pittsylvania, Norfolk, and Spotsylvania, also were against Mahone. The appeal to the state's protectionists had been ignored.[66]

Press comments, regardless of party, were harsh. According to the Democratic New York *World*, McKinney's victory showed that "the famous scheme of building a white republican party in the South" had "taken a wrong turn at the crossroads." To the Negro New York *Age* the defeat of Minor in Louisiana and of Mahone in Virginia, "both of whom, with the sanction of President Harrison's Administration, fought the fight on the 'White Man's Party' idea," proved that the South was "wedded to the Democratic Party, and that any Republican policy which ignores the position of the Afro-American" would end disastrously. The Mugwump New York *Times* agreed. "Mahone," it revealed, "was to lay the foundations of a protection party in the South. The negro leaders," although "furnished plenty of money," were to be "kept in the background." Whites were to be tempted by "profits from the tariff and by the gift of offices"; they were "not to be offended by the obtrusive race issue." The scheme, the *Times* went on, "has failed. The people of Virginia are not to be bought." Having "failed ignominiously" in the Old Dominion, the administration's policy was "not likely to succeed elsewhere." [67] Repudiated by both protectionists and Negroes, the Republican dream for the South came to a sorry end.

9

The Lines of Sectional Battle Are Drawn

I

During the first half of 1890 interest in the Negro problem ran high. In one form or another the subject was almost constantly before Congress and the public. And for the first time in sixteen years the Republicans, who controlled both the executive and legislative branches of the government, were in a position to pass bills aiding Southern education and strengthening federal control of elections.

A series of Democratic blunders early in the first session of the Fifty-first Congress helped bloody shirt Republicans. Three Bourbon Senators provided the Republicans with needed ammunition when they demanded that Southern Negroes be deported from the United States. Wilkinson Call of Florida wanted this country to offer Spain $50,000,000 or $70,000,000 for Cuba, which could be used as a dumping ground for discontented Negroes.[1] A resolution sponsored by Randall L. Gibson of Louisiana instructed the Senate Committee on

Foreign Relations to investigate the feasibility of setting aside or acquiring territory to which Negroes could be sent and asked the committee to suggest possible methods of transportation. Under the terms of a bill presented by Matthew C. Butler of South Carolina, Negroes from any Southern state could apply to a United States commissioner for permanent emigration. Travel accommodations for poor Negroes would be provided by the Quartermaster General of the Army. An initial appropriation of five million dollars was to cover expenses.[2]

Although Butler's act never came to a vote, it was vigorously debated in the Senate. John T. Morgan, an Alabama Democrat, said that the measure closely resembled the resolution introduced in 1879 by the present Secretary of the Treasury, William Windom, then a Senator. There was, Morgan believed, "a natural incongruity, 'an irrepressible conflict,' between the races," for which there was no solution except separation. Colored men were inherently and innately inferior. Quoting extensively from the writings of Henry M. Stanley, the explorer, he argued that the American Negro, if returned to the Dark Continent, would help his African brothers achieve a higher degree of civilization. Butler insisted that he was presenting the only possible solution to the race problem. His measure was nonpartisan and would produce results which would unquestionably justify the outlay of money.[3]

Northern Republicans rallied to the colored man's defense. To them Call, Gibson, and Butler appeared to be motivated by the worst impulses. George Frisbie Hoar scoffed at the idea of Negro inferiority, citing the long and honorable service of colored Representatives and Senators. He was convinced that only a system of universal education could permamently solve the race problem. White people had no right to ask anyone to emigrate. John J. Ingalls of Kansas made the key Republican speech. He was sure that the Bourbons could not prevent the colored man from achieving social and economic equality. As Ingalls saw it, there were four suggested solutions to the race problem: amalgamation, extermination, separation, and disfranchisement. He offered a fifth: justice. "I appeal to the South to try the experiment of justice," he cried. "Stack your guns, open your ballot-boxes, register your voters, black and white; and if, after the experiment has been fairly and honestly tried, it appears that the African race is incapable of civilization, if it appears that the complexion burned upon him by a tropic sun is incompatible with freedom, I pledge myself to consult with you about some measure of solving the race problem; but until then nothing can be done." [4]

The Republican press seconded Ingalls's views. The Cleveland *Gazette*, a Negro newspaper, called the Butler bill the "merest nonsense" and believed that the colored man, here to stay, should be better treated. The Portland *Oregonian* explained that the deportation of Southern whites would solve the racial question as adequately as the expulsion of Negroes would, and the Newark *Daily Advertiser* commented, "It is difficult to entertain seriously as ridiculous a project as this." [5]

These emigration schemes did the Redeemers far more harm than good. By focusing national attention upon outrages in their section, Southerners created a good deal of sympathy for the Negro and gave Republican orators a platform from which to condemn Bourbonism.

II

A far different aspect of the Southern question also received attention early in 1890. The education bill sponsored by Henry W. Blair of New Hampshire once more was before Congress. It had passed the Senate and had been bottled up in the House in 1884, 1886, and 1888. [6]

As amended, the measure provided for government aid to

common schools for ten years. Starting with $7,000,000, the annual appropriation was to be increased gradually to $15,000,000, kept there for one year, and then decreased to $5,000,000. The states and territories were to receive payments for each illiterate over ten years old within their boundaries as of 1880. Separate schools for whites and Negroes were permitted and state governors were required to submit annual reports on the distribution of funds. Since nearly three-fourths of the nation's illiterates were in the sixteen Southern states, and 69.7 per cent of these were colored, there was little doubt about whom the bill would primarily aid.[7]

From the first there was a good deal of opposition to Blair's bill, even among Republican Senators. John Sherman believed that the government should have a stronger voice in determining the curriculum of the schools aided. "What kind of education, what kind of ideas, is to be promulgated?" he asked. "Who is to control that matter?" John A. Logan of Illinois disliked the fact that illiterates of all ages, even those ninety or one hundred, were counted in the census, although only children from five to twenty went to school. Charles H. Van Wyck of Nebraska did not trust the Southern states to administer the funds. The Bourbons had violated the war amendments and would not observe the spirit and letter of this act either.[8]

Southern Democrats found fault with the measure, too. Richard Coke of Texas said that it would extend federal interference into still another sphere. The bill would "add another element to the various others growing out of the race question to be agitated in the political arena and foment discord and trouble." Zebulon Vance of North Carolina felt the measure was a partisan one brought forward by the Republicans solely for political gain. Its passage would merely complicate an already involved issue.[9]

In the middle 1880's much of the opposition to the Blair bill came from those who feared that it would eliminate the surplus in the federal treasury and pave the way for an even higher tariff. Republican papers like the Chicago *Tribune* and Senators like Joseph R. Hawley of Connecticut joined Democrats like Representative Henry S. Van Eaton of Mississippi in fearing the act for this reason. In 1886 Blair was thoroughly convinced that free traders were primarily responsible for the defeat of his pet bill in the House.[10]

After 1889 Blair could count upon the strong support of President Benjamin Harrison, who had long favored the measure. As a senator he had voted for it in 1884 and two years later had been paired in favor of it. A paragraph in Harrison's letter accepting the Republican presidential nomination in 1888 strongly endorsed national aid to education.[11]

In his first annual message to Congress, delivered in December, 1889, the President dealt at length with the subject. The federal government had long aided education, he said. Heretofore, help had consisted primarily of land grants to the states, but a direct appropriation of money would be just as legal, he believed. The sudden emancipation of the slaves and the inability of the states to care adequately for them prompted national interest in the problem. But federal aid should supplement, not supplant, local efforts. The President recommended that any allotment of funds "be so limited in annual amount and as to the time over which it is to extend as will on the one hand give the local school authorities opportunity to make the best use of the first year's allowance, and on the other deliver them from temptation to unduly postpone the assumption of the whole burden themselves." [12]

More than counterbalancing Harrison's enthusiasm, however, was the new and powerful opposition which had developed. In the late 1880's by far the most important enemy of the Blair bill was the New York *Evening Post*. Strangely enough, this influential publication had barely noticed the measure when it was first introduced; it seemed more to straddle the issue than to take a stand on it.[13]

Then in 1885 a new editorial writer, Edward P. Clark, joined the staff of the paper and of its weekly edition, the *Nation*.[14] As soon as he entered the scene, he savagely and continually attacked the education bill. In the *Evening Post's* office Clark ruled over a little section known as the "Bureau of Mendicancy," which issued four editions of an anti-Blair act pamphlet appropriately entitled *A Bill to Promote Mendicancy*. Consisting primarily of his blistering editorials, the booklet was sent to all Congressmen, regardless of party, to prominent newspaper owners, and to important educators. Copies were also sold at newsstands. Because of his antipathy toward the act, Clark soon became known to his colleagues at the *Evening Post* as "The Blair Bill Editor." [15]

The journalist opposed the measure because he feared that it would lead to complete federal control of education. "During the past year I have given much time, study and thought to the present tendency toward paternalism in government," he told President Grover Cleveland in 1887. "My investigation of the condition of Southern education when the Blair bill was up—which I think I may say without egotism was the most thorough ever made—resulted in profoundly impressing me with the conviction that recourse to Washington for school money would inevitably harm the schools in the States by weakening the spirit of self-reliance." Clark believed that "the disposition to fall back upon the General Government for everything" was "the most alarming tendency in American character at the present time. Unless it is arrested there is, it seems to me, grave danger for our future as a nation." [16]

As part of his anti-Blair bill campaign Clark implored James B. Angell, president of the University of Michigan, to come out against the measure. The Southern states, he was convinced, were prospering as never before and were thoroughly capable of perfecting their own educational systems. "It seems to me," Clark told Angell, "that any candid person, making to-day an unbiased study of the question will be forced to the conclusion that, if there ever was any excuse for Federal interference in this matter of education, on the ground that the South was poor and could not raise sufficiently large school funds, that time has passed in view of the overwhelming evidence that the South is rapidly growing in prosperity, and that the people in most parts of the section are as rapidly of their own accord increasing taxation for the purpose of public education." The editor, early in 1889, admitted that he was asking important men throughout the country to write Harrison of their dislike for the Blair bill. "I think that a letter from the President of the chief University of the West would be regarded by General Harrison as entitled to great weight," he flattered Angell, "and that the writing of such a letter might well be regarded as in the light of a public duty. . . . It is quite unnecessary for me to add that any reference to the *Evening Post*, which so strongly opposed Harrison's election, would be calculated to prejudice the end in view." [17]

Supporters of the education measure readily admitted that the *Evening Post*'s campaign was a potent factor in shaping public opinion. Waving a copy of Clark's pamphlet in his hand, Blair on the Senate floor complained that the influence of the Bureau of Mendicancy seemed to be everywhere. Imitating the *Evening Post*, scores of papers were now calling the Senator's pet measure the Bill to Promote Mendicancy.[18] John Jay, an ardent advocate of the bill, noted that some Republicans had voted against it "in accord with the advice of the Evening Post which is an unsafe guide for the Republican party." He suggested that Republicans in this instance might do well to follow one of Napoleon's maxims: "If your enemy wishes you to do a thing, do not do it for the reason he wishes you to do it." [19]

When Clark died in 1903, many newspapers recalled the defeat of the education bill as his most glorious achievement. His own journal commented:

> Perhaps the best instance of Mr. Clark's resources was the campaign against the Blair bill, which he carried on in the columns of the *Evening Post* for all the years in the eighties when that measure was to the front in Congress. This scheme to take millions from the Federal Treasury in aid of public education in the South he opposed with a fertility of argument and a mastery of detail which were universally conceded to have been the main cause of its final defeat. Amassing his evidence indefatigably, he bombarded State Legislatures and Congress with it until their surrender was forced.[20]

The Indianapolis *News* agreed:

> No man in the country did as much as he did to defeat the vicious Blair education bill, which came so near passing during Mr. Harrison's Administration. Mr. Clark not only denounced it in the columns of his paper, but he established a sort of private literary bureau, through which he conducted a personal and private warfare against it.[21]

Similarly, the Brooklyn *Daily Eagle* noted that Clark was responsible for "the articles as extraordinary for number as for ability, which appeared" in the *Evening Post* "against the Blair Educational Bill. Those articles by attrition, by reproduction and by the influence which they exerted upon writers on other papers, wrought the defeat of the measure, and changed a majority for it in Congress to a strong majority against it there." [22]

As if Clark was not enough, Blair and his followers also attributed the education bill's growing unpopularity to a systematic campaign of the Jesuit order. To the Senator many of the journals which disliked his measure were merely "organs of Jesuitism in this country." He swore that after his bill had passed the Senate and was in the House in 1886 "a Senator showed me, and I read it with my own eyes, the original letter of a Jesuit priest, in which he begged a member of Congress to oppose this bill and kill it, saying that they had organized all over the country for its destruction, that they succeeded in the committee of the House, and they would destroy the bill inevitably, and if they had only known it early enough they could have prevented its passage through the Senate." The Jesuits were "engaged in that nefarious and wicked work" of gaining control of the country by destroying the public school system. They were, according to Blair, more of a threat to the security of the United States than the anarchists.[23]

During the years his measure was before Congress, Blair frequently denounced the Jesuits and cited articles in two of their leading magazines, the *Church Progress and Catholic World* of St. Louis and the *Catholic Review* of New York, as proof of the group's hatred for his act. "The Blair bill is dying! 'Ring out, wild bells to the sky,' " proclaimed the *Catholic Review*. "Its proposal to spend millions in Southern education has been definitely rejected by the South which it purposes to benefit. It outraged, first of all, the independent spirit of the States it considered paupers; it violated the spirit of the Constitution, which forbids the Federal Government to offer and the States to take bribes . . . and it was above all a blow aimed at Catholicity in America. Therefore, it deserved to fail." The principle embodied in the bill would eventually mean "death to parochial schools! But the South will not have it, and the great parties fear it. Mr. Blair can go back to New Hampshire." The *Church Progress and Catholic World* expressed similar sentiments.[24]

Blair might also have pointed to the violent opposition of *The American Catholic Quarterly Review* to his act. John

Gilmary Shea, a prominent writer for the publication, charged that the idea of federal aid to "education of the Southern Negro" had been conceived by Reverend Amory Dwight Mayo, a Unitarian minister. This "scheme thus generated in the brain of a New England Protestant clergyman required some one to take it up and push it in Congress. Such a person was found in Senator Blair," who was in reality a mere tool of more powerful forces. Under the education act sectarian institutions would receive no money, the term "sectarian" being "aimed especially at Catholic schools," Shea argued, "for it is the only church which has any extensive system." The bill, moreover, would create an army of federal officers "who will debauch the public morals." Congregationalists, Methodists, Baptists, and Presbyterians strongly favored it because they realized it would benefit them. Defying Blair to produce the "letter of a nameless Jesuit priest to a nameless member [of Congress] asking him to kill the bill," Shea warned Catholics that only evil could accompany passage of the measure.

Education when based on religion and morality is a good; without such control it may be and must be a curse and not a blessing to any community. . . . Even now all reference to God and prayer and eternity is carefully expunged from books adopted in the common schools of the country. . . . If control of all the public schools in the country is allowed to be grasped by the Federal Government, the rationalizing process becomes comparatively easy. Instead of laboring to effect the dechristianizing scheme in State after State, the whole effort can be concentrated at Washington.

Here is one great danger which it behooves all men who still believe in Christ the Redeemer and God the Creator to labor to avert.[25]

The long struggle over the education bill came to an end in March, 1890, when by thirty-one to thirty-seven the Senate rejected it. At that time twenty-three Republicans and eight Democrats were for the measure and seventeen Republicans and twenty Democrats were against it. Of the eight Senators who changed their votes from affirmative in 1888 to negative in 1890, three, Sherman, Philetus Sawyer of Wisconsin, and J. Donald Cameron of Pennsylvania, were Republicans, four were Southern Democrats, and one, Henry C. Payne of Ohio, was a Northern Democrat. The *Evening Post* may have influenced Frank Hiscock, a New York Republican, who opposed the act, but it had little effect upon William M. Evarts, who favored it. While any analysis of the vote along religious lines is far from conclusive and certainly ignores many factors, most of the senators from the seven states with close to or over 250,000 Catholics—New York, Massachusetts, Pennsylvania, Illinois, Ohio, Minnesota, and Wisconsin—disliked the bill. Eight Republicans and one Democrat representing these regions voted or were paired against the act, while five Republicans endorsed it.[26]

Certain general patterns emerged from the four Senate votes between 1884 and 1890. In each instance a Republican majority wanted federal aid to education, although the size of the majority diminished considerably in these years. Moreover, except for 1890 a majority of Democrats always favored the bill. During these years the Far West was the only section which increasingly favored the measure; conversely, the South became most deeply opposed to it.[27]

After the defeat of his bill in 1890, Blair once again charged that the combined opposition of the *Evening Post* and the Jesuits had killed his measure. He knew that federal aid to education, unable to pass a Republican-controlled Congress, was dead.[28] Powerful and numerous foes had destroyed one of the colored man's chief hopes for social and political improvement.

III

Meanwhile, agitation for an election bill was being led by a group of young Republican Congressmen, headed by Henry

Cabot Lodge of Massachusetts. Interest in the Negro problem was a Lodge family tradition. As the Congressman later wrote, he had been reared before the Civil War in a "Free Soil, Republican household." Both his father, John Ellerton Lodge, and his grandfather, Henry Cabot, had left the Whig party in 1850, when Daniel Webster had espoused compromise with the South. "Profoundly stirred" by the sectional issue, John Ellerton Lodge, a former New Orleans cotton factor, in 1856 "went down to the wharves, where his ships were lying, and made a speech to the sailors, longshoremen, and stevedores in behalf of Fremont," the Republican presidential candidate.[29]

Wendell Phillips occasionally and Charles Sumner frequently visited the Lodge home. Greatly influenced by Sumner, Henry Cabot Lodge always believed he "stood for human freedom" and was "among the first of those who have been well called the human rights statesmen of that period." [30]

The Civil War deeply affected young Lodge. Although only ten in 1861, he strongly hoped that the North would fight to defend Fort Sumter. He was enraged when a hostile mob killed four and wounded thirty-six members of the Sixth Massachusetts Regiment as it passed through Baltimore shortly after the outbreak of hostilities. And the sight of Robert Gould Shaw's Negro regiment marching off to battle was something the youngster never forgot. So moved was he that he even contemplated enlisting in the army as a drummer boy. "The war," he wrote in 1913, "left me, as I think it left those of my time generally, with certain profound convictions which nothing can shake." He viewed the struggle chiefly as a moral conflict: "the North was right and the right won." [31]

Coupled with this heritage was Lodge's strong belief in the sanctity of the ballot. One of the first Ph.D.'s in Congress, he had long entertained notions about purity in politics. In 1879 Lodge wrote an article for the *Atlantic Monthly* favoring the reform of both state and local electoral procedures, and

the next year he urged Governor-elect John D. Long of Massachusetts to enforce strictly and impartially the Bay State's
voting laws.[32]

After Harrison's victory Lodge became one of the public
champions of a national elections act. He admitted in February,
1889, that he was "perfectly willing that there should be a
United States supervisor and, if necessary, a file of United
States soldiers at every polling place in my district" in order
to guarantee fair elections. During the campaign of that year
he frequently advocated a Force bill "for every district" in
the country.[33]

As December, 1889, the time for the assembling of the first
session of the Fifty-first Congress, drew near, Lodge became
more and more disgruntled. The Bourbons had stolen a large
number of House seats in the last election, he fumed. Something must be done.[34]

The Congressman readily admitted that the success of his
plans depended largely upon the committee designations of
the Speaker of the House. He worked feverishly to secure the
election of his close friend and fellow New Englander, Thomas
B. Reed, as Speaker and after Reed's victory was appointed
chairman of a Select Committee on the Election of the President, Vice-President, and Representatives in Congress.[35]

A short while later, Lodge, in an authorized interview with
the New York *Herald*, stated that two main suffrage problems
faced the national legislature. First, contested election cases
were becoming far too numerous; they occupied from thirty
to sixty working days in each session and created much bitter
feeling. He suggested that the courts might be able to decide
these disputes better than Congress could. A more important
problem was the open suppression of the ballot in the South.
A bill to regulate the election of Congressmen was needed. In
spite of the vast amount of confused and confusing talk on
the subject, Lodge advised that "there is nothing in the least

violent or revolutionary in what is proposed and at the same time nothing can disguise its importance." For many years, he said, the people in the Northern states had favored an election act. Whether either political party benefited from such a law was beside the point; fair elections were essential to good government. "It is a very narrow view of the subject which sees in the protection of the ballot at Congressional elections a mere partisan measure," he continued.

If honest voting all over the country is going to give the republican party additional seats in Congress it is because they are now cheated out of seats which belong to them. If they are not cheated out of seats which belong to them an absolutely fair system of elections will give them no advantage. . . . We must have fair elections if we are going to carry on our system of government successfully, but we must have something more. We must have an absolutely popular belief that the elections are fair and the verdict of the ballot box honest.[36]

Speaking in Newark to a Lincoln's Day gathering, the Congressman once more insisted that frauds must be ended. "Every man who is an American citizen has a right to vote, and a right to expect that his vote will be counted. The Republican party has made the promise, and if it fails to make an effort to give him that right then it is a case of misplaced confidence." [37]

As the session wore on, some Republican members of the House Committee on Elections became convinced that a Force bill must be passed. During the many contested election cases which the committee investigated in early 1890, abundant evidence was produced that Southerners were violating the Constitution. "No fair man can sit in Committee as I have done and hear the testimony and arguments in seventeen contested cases without becoming thoroughly *convinced* of the absolute lawlessness in elections in a large portion of the South," wrote Nils P. Haugen of Wisconsin. In the South, he commented on another occasion, "It is no wrong and is rather a credit to a man to defraud the negro of the suffrage, and still these people are flattering themselves that they are honorable and honest. They are certainly breeding a contempt *for* the law that must end disastrously to themselves in the end." John F. Lacey of Iowa, another member of the committee, came to a similar conclusion.[38]

With the Republicans in control of both the Congress and the presidency, bloody shirters spurred their fellow party members on. "That some law must be passed is now apparent," Chandler told Reed. "The necessity is upon the Republican party, and the sooner the shock of conflict begins in the House or the Senate, or both, the better for us all." Chandler remarked to a reporter that nothing was more important than the Force bill. "To pass the measure is the first duty of the Republicans in Congress, and it ought to be given precedence over everything," he said. Spooner also vowed to push the issue forward until a bill was enacted.[39]

Northern Republicans presented a large number of election bills in the new Congress. Senators Hoar, Sherman, Spooner, Chandler, and Representatives Lodge, Jonathan H. Rowell of Illinois, and Harrison Kelley of Kansas sponsored measures.[40] Late in April, 1890, House Republicans instructed Lodge to make order out of chaos.[41]

In its final form the Lodge bill was a strong measure. A chief supervisor of elections was to enforce it in cities with 20,000 or more inhabitants, in entire Congressional districts upon the application of one hundred voters, and in counties and parishes forming a part of Congressional districts when requested to do so by fifty voters. He was to be assisted in each Congressional district by three regional supervisors, representing both major parties, who were to be appointed by United States district judges. The regional supervisors were empowered to inspect registration books, attend elections, and perform a variety of other functions. In towns of 20,000 or more they were required to make a house-to-house canvass before each election and inform registrants of the mechanics, place, and time of voting. Finally, a three-man board of canvassers, appointed by United States circuit courts, was to certify the results in, and check the count of, each Congressional district every November 15.[42]

Far from receiving universal approval, the measure was fiercely debated in a Republican caucus for three days. Opposition to the bill was led by Hamilton G. Ewart of North Carolina, who denounced it as a partisan measure which would hurt the South. Arguing that in his state most elections were as fair as anywhere, he declared that the Lodge bill would intensify race prejudice and sectional hostility. If the South was left alone, the Negro question would eventually settle itself. Western Republicans, who were pushing for a free silver measure, also had little desire to pass the bill. And Joseph G. Cannon of Illinois objected to giving it priority over other important legislation. After the debate, the caucus voted by a majority of only one to report the bill. Cannon illustrated the complete submission of party members to the decision by agreeing to present the order giving the bill right of way in the House.[43]

The day after the caucus, Lodge introduced in the lower chamber the measure bearing his name.[44] The lines of the fiercest sectional battle since Reconstruction were drawn.

IV

While these events were taking place, pressure for the Lodge, or Force, bill was building up among the Northern Republicans who had tried to break the Solid South during 1889 with a high tariff platform. The defeats in Louisiana and Virginia finally convinced these men that the Bourbons were not to be trusted and that only federal regulation of elections could solve the sectional problem.[45]

This group of converts contained some of the best-known and most important Republicans. It included President Benjamin Harrison; Senator John Sherman of Ohio; Thomas B. Reed, the newly elected Speaker of the House; Representative Julius Caesar Burrows of Michigan, a key member of the House and one of Reed's chief rivals in 1889 for the speakership; James S. Clarkson, the First Assistant Postmaster General, vice-chairman of the Republican National Committee, a skilled political organizer, party boss, and patronage dispenser; and Grenville Dodge, the New York railroad engineer, businessman, lobbyist, and a former Congressman from Iowa. During the first six months of 1890 these men helped lead the Republican fight for passage of an election bill; on this issue Reed and Clarkson became even more Stalwart than Chandler and Ingalls.

The sharp revision in the administration's policy became evident when Harrison delivered his first annual message to Congress on December 3, 1889. In his inaugural eight months before, the President had openly invited Southern high tariff men to join the Republican party, had strongly implied that he would not press the race issue, and had suggested that he would appoint only whites to high Southern offices. Far different, this address contained a firm statement on the Negro question. To the disgrace of the entire nation, he said, colored people in many areas were "by various devices deprived of any effective exercise of their political rights and of many of their civil rights." The President asked what Southern communities were doing to solve the problem and wanted to know when the freedmen would be given full social and political equality. The present generation, he believed, should settle the issue once and for all and should not leave it for those to come. Harrison then called Congress's attention "to [a] consideration of such measures within its well-defined constitutional powers as will secure to all people a free exercise of the right of suffrage and every other civil right under the Constitution and laws of the United States." The Negro should be protected "in all his relations to the Federal Government, whether as litigant, juror, or witness in the courts, as an elector for members of Congress, or as a peaceful traveler upon our interstate railways." [46]

Reviewing the message, the New York *Age,* the nation's leading colored paper, noted the radical change in the President's views. He had definitely abandoned the idea of fostering a white man's party in the South and was demanding the enactment of a Force bill.[47]

Soon after, Blanche K. Bruce, the Negro who formerly served as Senator from Mississippi, conferred with Harrison and reported that the race problem was "giving the President more anxiety than anything else, and he is exceedingly desirous of securing some solution of it." [48] So confident a year ago that he could break the Solid South, Harrison was now disillusioned.

Perhaps Julius Caesar Burrows of Michigan best described the shifting Republican attitude. "For some time," said the Congressman, recalling his role in the Virginia election of 1889, "I was strongly of the opinion that the best way to solve the race question was for the Republican party to push the industrial problem in the South, and, if possible, turn the attention of the people" of that region "away from the outrages incident to race prejudice" and onto economic themes. It was with that belief, Burrows revealed, that he had entered the Virginia campaign and had supported an ex-Confederate general, William Mahone, for governor. He had delivered speeches on the tariff question which were enthusiastically received by large audiences all over the state, even in the Democratic stronghold of Richmond. The sole issue of the canvass should have been free trade versus a high tariff. But as the campaign progressed the Democrats, to a man, raised the dreaded cry of Negro supremacy to divert attention from the real issue. This charge, Burrows continued, was foolish, since in Virginia whites outnumbered Negroes two to one. Its only purpose was to prevent the Solid South from splitting on the rock of protection to American industry. "The cry, ridiculous as it was, was successful," he noted. "I then became convinced that all efforts to build up a party of protection, even in Virginia, would be futile unless some security could be given for a free ballot and an honest count." [49]

Sherman went through a corresponding transformation. In September, 1888, he insisted that the tariff was the only subject worthy of political consideration. The South should be allowed to handle the race problem without Northern interference. Bloody shirt speeches merely hindered sectional reconciliation. Yet in the summer of 1890 the Senator told the Cincinnati *Enquirer:* "I favor the election of members of Congress under Federal authority. The Government ought to take supreme control of such elections, even to the extremity of defraying every expense incident thereto, including the printing and furnishing of tickets." According to him, Congress had been given the power by the Founding Fathers, "and it should exercise it." [50]

Dodge by 1890 also favored a strong measure. His statements then were the exact opposite of those made two years before.

Dodge in 1888 [51]	*Dodge in 1890* [52]
. . . I think if you keep on with this [bloody shirt] policy [he told William E. Chandler] that you won't lose 8 or 10% of the Republicans . . . but will lose 25% of them. . . . We have got to appeal to new interests; to the business interests of the country,	I look upon the Election Bill as bringing peace and harmony between the races beyond any measure which I have heretofore seen. My reasons are simply, that as soon as it is passed, the South will immediately give the negro his rights and go for his

and if we can't carry the country on a protective tariff I don't see upon what we can carry it.

vote, and they will get at least one-half of them, but we will get a large white vote on account of it. If we allow the Republican party to go on as it has been doing for several years past, without defending what we won in the war, we need never expect any white vote in the South.

A similar change took place in the thinking of Clarkson, who, like Burrows, had recently canvassed Virginia for Mahone. Reversing his previous attitude, he pressed for passage of a Force bill in April, 1890, when he addressed a group of Pittsburgh Republicans.

Clarkson in 1888 [53]

As the war has receded, and the issues of a time of conflict and great events have cooled, the party has come forward to peace issues, and has had to learn to rely on its own daily strength of Republican or partisan sentiment, as distinguished from the spontaneous moral support it received from all patriotic people when engaged in suppressing treason and healing its wounds. The heroic days are over, the unheroic days succeed. A million first voters, to whom the war is history and not a personal experience, are added to the voting population every four

Clarkson in 1890 [54]

The southern question is the great and luminous of all, no matter how it is ridiculed. . . . The Republican party itself is a sentiment, as everything good in life is a sentiment. There is much of sentiment to attract young men to a party and to make old men more earnest in it, in putting above all other issues, the paramount thing that there must be honest elections, fair ballots and fair counts. . . . Let us teach always and ever, that first above everything, first above the tariff and all other issues, the great Republican doctrine is the duty of standing resolutely years. They are not swayed by sentimental issues nor the historic grandeur of the Republican party. They turn to the future and want to fight present politics on present issues.

now and always for absolutely pure elections. . . . It is now time for action in the Southern question. If the states cannot or will not settle it the United States can and will. Neither the present time nor the future will forgive the Republican party if, while it has complete control of the Government, it does not provide for fair election of Congressmen and Presidential Electors in the South.

Clarkson became one of the most persistent advocates of an election law. In May he spoke in Boston and again demanded justice for the colored man. "With the Republican party having full control of the Government—Congress and the Executive Departments—it will be as false to posterity as to itself if it does not exercise its power under the Constitution to make American citizenship equal and complete in all parts of the Republic," he stated. Soon thereafter, Clarkson told Louis T. Michener of Indiana that the speech expressed sentiments close to his heart. "I feel deeply the situation," he explained. "If we do not protect the Republicans of the South at the polls and in their homes we shall show ourselves too cowardly as a party to be worthy to live. . . . There is no other real question in present politics but this." He termed civil service reform "the toy of a child, the trifling thing of hobby riders" in comparison to "this great overshadowing question." If the party took "counsel from cowardice . . . it would die, and it ought to die." [55]

The case of Reed, another Republican who had campaigned for Mahone in 1889, was like that of the others. "I have not for years been one of those who have talked about the South," he told the same Pittsburgh audience that Clarkson addressed in April. "For the past eight years no man has heard me in the house or in the campaign discourse upon outrages or wrongs, murders, or shootings, or hangings." But after the Virginia fiasco he suddenly became a strong and relentless supporter of a Force bill. Reed noted that in the South terrorizing was becoming less frequent but "ballot-box stuffing and cheating in the count have taken their places." The only remedy was federal supervision. "Let us cut loose from the State elections, do our own registration, our own counting and our certification. Then the nation will be satisfied." [56]

The Speaker published a long defense of the Force bill in the June, 1890, number of the *North American Review*. "The object of assembling the Congress together is to declare the will of the people of the United States," he wrote. "How can that will be declared if there be more than twenty men returned to the House who never were elected, whose very presence is a violation of the Constitution of the United States and of the law of the land?" That Negro domination might accompany honest elections was no excuse. "Violations of law and disregard of statutes are not needed to save the United States." He asked only "that in national matters the majority of the voters in this country may rule. Why should any Southern man object to this?" [57]

The importance of this Republican change of heart can hardly be exaggerated. The power and influence of men like Reed, Clarkson, and Sherman made passage of the Lodge bill a strong probability.

v

On the floor of the House the Force bill debate was unusually bitter. Democrat after Democrat arraigned it. Representative Benton McMillan of Tennessee called it "centralization run mad. Despotism is sure to follow if it be enacted," he prophesied. "Why try this dangerous experiment? Why not continue to trust the people? If they can not be trusted, our institutions are a failure." Under Lodge's measure, McMillan argued, the legislative branch of the government would be manacled to the judiciary. John J. Hemphill of South Carolina complained that the Republicans were setting up an army of officials who had life tenure and were responsible to no one. The bill would revive the intolerable conditions under which the South had labored during Reconstruction. Northern carpetbaggers would once more be "sent South to oppress the people." He argued that the nation did not need a New South; "What this country needs is a new North. It needs a North that will take a view of all the facts and not be guided by their own preconceived prejudices." According to Roswell P. Flower of New York the bill was un-Republican, un-democratic, and un-American. Any court which enforced it deserved the censure of the people. The measure would completely subject state officers to the will of federal officials. James W. Covert of New York warned that Lodge was undoing the glorious work of the republic's Founding Fathers. Puzzled by Reed's motives, he recalled that now, after many years of silence on the subject, the Speaker had suddenly become an ardent, and relentless, supporter of the elections measure.[58]

Lodge presented a long historical defense of his brain child, citing the Constitutional Convention, the Constitution itself, and a batch of legal cases to prove his point. His bill was national, not sectional, in scope and would touch Northern cities as well as Southern. "If," he said, "as I have heard it stated in this chamber, Southern elections are perfectly fair, and the black man goes carolling to the voting place by the side of his employer, seeking to cast his vote for those whose interests are identical with his own, then sir, it is the duty of the United States Government to uncover this pleasing picture and display it to the country so that confidence may be restored, and no man suspect that Southern elections are open to criticism." The Congressman demanded that the government "extend to every citizen equal rights." [59]

Although most Northern Republicans agreed with Lodge, some Southern party members did not. Hamilton G. Ewart of North Carolina shuddered at the thought of Negro election supervisors and marshals. This bill, he stressed, would solidify the white vote of the South and retard the growth of industry and commerce in that section. It was a wicked piece of legislation, "damnable, illogical, inequitable, and vicious." But because of the "keen sting of the caucus lash," even those Republicans who hated it were forced to vote for it. Just as significant were the comments of Hamilton Dudley Coleman of Louisiana, the foremost Southern advocate of the policy which Henry C. Minor and Mahone had followed in 1889. Unlike Burrows and Reed, he still favored appealing to Southern industrialists and planters on a high tariff platform. Insisting that ninety per cent of the Republican businessmen of the nation opposed the Lodge bill, he argued that "every furnace and every rolling-mill and every factory established in the South makes friends and recruits for the Republican party of protection, internal improvements and the enforcement of the law." Much of Louisiana, including his district, had been strongly Whig before the Civil War. "Now, as a matter of fact, when these old Whigs in the South vote the Democratic ticket they do so with more or less compunction," he said, "and they would be glad to vote against their old political opponents if they could do so without fear of Negro supremacy." The Force bill was playing right into Bourbon hands.[60]

With the lower chamber under the firm rule of Reed, the debate, despite its bitterness, proceeded in a most orderly fashion. Changing the House rules throughout the session to suit himself and his party, Reed limited each speaker to forty minutes, brooked no delays, and rigidly controlled his fellow party members. As a result on July 2, 1890, the House passed the Lodge act, 155 to 149. All the affirmative votes, except that of Lewis P. Featherstone of Arkansas, a Union Laborite, were cast by Republicans. Only two members of the party, Coleman and Herman Lehlbach of New Jersey, opposed the measure.[61]

The balloting was an amazing display of party regularity, a tribute to Reed's engineering and skill. But some enemies of the bill still were hopeful that it would be defeated. The New York *Evening Post* commented, "Speaker Reed has forced through the Federal Election Bill, as it has been expected that he would do ever since he had it made a caucus measure." While Reed "is the House of Representatives, happily he is not yet the whole United States Congress." [62] As the paper suspected, the crucial struggle was to take place in the Senate.

10

Factions

THE STORY of the Lodge bill in the Senate was one of battling
Republican factions and of skillful Democratic exploitation of
Republican weaknesses. Mugwumps, silver interests, commercial groups, and those who still believed that Southern
high tariff men would be drawn into the Republican party if
the race issue was dropped all took part in the struggle.

After the Force bill passed the House, its sponsors were
determined to make it a law. "We must pass the bill in the
Senate or our defeat is certain," Thomas B. Reed advised
William E. Chandler. Henry Cabot Lodge felt that members
of the upper chamber would "make a terrible mistake if they
failed to act now." To Chandler the measure was a party
rallying cry. "There's no sentiment about the tariff," he told
Lodge, but there was "much of it about human rights and
the negro." He wanted "to see an old fashioned appeal . . .
made to that sentiment." [1]

Unlike these Republicans, Mugwumps intensely disliked the Force bill. E. L. Godkin said that the key question to be considered was, "what would be the effect on southern society of *not* suppressing the Negro vote?" The "ignorance with which the South has to contend surpasses the ignorance with which any other popular government has had to contend." In opposing Negro suffrage, Southern whites were "resisting the restoration of a regime which they intelligently believe would not only prevent industrial progress, but put their civilization itself in some peril." Since Northerners did not face the problem, they could not adequately understand it. "Nothing but education will make the southern Negro a free voter in the American sense of the term." Republican interference in Southern affairs should cease.[2]

Other Mugwumps stressed different arguments. *Harper's Weekly* believed the Force bill would interfere with the principle of state control of elections, which was an "unbroken tradition in America." While admitting that the disfranchisement of the colored man was a great wrong, the magazine argued that the remedy provided by the Lodge bill was even worse. Lodge and Chandler would hurt the Negro 364 days a year to help him on the 365th. Former Secretary of the Treasury Benjamin H. Bristow was just as bitter. "It seems to me monstrous that intelligent men can look with favor upon such a measure," he wrote. "It is pregnant with evil consequences & ought to cause the death of any party that is responsible for it. *And it will.*"[3]

Even more vigorously opposed to national control of elections were Northern merchants engaged in Southern trade. Without exception, the newspapers representing these men detested the Force bill. The New York *Commercial Bulletin*, for example, believed that Northern capital in the South "would be put in jeopardy by legislation that tends to provoke retaliation and distrust." Already an important venture proposed

by Baltimore capitalists had been abandoned because they
feared the Force bill would hurt business. The South was
booming, noted the *Bulletin*. In the past ten years the population of Fort Worth had grown 360 per cent; of Birmingham,
270 per cent; of Dallas, 280 per cent; and of Atlanta, 100 per
cent. Northern factories and capital were moving southward
at a great rate. During the last decade Negroes, supposedly
mistreated and abused, had accumulated more than $150,-
000,000 worth of property. In view of these facts, the paper
argued, Congressional solutions to the race problem were not
needed. The New York *Commercial Advertiser* agreed that
Northern capital had made the South prosperous. Businessmen, it stressed, desired "a tranquil atmosphere" and stood
"in mortal dread of everything in the shape of political turmoil
and intestinal commotion." The Lodge bill "would imperil confidence . . . and would certainly dry up the stream of investments to come." The New York *Journal of Commerce* warned
its readers that the measure was a step toward centralization,
that it would interfere with intersectional relations, and that
it had been drafted by intensely partisan Republican politicians whose sole interest was to keep themselves in power.[4]

Of the trade papers the *American Grocer* of New York
shouted the loudest. "As a general rule," it stated, "we think
that business journals should not interfere with partisan
politics but there are political measures which are so intimately associated with the welfare of the whole country that
it becomes the duty of every business man to speak out and
let himself be heard upon them." The publication complained
that "just as the New South is emerging from its darkness
with its labor contented and its resources developing by a
union of Southern efforts and Northern capital, certain politicians now come forward and for partisan purposes seek
again to stir up strife between the North and the South" and
to pit section against section. The giants of the Republican

party, Lincoln, Grant, and Garfield, if alive today, the *Grocer* continued, would shudder with horror at the thought of the Force bill. The South was prospering; taxes were being levied for education; and giant strides were being made in solving the race question. The Republicans now proposed to disrupt all this. "It is time for the business men of the United States to protest in the name of the country's welfare against such legislation as the Force bill," the article concluded, "and that they *will* protest earnestly and vigorously, the leaders of the Republican party will find out in 1892, if they do not before." [5]

The Atlanta *Constitution* skillfully played upon the fears of commercial interests when it advised Southerners to boycott Northern products if the Lodge bill was passed. The journal vowed that as soon as word was received that President Harrison had signed the measure it would "call a mass meeting to organize a Home Rule League," which would supervise the boycott of Yankee goods. "With every white man, woman and child in the South behind it," the League would "be mightier than all the armies whose marching feet shook this continent from sea to sea" in 1861. From Texas to Maryland loyal men would follow Atlanta's example. "Home Rule Leagues will be organized everywhere in the South, and the members will pledge themselves to buy not a dollar's worth of anything that is produced or manufactured in the north. Commercially speaking, an impassable wall will rise between the sections." As during the Civil War, industry would spring up throughout the South. Farmers would cease buying corn and meat from the West and raise their own. Southern ladies would proudly wear homespun dresses, while Southern men would put "aside their costly attire" and array themselves "in home-made jeans."

In the boycotted North, on the other hand, suffering would be intense. "Paralysis will seize the congested capital, the industries, the commerce and the railway lines running from the north to the south, and hundreds of thousands of desperate and idle workingmen in the great cities of the north and west will fiercely turn upon society and raise the cry 'Bread or Blood.' " The business community of the North would soon be gasping for breath; slowly and agonizingly it would strangle. "Blessed be the boycott!" roared the *Constitution*. It would be "the salvation of the solid south," and once and for all time end "the foul domination of the revolutionists who are trying to make an Ireland or an India out of the land of Washington, Jefferson and Lee—a land of sovereign states with millions of freemen who know their rights and dare to maintain them at any cost." [6]

Two days later, the paper happily reported that the response to its scheme was overwhelming. Businessmen all over the South endorsed it. Many Northerners did, too. A boycott, bragged the *Constitution*, had worked in 1860. Then, an Atlanta journal had published a black list of pro-Republican Northern merchants. Loyal Southerners had banded together and ruined these warmongering Yankees, sending "a chill through north-ern commercial circles" in the process. So afraid had some Eastern businessmen been that they had advocated seceding from the Union themselves and had talked of forming free cities like Hamburg just to keep their Southern trade. Now intersectional commerce was even larger and more vital to the North. The Yankees would be even more responsive to this type of pressure.[7]

The *Constitution*'s proposal received a tremendous boost when Governor John B. Gordon of Georgia endorsed it. He announced in a public letter to the New York *Herald* that if the Force bill was passed he would "use what ever influence and ability I may possess to arouse the southern people to the necessity of looking only to their own exhaustless resources." [8]

In answer to these threats the Republican press invariably compared 1890 with 1860. Then as now, the Concord *Evening Monitor*, Newark *Daily Advertiser*, and the Philadelphia *Press*

predicted, the attempt to intimidate the North would fail. Even
the Mugwump New York *Herald* denounced the scheme. "The
Northern people will simply not endure it," the paper stated.
"Their opinions are not for sale. Their goods, not their principles, are in the market." [9]

But Northern businessmen of both parties sympathized with
their Southern customers. New York City's wholesale grocers,
led by Francis B. Thurber, of the firm of Thurber, Whyland,
and Company, "the largest manufacturers and dealers in food
products in the world," a stanch Republican and for years one
of the most influential members of the city's Board of Trade,
actively campaigned against the Force bill. According to a
petition drawn up by a score of grocers, the measure would
"fan to life the smoldering embers of the race question, which
time and education are gradually extinguishing," and would
alarm "capital and injure alike the whites and blacks, the
South and the North."

Thurber explained to a New York *Times* reporter that politics played no part in the anti-Lodge bill drive. His associates
included men of all parties: Stalwart Republicans, Democrats,
Mugwumps, and even Prohibitionists. The grocers were packing thousands of copies of their petition in with their merchandise being shipped all over the North and West. Thurber
was confident that the plan would be effective and that Congress would listen attentively to the voice of business. [10]

A few days after the movement got underway, Frank Hiscock of New York and Samuel Pasco of Florida showed the
Senate the first two commercial protests against the election
bill. Hiscock's petition was signed by one hundred and seven
grocers, hatters, manufacturers, and retailers, who, collectively, were worth over $50,000,000. About half of them were
Republicans. Important signers included Thurber and his partner, Albert E. Whyland; Henry B. Kirkland, Alex Wiley, and
William N. Woodman, three other large wholesale grocers;

Luman R. Wing, a wholesale fruit merchant; A. D. Cowan and
Company, seed dealers; John Early and Company, a hardware
firm with three New York stores; and Louis Hymes, a Broadway clothier. The sponsors of Pasco's memorial complained
that the Force bill had been drawn up "for partisan and not
for public benefit and that it does not embody the spirit of the
great leaders of the Republican party, Lincoln, Grant, and
Garfield." Among its twenty-six signers were Albert G. Wood-
ruff, a Broadway hatter, and Jonathan Broome, a New York
dry goods merchant.[11]

Anxiety over the Lodge bill was not limited to New York
merchants. St. Louis dealers of both parties also warned that
the measure was "destructive of the business interests of the
country." They were headed by Edwin O. Stanard, a flour
miller and a former Republican lieutenant governor of Missouri, who in 1875 as a United States Representative had opposed the Civil Rights bill, and by George Bain of the Regina
Flour Mill Company.[12]

Senate Republicans reacted swiftly to the *Constitution*'s
threats and to the complaints of Northern businessmen. According to John J. Ingalls of Kansas, the Elections Committee
decided to tone down the House version of the Lodge bill
largely because of commercial pressure. The Senators prohibited the use of troops at the polls and modified the sections
empowering supervisors to make a house-to-house canvass to
learn if voters were really residents of the cities and counties
in which they were registered.[13]

A number of Republicans frankly admitted that they had
turned against the bill because they believed it would injure
trade. After visiting New York, Boston, Providence, Fall River,
and Philadelphia, and listening to businessmen who feared a
boycott, Algernon S. Paddock of Nebraska vowed to oppose
the bill. William D. Washburn of Minnesota said that the
people in his region had no interest in a federal election law

and revealed that he, too, would vote against it. The Republican merchants of Providence, who traded with the South through steamship lines which ran to important cities like Savannah, made Nelson W. Aldrich of Rhode Island promise to do the same. J. Donald Cameron of Pennsylvania also argued that the election law would disturb commercial relations between the sections.[14]

The Republicans influenced by the business argument were challenged by the bloody shirt Republicans.* During a caucus on July 28, 1890, the two groups clashed. Aldrich and Cameron reminded their fellow senators that a boycott was sure to follow passage of the Force bill. Refusing to heed these warnings, George Frisbie Hoar, one of the sponsors of the bill, answered "that rather than have Constitutional Government overthrown and be governed by minorities for the sake of protecting their Southern investments, the people of Massachusetts would prefer to have their factories burned and to live on codfish and 50 cents a day." [15]

Chandler endorsed Hoar's words. In an article on "National Control of Elections" published in the August, 1890, number of *Forum,* he repeatedly attacked the businessmen of his own party for abandoning the Negro. It was, he wrote, "through Northern commercial timidity" that the threats and vituperations of the South were permitted to go unchallenged. "As in the days of slavery," he pointed out, "southern trade is precious to northern merchants." Democrats continually boasted that the North would do nothing about violations of the Constitution because "enough Republicans who fear business disturbances and the loss of trade will abandon their party" and

---

* Both the bloody shirt and the pro-business groups defy analysis. Both factions included Republicans from all regions. Although one might suspect that Hoar, representing a state which had a large amount of Southern trade, would be more inclined to oppose the Force bill than Paddock of Nebraska, the reverse was true.

vote with the Redeemers. The time was coming, he warned, when the North, "overcoming commercial cowardice and dough-face subserviency," would once and for all put an end to political murders and other Bourbon abuses.[16]

Other important supporters of the Lodge bill felt the same way. Grenville Dodge, unlike most businessmen, was "pretty well disgusted with the entire South. I have put an immense amount of money in there; the more we put in the colder they grew and the less well disposed they were to respect the rights of property and the citizen. If Congress will pass the Force bill," he went on, "it will settle the Southern question in less than a year; but we have so many men in our party who care more for their pockets than for principle, that I doubt whether it becomes a law." He reaffirmed his "right to speak upon this question, for I do not know of anyone who has solicited and invested more millions in the South than I have." [17] Senator John C. Spooner, too, believed that there were "two or three Republican Senators who do not like to vote for any federal election bill. The almighty dollar obscures their vision. I mean by that," he explained, "that the commercial spirit which held back the anti-slavery men is holding them back against anything which might sacrifice commerce to the rights of citizenship." [18] As so often since 1877, Republican businessmen and bloody shirters were again at odds.

II

A small but important group of Republicans, led by James G. Blaine and Murat Halstead, disliked the Force bill for an entirely different reason. They still believed that the party should ignore the Negro and appeal solely to Southern tariff interests for support. Their position in July, 1890, was exactly that of James S. Clarkson and Dodge in January, 1888, and of the National Committee during the 1888 canvass.

Blaine could see little of value in the election bill. To him it was folly for the party to stress anything but economic questions. He was convinced that the Negro issue was, in effect, dead.[19]

Like Blaine, Halstead desired to "put aside the sword." In the columns of his new paper, the Brooklyn *Standard Union,* he preached that "victories may be won without it."

Aye, the victory has been won—that of the year 1888—which witnessed the election of a Republican President and Congress. The nullification of the Constitution was going on then, there was the same state of affairs that exists to-day. Was the great victory of that year won upon the question of the enforcement of the Constitution? It was not. On the contrary, that subject if not entirely ignored was largely evaded. The campaign was a success through the persistent discussion of the economic questions. That was the advice and initiative of Mr. Blaine when he came home, and the course of his speeches, and General Harrison's letter of acceptance and speeches beginning earlier than those of Mr. Blaine were in the same line. . . . The way to run the next Presidential campaign is not on the Lodge bill—the principle of it however correct, the history behind it however monstrous—but the tariff, with its enlarged free list and other provisions, and the settlement of the silver question on sound principles.[20]

Halstead's views found no favor with Chandler. Strongly hinting that the Lodge bill would distract Northern and Western voters from Republican attempts to increase further the already high tariff and to prevent the coinage of more silver dollars, the Senator termed the editor's argument apostasy. Should the party follow Halstead's advice, it would continue to be defeated in every Southern state and in addition would lose two-thirds of the North. Chandler compared the editor's counsel to that of the traitors who in 1861 had advised against re-enforcing Fort Sumter. "The forebearance did not prevent the war of secession, neither will an abandonment of the Fifteenth Amendment now through commercial and political timidity save the Republican party. Our only hope," Chandler insisted, "is the manly and honorable course of an effort to enforce the Constitution by all appropriate and suitable laws." The next few months would determine "whether the Republican party cares more for humanity than for money, more for principle than for self." [21]

Defending himself, Halstead showed little sympathy for the policy of using the Force bill to cover the tariff and currency issues. "The people at large," he replied to Chandler, "have been weary of what may be called sectional political questions, and prefer business—and it is the first necessity for a practical politician to understand the temper of the people, which we may be sure has not changed much in two years." [22]

In the South the men who had fostered the white, high tariff movement during 1889 shared the feelings of Halstead and Blaine. They still believed that they could break the Solid South if the race issue was dropped. On July 23, several hundred protectionist Republicans met in Birmingham and approved a platform, later sent to the Senate, which called the Lodge bill unconstitutional, asserted that it would injure commercial relations between the sections, and said that it "may lead to a race conflict, and thus imperil our present grand industrial system, which is just starting its career of unequalled progress." Ex-Governor William H. Smith of Alabama, president of the white Republican league which Harrison had recognized the year before, presided over the gathering. Later, one hundred and seventy-three men from the high tariff center of Anniston, Alabama, also urged Congress to reject the Force bill.[23]

Although the protectionist Republicans of Alabama disliked the election bill, the regular state organization, headed by R. A. Mosely, who the previous year had led the enemies of the white men's party, endorsed it. Mosely protested that the resolutions of the recent Birmingham meeting had been drawn up by Bourbons who posed as Republicans.[24] Clearly, the Republican machine politicians of the South stood to gain a great deal from the enactment of the Force bill.

III

The Senate, which contained forty-seven Republicans and thirty-seven Democrats, was a busy place in August, 1890. The McKinley tariff, for which manufacturers were clamoring, and the Lodge bill, although both Republican-sponsored measures, were actually competing with one another for space on the crowded calender of the upper chamber. For a while it seemed as if neither would have a chance to pass.

The Democrats were determined to exploit this situation. As papers like the Philadelphia *Press* and the Philadelphia *Inquirer* and men like Spooner suspected, they had voted in July for legislation increasing the amount of silver coined in return for a pledge that Western Republicans would oppose the Lodge bill. Now the Democrats, preferring protection to controlled elections, were anxious to come to some sort of understanding with the supporters of the McKinley bill.[25]

Their efforts met with success. On August 12, after conferring with Democratic leaders Arthur P. Gorman of Maryland and Isham Harris of Tennessee, Senator Matthew S. Quay of Pennsylvania introduced a resolution which called for a vote on the tariff on August 30 and, in effect, put the Force bill over until December.[26]

The day after introducing his resolution Quay explained to the Philadelphia *Press* that he did not intend to defeat the election bill. His sole object was to protect American industry. The Force bill did not stand a chance of passing during this session anyway. A Democratic filibuster would surely kill it unless the Senate rules could be changed. Why should the Lodge bill carry the tariff down with it? He then read a letter from President Thomas Dolan of the Philadelphia Manufacturers' Club, who had raised $300,000 for the party in 1888 on the expectation that higher rates would accompany a Republican victory. If the McKinley bill was not enacted at once, Dolan pointed out, foreign manufacturers would flood the country with cheap goods. As chairman of the Republican National Committee, Quay had to fulfill the promises he had made during the last presidential campaign. If the party expected to fry the fat out of industrialists in the future, it would have to keep its word now.[27]

Just as important as the tariff in shaping Quay's ideas were the complaints of Hamilton Disston, a prominent and wealthy Philadelphia Republican who hoped to run for the Senate in 1891. Disston and his associates of the Atlantic and Gulf Canal and Okeechobee Land Company had been draining the Florida swamps, settling people, and building railroads since 1880, when they had paid the state $1,000,000 for the right to clear a four-million-acre region. Owning 13,000 acres in the Everglades outright, Disston had repeatedly urged Quay to prevent passage of the election bill because he feared it would injure commercial relations between the North and the South and, in turn, would lower property values in the South.[28]

The Florida land investors possessed enormous influence. They were intimate with many leading Pennsylvania Republicans, including Cameron. Two important Philadelphia Congressmen, Alfred C. Harmer and John E. Reyburn, both of whom had enthusiastically voted for the Lodge bill in early July, came out against the measure in August after they had talked to Disston.[29] In a public letter to his constituents explaining his new stand, Harmer now called the Force bill "very bad politics." It would undoubtedly hurt business, he argued. Now was the time "to call a halt in this line of legislation. We have at best too much of it." Harmer noted that every

Mugwump and many Republican papers supported his new position, "and with almost no exceptions the business men of my city . . . give me credit." [30]

Discounting the roles of both Dolan and Disston, the New York *Times* attributed the Quay resolution to Blaine and his chief supporter, Benjamin Franklin Jones, president of Jones and Laughlin, Limited. The paper pointed out that Jones, a steel manufacturer who desired higher tariff rates, had been an immediate, warm, and open advocate of the Pennsylvania Senator's proposal.[31]

This story deeply hurt Blaine. Insisting that he would stand by the election bill if he were in Congress at the moment, he pleaded his innocence in long letters to the President and to the wife of his good friend, Henry Cabot Lodge. To him the New York *Times* was "the meanest of all newspapers" and its story was pure fabrication.[32]

Shocked by what seemed to him a mutiny within the ranks of the palace guard, Harrison acted. He called Senators Aldrich, Spooner, and a half-dozen others to the White House and urged them to do all they possibly could to pass the Lodge bill.[33]

The President's efforts were of no avail. At a Senate caucus a few days later eighteen of the thirty-five Republicans present voted to support the Quay resolution.[34] Although on the surface the caucus struggle seemed to be a battle between protectionists and bloody shirt wavers, it was far more than that. Of the eighteen Senators who voted with the majority, ten represented Western areas favoring increased coinage of silver. Led by Preston Plumb and John J. Ingalls of Kansas and by John P. Jones of Nevada, they remained true to the bargain struck with the Democrats two months before and opposed controlled elections, even though they hated the McKinley bill and fought increased tariff schedules on such items as iron ore, earthenware, and tin plate. So against the McKinley bill was Plumb that at one caucus in which he upheld the Quay resolution he went out of his way to denounce Eastern industrialists, "the power in the American Congress," who were determined at all costs to get the protection which they had purchased in 1888. On one occasion Hoar, the Senate sponsor of the Lodge bill, publicly arraigned Plumb for attacking the tariff.[35]

Although those who had no use for the tariff voted for the Quay resolution, some of the party's most ardent protectionists voted against it. This group included Sherman, William B. Allison of Iowa, and Connecticut Senators Joseph R. Hawley and Orville Platt, the first two of whom, as close friends of James M. Swank, were as deeply concerned with iron and steel rates as Quay.[36] Julius Caesar Burrows, a member of the House Ways and Means Committee, whose devotion to a high tariff was second to none, in attacking the Quay resolution helped explain why these men wanted federal control of elections:

It is of little avail to pass a measure protecting the iron industries of Pennsylvania, the copper industries of Michigan and the interests of all the States, if we permit Congresses and Presidents to be elected by fraud. . . . [The Bourbons] will conspire at the first opportunity to overthrow our protective system, and launch us on the perilous sea of Free Trade. Protection to American industry will not long endure if we do not protect the American voter at the polls.[37]

The New York *Tribune*, which always supported the tariff designs of Pennsylvania industrialists, said the same thing in a different way:

The Election bill carries within itself the assurance of future Tariff bills by the hundred. A Congress elected by the people, and not by fraud, would uphold the American policy of Protection and shrink from no change that might be necessary to make it effective.

. . . But a Congress elected by ballot-box stuffers at the North and bulldozers at the South cannot be trusted to sustain Protection in any form.[38]

The influence of commercial groups was also felt in the caucus. Aldrich, Cameron, Paddock, and Washburn, all of whom had vowed to oppose the Lodge bill because it would hurt intersectional trade, kept their pledges. On the day of the caucus Elijah W. Halford, Harrison's private secretary, noted in his diary that Aldrich "opposes the election bill on the ground of the business interests being against it." [39]

Further conferences and discussions gained nothing for the supporters of controlled elections. The Republicans decided to hold the Lodge bill over until the second session of Congress and to vote on the tariff in accord with the Quay resolution.[40]

In reviewing the first phase of the struggle, the advocates of the Force bill attributed the defeat of the measure to a variety of sources. George F. Edmunds and Orville Platt blamed the Silver Republicans, who had deserted their party and bargained with the Democrats. Lodge felt that the campaign of the commercial interests was most important. He denied that his measure would "endanger Northern property and affect Northern business in the South." This was, he argued, the doughface cry of 1860. What the Redeemers and their allies were really saying was "that fair elections of Congressmen would endanger business and prosperity in the Southern States; and the mere statement of the proposition is its complete confutation." Led by "the gallant Governor Gordon," the Bourbons had threatened and blustered "as if we were in the days of South Carolinian nullification." The Republicans, Lodge asserted, would see to it that all the laws of the United States were obeyed. The boycott threats were "unworthy the use or notice of intelligent men." [41]

The conclusions of the Washington *Bee,* a Negro journal, resembled those of the Massachusetts Congressman. The paper lamented that the former Confederates had cleverly relied "upon the tactics which had served them successfully before the war—defiance and insolence—thoroughly understanding the cowardice of the commercial spirit of the North and counting confidently upon it for success." The editorials of the Atlanta *Constitution* in 1890, it declared, resembled those of the Charleston *Mercury* in 1860. The Southern plan "was not without influence then in terrorizing the commercial classes of the North into submission, and it is not expected to accomplish less now." [42]

IV

The results of the Maine election of September 8, 1890, held six weeks earlier than that in the rest of the country, gave the Force bill advocates great hope. Reed was easily re-elected on a platform stressing the bill, his plurality being the largest ever given to a Congressional candidate in his district.[43]

But the November results, after a canvass centering principally on the McKinley tariff, proved disastrous for the Republicans. The party's margin in the Senate was reduced from fourteen to eight, while the newly elected House contained 235 Democrats, eighty-eight Republicans, and nine Farmers' Alliance men.[44]

Some observers were sure that the verdict in part reflected the public's dissatisfaction with the Force bill. Benjamin Bristow crowed, "We have had more than enough of high tariff nonsense, and force bills and reckless pension bills," while Stephen B. Elkins of West Virginia believed that "Reed's rulings and position as Speaker had something to do with bringing about the result as did the Force bill." [45]

Realizing that this would be the party's last chance in a long while to pass the Lodge bill, the President went to work. In his annual message to Congress of December 1, 1890, he reiterated the need for a federal election bill. Such a measure was legal and constitutional, he argued. It should be "absolutely non-partisan and impartial," should insure fair elections, and should guarantee that henceforth majorities would rule. Harrison promised to do his utmost to safeguard the rights of all citizens.[46]

In the reconvened Congress the Negro question was again prominent. Early in the session Republicans attacked the recently adopted Mississippi Constitution, which required all voters, when requested, to demonstrate their ability to read and interpret any section of the new document. Angered by this obvious attempt to stop the state's colored population from voting, party members in both branches of Congress introduced resolutions to punish the Redeemers. Representatives Lucien B. Caswell of Wisconsin and Leonidas C. Houk of Tennessee authorized the House Committee on the Judiciary to inquire whether Mississippi's scheme constituted an illegal disfranchisement of Negroes and whether the Congressional representation of the state could be lowered in accord with the second section of the Fourteenth Amendment. In the Senate Joseph N. Dolph of Oregon introduced a similar motion. Senator George G. Vest, a Missouri Democrat, countered by demanding an investigation of the racial discrimination practiced by Oregon officials hiring laborers for public works projects.[47] The busy upper chamber paid little attention to either the Dolph resolution or the Vest amendment.

The Lodge bill received far more attention. Now those Republicans who favored the coinage of more silver dollars led the opposition to it. Like Quay during the previous summer, the Silver Republicans did not really hate the Force bill; they merely loved free silver more and were willing to do anything to pass an act embodying this idea. Having successfully bargained with the Democrats during the first session of the Fifty-first Congress, they were ready to do the same in the second. On December 15, 1890, the Chicago *Tribune* warned of this possibility, and a few days later Spooner was "quite sure that such a move is in contemplation." [48]

Republican party leaders hoped to stave off a Silver Republican-Democratic alliance by concessions to the Western Senators. In the middle of December a Republican caucus approved a bill calling for the purchase of an additional 12,000,000 ounces of silver during 1891. Although Sherman reported this act from the Finance Committee, Senator William Stewart of Nevada was not moved. He announced that he would introduce a free coinage bill. [49]

Events played into the hands of the silver faction. By January 5, 1891, it was in a strong position, having been bolstered by the recent addition of four new Senators from the mining states. On that date Stewart, after consulting with Gorman, moved to replace the Lodge bill on the Senate docket with his coinage bill. The motion was passed by thirty-four to twenty-nine, eight Silver Republicans voting with the Democrats. [50]

Still the Lodge bill was not dead. After the Senate passed the silver bill on January 14, Hoar moved to reconsider the Force bill. When the favorable vote of Vice-President Levi P. Morton broke a thirty-three to thirty-three tie, the Democrats began to filibuster, even though the session still had six weeks to run. On January 20, the Republicans attempted to close the debate, but the Democrats foiled the scheme by leaving the Senate chamber and preventing a quorum from assembling. Two days later, six Silver Republicans, repaying their debt to Gorman, again joined with the Democrats, and with Cameron, who was speculating in silver at the time, and voted to sidetrack the election bill and consider an apportionment act. [51] The Lodge bill had been buried by a bargain between the Democrats and free silverites.

V

Many groups were responsible for the defeat of the Force bill, and the supporters of the measure blamed them all. Senator George F. Edmunds of Vermont, in an interview with the New York *Tribune*, classified the enemies of the bill as the four D's. "First, the Democrat pure and simple; second, the Dough-face of the North, who always sides with the Southern wing of his party; third, the Demagogue who, in the form of the Mugwump, always seeks to have peace at any price; fourth, Dives, the rich New York grocer, who thinks that if the Election bill were passed he might not be able to sell as much tea and sugar in the South as before." Like other Republicans, Edmunds believed that history was repeating itself. "We are now encountering the same situation, in some respects, that we had thirty years ago." Then, when "a small slave-holding oligarchy" attempted to run the country, "the Democrat, the Dough-face, the Demagogue and Dives advanced the same argument against any agitation of the subject, against anything which would impair the peaceful relations of the North and the South, that are heard now." [52]

Hoar's version of the story was slightly different. Writing on "The Fate of the Election Bill," he emphasized that "If the body of northern business men, the body of self-styled 'reformers,' the body of educated and wealthy men, who are indifferent to their political obligations, had acted for the past fifteen years with the Republican Party," fair elections would now be taking place throughout the South. The "overthrow of constitutional government in this country is due to the defection of the classes to which I have referred." The paradox to him was that the Southern Democracy voted for everything which Northern businessmen abhorred, including free silver and bankruptcy laws. And yet commercial interests endured all this for the sake of intersectional harmony.[53]

Other Republicans came to much the same conclusions. Grenville M. Dodge felt that the Southern wing of his party had been "sold out as a merchantable property" by Silver Republicans and Eastern merchants, who "haven't the nerve to stand up for a principle." James S. Clarkson lashed out at the "time-servers in the Republican party and out, who for commercial or other reasons of greed or cowardice have helped to betray the negro in his time of need and hope." He was especially baffled by the indifference of Northern clergymen, most of whom were Mugwumps, to the plight of the Southern Negro.[54]

For bloody shirt Republicans like Edmunds, Hoar, Dodge, and Clarkson, the defeat of the Force bill was disastrous. These men had vehemently insisted that a harsh policy alone could make their party powerful in the South. Now sectionalism, along with Hayes's appeal to ex-Whigs interested in internal improvements, Arthur's alliance with the Southern Independents, and Harrison's white, high tariff party, was a defeated and completely discredited scheme. Silver Republicans, Mugwumps, commercial groups, and tariff advocates had done their work well.

II

The "Good Fellow" Business

I

As EVENTS during the remainder of the Harrison administration illustrated, the defeat of the Force bill marked a sharp and significant change in the nature and degree of Republican interest in the Negro. Never again did the party leaders of this generation adopt an aggressive Southern policy. Aware that in the past fifteen years all of their plans to build Republicanism in the South had failed, almost all Republicans now conceded that their party was destined to be a Northern, not national, organization. The day of education bills, of election laws, of investigations of Bourbon atrocities, and of campaigns run on the race question was gone. The Southern problem hereafter became largely a matter of dispensing patronage and of obtaining delegates for national conventions.[1]

Even William E. Chandler mellowed after the Lodge bill fight. The conduct of the Negro, he told T. Thomas Fortune, editor of the New York *Age*, was now of greater importance

than ever before. It was not fair of colored men to expect
Republican aid after they had helped draft the Mississippi Constitution of 1890, which had disfranchised almost all non-
whites. Admittedly, a large segment of the Republican party
was indifferent to the Negro's plight, "but maligning the de-
linquents accomplishes little." Members of the colored race
should "as one man stand up and say that they will not allow
the suffrage to be taken from them directly or indirectly. . . .
The Lord helps those who help themselves," the Senator now
preached.[2]

Only the lynching problem still bothered Chandler. He was
convinced that every prominent Negro politician was "gotten
rid of" by this horrible method. With Frederick Douglass and
a few Republican editors, he began what proved to be a brief
and ineffective crusade against the practice. By giving Magnus
Robinson of the Alexandria, Virginia, *Weekly Leader* a subsidy, Chandler induced him to play up atrocities.[3] The desul-
tory protests of the Chicago *Tribune* and the Newark *Daily
Advertiser* added force to the Republican campaign. The
Tribune estimated that in the last ten years 856 Negroes and
378 whites had been lynched in the South. Of the 728 colored
men killed during the past eight years, 269 had been punished
for rape; 252 for murder; forty-four for robbery; thirty-seven
for incendiarism; thirty-two for unknown crimes; twenty-seven
for being colored; thirteen for quarrels with white men; ten for
making threats; seven for attempting to vote; five for mis-
cegenation; four for burglary; three for circulating scandals;
three for defending themselves when attacked; two for cutting
levees; two for turning state's evidence against whites; two
for gambling; one for drinking; and one for trying to poison a
well.[4]

Frederick Douglass continued the assault with an article in
the July, 1892, number of the *North American Review*. Con-
ceding that lynchings probably never would cease, he placed

the blame for these crimes "not entirely with the ignorant mob. The men who break open jails and with bloody hands destroy human life are not alone responsible. . . . They simply obey the public sentiment of the South, the sentiment created by wealth and respectability, by the press and the pulpit." If clergymen and newspapers would "unite their power against the cruelty, disgrace and shame that is settling like a mantle of fire upon these lynch-law States," these murders would become rarer. Since the North did not condemn them, it shared the guilt. To Douglass lynchings were the "common crime" of both sections.[5]

Disagreeing with this point of view, Harrison argued that he could do nothing to prevent atrocities. He swore that if he could punish lynchers he would. But, he pleaded, "as President, the constitution and the laws limit my power." [6] Faced with this attitude Republican agitators soon dropped the subject.

II

As far as the Negro question was concerned, the campaign of 1892 in the North differed radically from any since the Civil War. This time the Democrats aggressively and skillfully played up the sectional theme. By arguing that a Republican victory meant a Force bill, they created a powerful, unanswerable issue which helped them gain victory.

Just before the canvass began, Harrison hit upon a new scheme to deal with Southern outrages. In his annual message of December 9, 1891, he called for the creation of a "commission, nonpartisan in its membership and composed of patriotic, wise, and impartial men," to whom the entire question of election laws might be referred. He suggested that the Supreme Court be permitted to select the commission's members.[7]

Far from approving this proposal, the Republican national convention, which six months later renominated Harrison, worked against the President. At the insistence of Joseph B. Foraker of Ohio, chairman of the platform committee,[8] it adopted an unusually harsh plank which demanded "that every citizen of the United States . . . be allowed to cast one free and unrestricted ballot." The party vowed "never [to] relax its efforts until the integrity of the ballot and the purity of elections shall be fully guaranteed and protected in every State." Moreover, Republicans denounced "the continued inhuman outrage perpetrated upon American citizens for political reasons in certain Southern States of the Union."[9]

A short time later, the Democrats struck back. For the third straight time they nominated Grover Cleveland, a low tariff advocate, for the presidency and selected Adlai E. Stevenson of Illinois as his running mate. Their platform, approved after a bitter fight, called for reduced duties.[10]

Threatened with a bolt by protectionists, Democratic leaders searched for an issue upon which both high and low tariff men could unite. Charles A. Dana, editor of the New York Sun, a former antislavery Whig who had served as Assistant Secretary of War under President Lincoln, solved the problem. Realizing that he and Cleveland were at odds over economic issues, Dana also knew that he and the nominee agreed about the evils of the Force bill. The Republican convention had unwittingly played into their hands by strongly endorsing an election act.[11]

Taking full advantage of the situation, the Sun from June to November ran scorching anti-Lodge bill articles every day. "No Force bill! No Negro Domination in the South!" became its campaign cry. "This is the one all-important question of this election," its editor preached. "All else is trivial and petty in comparison." "We do not deny," Dana said on another occasion, "that in other elections the tariff has been a great issue," and it might well be an important factor in future campaigns. But "in the election of 1892 the tariff is of no importance and we may in truth say it plays no part at all." The "supreme duty of this canvass and this election is to beat the Force bill and Negro domination; and that is a duty to which Free Traders and Protectionists, however radically divided in economic ideas and convictions, can join heartily and earnestly in performing." Conjuring up visions of Reconstruction, Dana announced that the Republican "road . . . leads back to negro domination, the bloody shirt, the carpet bag, the Federal Lieutenant of infantry dispersing, under orders from Washington, the Legislature elected by the sovereign voters of a free state, visiting statesmen, fraud, force, legislation for plunder, taxation that is confiscation, disaster and ruin to the new prosperity of the New South. The blackest ink is not black enough to describe the consequences of the Force bill policy, once successfully put into operation by the politicians who have devised it." If victorious in this election, he warned, the Republicans would "turn the hands of the clock back to the South's midnight." [12]

Early in July the Democratic National Committee formally endorsed the *Sun's* tactics. Beginning with a gala Independence Day celebration at Tammany Hall, campaign leaders shifted emphasis from the tariff to the Force bill. The party now had an issue upon which all could unite. [13]

Cleveland eagerly adopted the new theme. On July 7, in a public letter he charged that the doctrines embodied in the Lodge bill were "a direct attack upon the spirit and theory of our Government, and while such a measure especially menaces the welfare and prosperity of the South, it must be condemned and denounced by all those everywhere who love their country and have the least claim to be numbered among those who believe in the principles of true Democracy." Two days later, Cleveland called the act "a most atrocious measure." He did "not see how any Democrat can think otherwise." [14]

Almost immediately, Republican papers complained that

the Democrats had unfairly injected the subject into the campaign. "The New York Sun," fumed the Brooklyn *Times*, "having failed most ignominiously to prevent the nomination of Grover Cleveland, and having to some extent impaired its influence as a Democratic organ by its frantic efforts in that direction, has been laboring, ever since the Chicago convention completed its work, to make amends . . . by providing the Democratic party with a new issue." It "calmly ignores or ridicules the leading points in the Chicago platform and exhausts its editorial energies in fierce denunciation of a mythical 'Force Bill.'" According to the Pittsburgh *Commercial-Gazette*, "The Force bill scarecrow is merely a device of Democrats who fear the result of a straight fight between protection and free trade, and seek by this means to hold the South solid through one more campaign." The Redeemers realized that the race question kept their section Democratic; "when a Southern State shows signs of faltering in its Bourbonism, as several did in 1888, the ultimate appeal is to the 'horrors of negro rule.' If that does not bring the answer nothing will." [15]

The bewildered President sought for a solution to the problem posed by Dana's campaign. One Saturday night late in July, Harrison and Senator Joseph R. Hawley of Connecticut chatted informally about the colored problem and the forthcoming letter of acceptance. Worried by the President's wishy-washy remarks, Hawley later implored him to take a firm stand on the race issue. Southern election frauds must be opposed.[16]

Disregarding this advice completely, Harrison in his letter repeated his plea for a nonpartisan commission. This plan, he believed, would prevent a repetition of the recent Alabama election, in which the Republicans had not dared to run candidates, and would safeguard the ballot box for all.[17]

Many Republican journals hoped that Harrison's mild statement would end the Force bill fuss. The Chicago *Tribune* remarked that the "Democratic clamor, in which Grover Cleve-

land, Adlai Stevenson, and Charles A. Dana have been conspicuously vociferous that the President would advocate the
imposition of a rigid force bill on the South, is silenced by
the latter's recommendation in his letter of acceptance." The
Iowa State Register insisted that "There is no such issue left
now that the president has written his letter of acceptance." [18]

James G. Blaine and Murat Halstead also endorsed the chief
executive's tactics. They were still convinced that if the race
question was dropped from politics four or five Southern states,
including Virginia, Tennessee, West Virginia, and Alabama,
would go Republican. Bloody shirt waving would do no good,
they felt.[19]

Many important Republicans hoped that the public would
forget Dana's charges if they ignored the Southern problem.
Party leaders like Henry Cabot Lodge, Thomas B. Reed, and
John A. Cockerill, editor of the New York *Commercial Advertiser*, were among those who now said nothing about the
issue in their speeches.[20]

The *Nation* was shocked. "Such silence," it commented, "does
not help the case of the Republicans at all, because nobody
believes for a moment that it signifies anything beyond their
desire to deceive the public. Lodge, and Reed, and the rest of
them might much better stand up like men." [21]

Frederick Douglass also disliked the Republican policy. To
him Blaine was the "marplot of his party. . . . In his studied
attention to economic questions," complained the Negro, "he
has succeeded in diverting from us the natural flow of Republican aid and comfort. He has continually kept us in the
background as a result of his influence upon the party." [22]

Meanwhile, the Democrats were making the most of the
Force bill theme. Cleveland's letter of acceptance argued that
the measure would rob the people of their basic rights. It was
the duty of the Democrats to oppose such a scheme.[23] In a
like tone Senator David B. Hill of New York, formerly the high

tariff rival of Cleveland and Dana's original choice for the nomination, in endorsing the former President told a great Tammany Hall rally: "The danger of a Force bill has not yet passed away, and we should not be lulled on into security by the silence or apparent apathy of its former advocates. A Democratic President and a Democratic Congress are needed to effectually give it the sleep that knows no waking." [24]

Using familiar tactics, Stevenson tried to scare businessmen. Late in October he told a Brooklyn audience that industry and commerce were languishing in eight Southern and Southeastern states because their people feared controlled elections. A Harrison victory and passage of the Lodge bill, he warned, "would undoubtedly retard the growth of the States at which it is aimed; would excite in many communities race troubles and invite retaliatory legislation which would disturb property values and discontinue and destroy the value of Northern investments. And its reflex action upon the North and the Northeastern States would result in consequent loss of commercial and trade relations with the vast territory now becoming tributary to their wealth and prosperity." So effective was this theme that Stevenson repeated it in full in his letter of acceptance, released a few days later.[25] Recognizing Stevenson's aim, James S. Clarkson later acknowledged that "the cry of Force bill and Negro domination was . . . made in the North to frighten northern merchants about southern trade." [26]

The Democrats employed various means to spread their gospel. Of the approximately three hundred pages in their campaign textbook for 1892, about forty were devoted to the election bill.[27] Moreover, the National Committee plastered huge, yellow anti-Lodge bill posters all over the South. A typical one, entitled "What the Force Bill Means," drawn by cartoonist Constantine de Grimm, depicted two colored elections marshals, guns in hand, stopping a white Southerner from casting his ballot.[28]

The nation's most prominent Mugwump, Carl Schurz, also denounced the Lodge bill. He termed it "one of the most reckless, most cruel, most revolting partisan contrivances ever devised." Although the Republicans were denying that the Force bill was a campaign issue, Schurz pointed out that their party's platform endorsed the measure. At one time or another "every prominent Republican of influence," including the President, had favored it. He warned that if the Republicans swept the election they would pass the bill.[29]

The Republican party was not given a chance to enact the Lodge bill. In November, Cleveland won a sweeping victory, amassing 277 electoral votes to 145 for Harrison. The New York *Sun* was ecstatic:

> The message which went over the wires this morning is worth a thousand millions of dollars to that section [the South] of our great republic.
> "No Force bill! No Negro Domination!"
> Every patriot in the land must rejoice that the black cloud which for several months has overhung the free and prosperous South is at last and forever dispelled.
> "No Force bill! No Negro Domination!"
> A new bond unites the Democracy of the Southern States with their brethren of New York, Indiana, and New Jersey. Together, they have won the great and final battle for home rule and honest elections, free from Federal bayonets and hired Republican bulldozers.
> "No Force bill! No Negro Domination!"
> . . . There will be no Force bill. There can be no return of the black days of Negro Domination.[30]

Looking back over the canvass, the Republican *Review of Reviews* concluded that the Lodge bill was an issue of great influence. The Republicans were rewarded for ignoring the Democratic charges that a Harrison victory meant controlled elections by losing the campaign. Far from keeping the subject out of the canvass, the Republican silence made the Democratic assertions seem more valid. "No Force bill! No Negro Domination!" became the Democratic rallying cry. Dana, the magazine went on, contributed more than anyone else to Cleveland's victory. Opposed to both the candidate and the party's tariff plank, he made the Lodge bill the key issue of the campaign. At first he was alone. Undaunted, he tirelessly stood his ground and attacked the Force bill. Those who in the beginning considered his crusade a joke later began to take it seriously. Hill, Tammany Hall, and the anti-free trade Democrats came to Cleveland's support on the ground that, if nothing else, they agreed with him on the Lodge bill question. The National Committee fell into line. Eventually, Southern papers like the Atlanta *Constitution* joined in. The victory for Cleveland was also, in a very real sense, a triumph for Dana.[31]

Other Republicans blamed the verdict in part on the Democratic tactics and on their party's failure to defend the Southern Negro. The President said that the *Sun's* editorials had done even more than just keep the South solid during the election; they had also brought the Democrats many votes in the North. Douglass once more attacked Blaine, at whose direction the Republican campaign had been "as cold and selfish as dollars and dimes could make it." According to Clarkson, Harrison did not "deserve to win, on the platform of commerce . . . that we had in this year. No party ever will win," he continued, "and never ought to win when it passively allows three quarters of a million of its own voters to be disfranchised." The growing industries of the South, needing protection, would be very seriously hurt by the free trade triumph; in the long run Cleveland would damage the section which had done so much to elect him.[32]

Undoubtedly Clarkson, Harrison, and Douglass were correct in assuming that the Force bill played a vital part in the 1892 campaign. Yet it was not the only cause of Harrison's defeat.

The McKinley tariff and the liberal Republican pension policy were still unpopular with many people. The strike in July, 1892, at the Carnegie steel plant at Homestead, Pennsylvania, also hurt Harrison. During the conflict ten men were killed and over sixty were wounded. Cleveland denounced the steel men for cutting wages after they had obtained a higher tariff, as they said, to better the condition of labor.[33]

During his remaining days in office Harrison refused to take a strong stand on the Southern question. In his fourth annual message to Congress, delivered in December, 1892, he repeated his request for a nonpartisan commission. "Is it not time," Harrison asked, "that we should come together upon the high plane of patriotism while we devise methods that shall secure the right of every man qualified by law to cast a free ballot and give to every such ballot an equal value in choosing public officers and in directing the policy of the Government?" The President also denounced lynchings but could not suggest a possible solution to this problem.[34]

III

As in the campaign of 1892, Republicans during early 1893 showed that their enthusiasm for the Negro had cooled considerably. Harrison provided an illustration one month before he left office when he filled a Supreme Court vacancy with a former Confederate officer. Increasingly unpopular with his own party and realizing that his nominee would need Democratic support to be confirmed, the President chose Circuit Judge Howell Edmunds Jackson, an ex-senator from Tennessee, for the post.[35]

Clarkson was dumfounded. In a signed article first published in his own paper, the *Iowa State Register,* and later reprinted in such journals as the New York *World* and the New York *Sun,* he declared that, although Negroes were still being murdered and intimidated, the President was surrendering the last refuge of the freedmen to the Redeemers. Just a few days before, a Paris, Texas, colored man had been burned at the stake by a mob for allegedly killing a four-year-old white girl. "That a Republican president, when the South neither in its press, nor by any public utterance of its people condemns such cruelties, should in selecting a supreme judge from the South, choose a man who represents such cruelty to the negro, and that he should do it on the very day after a negro has been burned alive and tortured with the passive consent of the state and local authorities in a Southern state, makes it stranger and more unaccountable and more to be condemned," Clarkson argued. Whether this act—"the greatest solecism in party politics ever committed by any President, and the first instance since the foundation of the Republic of a president selecting for the supreme court a man of the opposite political faith—was done in personal pique over his defeat or from whatever motive or cause, the Republican Senate owes it to the party of Lincoln, Grant and Blaine to condemn it," he pleaded. "To accept and confirm it would be to confess Republicanism a sham and all of its glorious principles canting hypocrisies." [36]

Tired of the race question, papers of both parties took issue with Clarkson. The selection of Jackson was "a just, high-minded, patriotic act," said the New York *World*. The journal did not expect Clarkson to applaud decisions of that caliber. Similarly, the once bloody shirt Chicago *Tribune* supported the nomination. Harrison, it believed, had once more risen above party politics.[37]

In a long letter to the *World* Clarkson fought back. The Republican party was now showing the same "moral cowardice" that it had exhibited during the 1892 campaign, he charged. Concessions to a party which disfranchised Southern Republicans and stole Northern state legislatures would only bring more Republican defeats. He had "no liking for the 'good fellow' business which so many Republicans in power at Washington have been playing for so many years in trying to make themselves appear better and wiser than their party. They have played it so much that they have given away nearly the whole Republican estate." Republicanism was "better than any man and wiser than any President." Millions of men who had voted for Harrison in November would have cast Cleveland ballots if they had known that the President would betray his own party by placing a Bourbon in a high federal post.[38]

The lone Republican to come to Clarkson's aid was Jacob Sloat Fassett, an ex-state senator from New York who had served as secretary of the National Committee during the election of 1888. He regarded "the President's appointment of Judge Jackson as an abject surrender of all the principles Harrison is supposed to have represented when he sat in the United States Senate and pleaded for negro suffrage, and when he approved in his letter of acceptance of the platforms adopted by the Republican National Conventions in 1888 and 1892, at both of which he was nominated for the Presidency." [39]

The rest of the party ignored Clarkson and Fassett. The Senate unanimously approved the selection of Jackson without even the formality of a roll call vote and without a single Republican objection.[40]

To Clarkson the confirmation was another sign that his party had shamefully deserted the colored man. He warned the annual convention of the National Republican League, of which he was president, that it was making a grave mistake. There were many indications that Negroes and Democrats were allying: during his first term Cleveland had appointed scores of colored men to office; an Iowa Negro had been a member of the convention which in 1892 nominated Cleveland for the presidency; in 1891 and 1892 Tammany Hall had sponsored colored clubs; and recently members of the race had been elected to the Charleston city council and to the South Carolina state legislature on the Democratic ticket. While the Democracy was wooing the colored man, the Republicans were ignoring him.[41]

Even Clarkson's own convention refused to heed his plea. When a Louisiana Negro complained that the planks adopted did not denounce Redeemer outrages in the South, he was brusquely informed that a general clause favoring the platform of 1892 adequately covered the situation.[42]

By the summer of 1893 those still interested in the race issue dejectedly admitted that most party members no longer cared about the problem. Spooner wrote Clarkson that "the interest of the republicans of the United States in an honest ballot, in maintaining the rights of citizenship, and in holding sacred the pledge of Abraham Lincoln's proclamation to the colored men is dead, or in a slumber too deep for us to arouse it." A short while later, a North Carolina Negro, who with the help of Clarkson and Spooner had been trying to sell his book dealing with Democratic outrages, reported from Chicago that he had "little if any hope that it will ever be published, or that the people would care about reading it, in any event. There seems to be utter indifference on the part of the people here regarding the Southern question." [43]

Within a short time even the occasional complaints of bloody shirt Republicans ceased. Chandler wrote no more letters to New York editors about Southern affairs.[44] Hoar forgot about election acts and now advised Negroes to "cultivate the virtues of integrity, industry, frugality. . . . The negro question," he believed, "is to be settled in this country by the personal worth of the negro. When he attains that, all other things will be added unto him!" [45] Never again did Foraker conduct a sectional campaign in Ohio.[46] Platforms became weaker and briefer.[47] Far from making fiery speeches, the next Republican president, who for years had proudly called himself Major William McKinley, used words similar to those uttered by Mugwumps, by Northern merchants engaged in Southern trade, and by those who believed that agitation of the race issue kept Southern industrialists and high tariff planters in the Democratic party. He told the Georgia state legislature:

Sectional lines no longer mar the map of the United States. Sectional feelings no longer hold back the love we bear each other. Fraternity is the national anthem, sung by a chorus of forty-five States and our Territories at home and beyond the seas. The Union is once more the common altar of our love and loyalty, our devotion and sacrifice.[48]

As Republican political weapons, the war issues were dead.

12

The Party and the Negro

During the years after the end of Reconstruction the Southern question was an important issue in politics. If, as the Stalwarts claimed, the Republican party had deserted the Southern Negro in 1877, that abandonment was short-lived. By 1878 sectionalism was once again the official policy of a Republican administration. For fifteen years after that, the race problem played a key role in party affairs.

This period was not the nadir for the Negro.[1] Certainly a span of time marked by the Lodge bill, the Blair bill, numerous Congressional investigations of Southern atrocities, and a steady stream of Republican speeches in favor of equal civil and political rights for the colored race cannot be considered a low point. The bottom was actually reached after 1891, when Republican efforts for the Negro dramatically and suddenly stopped. A student of the period between the Force bill struggle and the First World War will search in vain if he looks for election acts, education bills, and other political measures designed to aid the Negro.

Far from being the exclusive work of social and intellectual forces,[2] the sectional realignment of the last quarter of the nineteenth century was largely the product of powerful economic forces. More than any other Northern groups, merchants engaged in Southern trade and Eastern industrialists frustrated Republican attempts to stress the war issues. As in the pre-Civil War era, the former argued that agitation of the race question would ruin their profits. The latter persuaded influential Republicans like James G. Blaine and Murat Halstead that if the Negro theme was dropped from politics Southern high tariff advocates would join the Republican party for business reasons.

The Mugwumps also played a major role in the story. They reasoned that the Negro was inferior and uneducated; that his ignorance made him an easy prey for voracious and unscrupulous machine politicians; that Reconstruction had proven the folly of colored rule; and that measures like the Force bill would unduly increase the authority of the central government at the expense of local and state authorities.

It was, perhaps, natural for the bloody shirt wavers to dislike the Mugwumps, who, they claimed, had deserted the Republican party in the face of enemy fire. But the opposition shown by men like James S. Clarkson, Grenville M. Dodge, William E. Chandler, John C. Spooner, and Joseph B. Foraker, all of whose public and private fortunes were intimately connected with big business, to industrialists and traders is more difficult to explain. Basically politicians, these Republicans were unwilling to subordinate the interests of their party to those of any single group. Chandler, Clarkson, Dodge, Spooner, and Foraker were not anti-business; they simply felt that, as party leaders, their prime duty was to foster Republicanism and that the best way to do this in the South was by aiding

the Negro. Although the sectionalists often criticized businessmen, they consistently supported business's demands for a
high tariff and a sound financial program. Moreover, they
seldom doubted that the true path of economic progress for
the United States followed the route charted by the same
manufacturers and merchants whose attitude on the Southern
question they denounced.

Advocating numerous approaches to the race issue, Republican leaders continually quarreled between 1877 and 1893.
Fundamentally, these arguments were over the methods to
be used in extending their party's influence in both the South
and the country at large. With national political power during
this period almost equally divided between the two great
parties, Republican officials realized that if they could not
carry some areas of the South they would frequently lose
control of Congress and the Presidency. Only too well did
they know that with the Democrats in power such cardinal
Republican doctrines as protection and a sound currency were
in constant danger. Faced with the problem of making their
party truly national, Republican politicians, when debating
the race question, were, in effect, fighting about the best means
of establishing such an organization.

Every Republican president between 1877 and 1893, com-
prehending that only a national party could wrest power away
from the Democrats, adopted a scheme which he hoped would
attract Southern white men to Republicanism. Hayes appealed
to former Southern Whigs on a platform stressing internal
improvements; Garfield was drawing up plans to foster Southern education; Arthur allied with the Independents; and Harrison tried to form a white, high tariff organization in Louisiana,
Alabama, and Virginia. Each of these plans, with the exception
of Garfield's, was denounced by those who believed that support should be given to the old pro-Negro factions in the
South. But despite their differences, both those who endorsed

bloody shirt tactics and those who advocated subtler methods agreed that Republicanism must win large segments of the South if it was to remain in office. This fact was readily admitted by such disputants as Hayes and Blaine in 1877, by William E. Chandler and Whitelaw Reid in 1883, and by Clarkson and Chandler in 1888.

Not knowing which way to turn, most prominent Republicans from 1877 to 1893 adopted and dropped plans of action with great rapidity. Hayes, Arthur, and Harrison all employed sectionalism after their schemes for attracting important white Democrats had been foiled by the Redeemers. Clarkson, Dodge, Chandler, Sherman, and Blaine were even more inconsistent. Chandler's checkered career is an illustration. He favored a harsh policy when Hayes was president; supported the Independent movements under Arthur; was strangely silent during 1885 and 1886; and returned to the political scene as a sectionalist in 1887, only to drop this approach completely after 1891. Clarkson's attitude changed almost as often. A fierce opponent of Hayes from 1877 to 1880, he favored a harsh policy until 1888, when he adopted the idea that Southern protectionists could be wooed away from the Democracy if the race issue was eliminated from politics. After the 1889 election he became the most outspoken advocate of human rights in the party. Sherman was an even more complicated case. In 1887 alone he altered his position twice. He started off early in the year by trying to persuade Alabama and Tennessee protectionists to become Republicans. Then at Springfield, Illinois, on June 1, he spoke of evil rebels, of brave Union soldiers, and of the wartime treachery and cowardice of Grover Cleveland. He returned to his original approach after his Springfield address was severely criticized. Sensitive to every political wind that blew, Republicans constantly searched for methods of building up their party in the South. Not until 1891 did they abandon the quest.

And when Chandler, Clarkson, and Sherman finally did lose interest in the race question, it was the Negro who suffered. Almost entirely without Northern defenders for the first time since the Civil War, colored men in the 1890's fell even more completely than ever under the dominance of the Redeemers. Northern merchants, Eastern industrialists, and Mugwumps had made the task of the segregationist that much lighter.

II

There is mounting evidence that some of the forces which helped bring about Northern abandonment of the Negro by the 1890's are still alive today and that they may, in the future, work to build a strong Republican party in the South and to moderate white opposition to integration of the public schools. Southern manufacturing is a prime example. Industrialization in the South since the Second World War has progressed at so rapid a pace that it has undoubtedly now reached a height far beyond the expectations of the most business-minded Southerner of the 1880's. The aluminum plants of West Virginia, the giant chemical works of Louisiana, the textile factories of the Carolinas, and the oil refineries of Texas and Oklahoma are but a few of the dramatic and conclusive reminders that the South is no longer an exclusively rural section. It is certainly reasonable, as John Sherman, Benjamin Harrison, James S. Clarkson, Grenville M. Dodge, James G. Blaine, and other Republicans pointed out in 1888, to expect the political and economic outlook of the Southern manufacturer to differ sharply from that of the cotton picker. Well might one remark about today's Southern industrialists what these Republicans seventy years ago said about the Alabama and Tennessee steel producers, the South Carolina and Georgia rice planters, and the Louisiana sugar refiners. On economic questions these Southerners are Republicans. With Civil War traditions disposed of, they would naturally gravitate toward the Republican party. Moreover, many Northern Democrats today have far less sympathy for the segregationist's position than did Grover Cleveland and David B. Hill in 1888 and 1892. With Northern Democrats today taking an even stronger stand on the race question than their Northern Republican counterparts, Southern industrialists certainly would feel more at home than ever in the Republican organization. Undoubtedly, a strong two-party system in the South would foster greater opportunity for the discussion of issues, including integration, and, by making it necessary for each party to appeal for support to a wider range of voters, would serve as a moderating force on the Negro problem.[3]

The tariff statement of the Southern Governors conference of 1960 illustrates the economic affinity between Southern industrialists and Northern Republicans. Issued by sixteen governors, fifteen of whom were Democrats, the pronouncement accurately reflected the change in Southern sentiment brought about by the shift of that section from agrarianism to industrialism. A triumph for big business, its recommendation of import quotas for textiles, apparel, seafood products, oil and refined commodities, and other items was directly at variance with the Democratic platform of 1960. Lobbyists for the Southern textile and petroleum industries, many of whom attended the conference in the guise of newsmen, departed from the gathering in a gleeful mood. As the New York *Times* commented, the "statement on trade and tariff policy . . . read as if it had been prepared by the right wing of the National Association of Manufacturers." Complaining that "Many foreign-produced goods continue to usurp the American market place," the governors, "in true McKinleyesque spirit," went "right down the line for the protectionist lobby. . . . No one even pretends any more that the South is a stronghold of liberal tariff policies as it was before its industrialization," the *Times* continued, "but in this pronounciamento the Southern

Democratic Governors lay it right on the reactionary line." [4]
Clearly, the Southern industrialist has little to like in the
economic policies of the Democratic party.

Like the manufacturers, commercial interests are as hard
at work today as they were in the 1870's, 1880's, and 1890's.
But, unlike seventy years ago, their influence is being felt
principally in the South and against the segregationist. One
need only point to the comments of Winthrop Rockefeller,
chairman of the Arkansas Industrial Development Commission,
who in 1957 charged that the violence accompanying integration of public schools in Little Rock had greatly injured his
state's economic prospects. Northern firms, he maintained,
would refuse to do business with, or to move to, Little Rock
if disorder continued. He hoped that the "goodwill and moderation" of the people of Arkansas would reassert themselves
before intersectional relations were permanently impaired. In
a like tone, the Atlanta Chamber of Commerce, in the interest
of trade, late in 1960 urged its members to put pressure upon
the Georgia state legislature to repeal the laws calling for the
closing of any integrated school.[5]

Moreover, there is a striking similarity between the statements in 1884 of James B. Schuyler, the chief clerk of the
Gibson House in Cincinnati, that agitation of the race issue
was killing business and the complaints of New Orleans hotel
and restaurant men in December, 1960, that the squabble over
desegregation of the public schools was ruining the hotel and
tourist trade. According to the Mayor of New Orleans and to
business leaders there, the restaurant and hotel trade, a "major
factor" in the city's economy, was off more than twenty per
cent during the school dispute. Hotel cancellations, which nationally averaged about ten or twelve per cent, ran well over
twenty-five per cent in New Orleans. "Taxi drivers complain
that fares are scarce after sunset," related a New York *Times*
story. The famed restaurants of the city were almost empty,

the paper went on, and "the voice of the pitchman outside the night spots of Bourbon Street carries a new note of urgency." The merchants of New Orleans were quick to point out that these results occurred despite the fact that there was relatively little violence.[6]

Certainly the troubles facing the South are not at an end. The race problem seems destined to dominate Southern life for a great many years to come. At present, despite the support of industrialists and of many upper-class urban areas, the prospects for the rise of a strong, grass-roots Republican party in the South seem almost as dim as they were under Hayes, Garfield, Arthur, and Harrison; at the precinct level the Republican organizations there are now as notoriously weak and disorganized as they were in the 1880's.[7]

But in the years to come the very same influences which forced the Northern wing of the Republican party to desert the Negro by 1893 and which paved the way for the rise of legalized segregation in the South in the form of Jim Crow laws could conceivably turn the tide in the colored man's favor. Pressure from Southern commercial leaders, such as those in Little Rock, Atlanta, and New Orleans, from Southern industrialists looking for support for their economic program, and from intellectuals who believe in moderate policies possibly could induce the segregationist to modify his position. If the color barrier should gradually give way, the dream looked forward to so eagerly by Hayes in 1877, by Garfield in 1881, and by Harrison in 1889 might eventually be realized. Southern political parties might well consist of men of both races who joined forces on the tariff, internal improvements, and other political, economic, and intellectual issues, and not on the race question.

Bibliography

MANUSCRIPTS

Charles Aldrich Collection, Iowa State Department of History and Archives, Des Moines, Iowa.

Nelson W. Aldrich Papers, Library of Congress.

Russell A. Alger Papers, William L. Clements Library, University of Michigan, Ann Arbor, Michigan.

William B. Allison Papers, Iowa State Department of History and Archives, Des Moines, Iowa.

James B. Angell Papers, Michigan Historical Collections, University of Michigan, Ann Arbor, Michigan.

Chester A. Arthur Personal Scrapbooks, Columbia University Library, New York City.

Attorney General's Files, National Archives.

James G. Blaine Papers, Library of Congress.

Benjamin H. Bristow Papers, Library of Congress.

John E. Bruce Papers, Schomburg Collection of the New York Public Library.

William E. Chandler Papers, Library of Congress.

Zachariah Chandler Papers, Library of Congress.

William Claflin Papers, Rutherford B. Hayes Library, Fremont, Ohio.

James S. Clarkson Papers, Iowa State Department of History and Archives, Des Moines, Iowa.

James S. Clarkson Papers, Library of Congress.

Grover Cleveland Papers, Library of Congress.

James M. Comly Papers, Ohio State Historical Society, Columbus, Ohio.

Thomas M. Cooley Papers, Michigan Historical Collections, University of Michigan, Ann Arbor, Michigan.

George William Curtis Papers, Harvard University Library, Cambridge, Massachusetts.

Henry L. Dawes Papers, Library of Congress.

Anna E. Dickinson Papers, Library of Congress.

Grenville M. Dodge Papers, Iowa State Department of History and Archives, Des Moines, Iowa.

Stephen B. Elkins Papers, University of West Virginia Library, Morgantown, West Virginia.

Lucius Fairchild Papers, Wisconsin State Historical Society, Madison, Wisconsin.

Hamilton Fish Papers, Library of Congress.

Joseph B. Foraker Papers, Historical and Philosophical Society of Ohio, Cincinnati, Ohio.

John Murray Forbes Papers, Massachusetts Historical Society, Boston, Massachusetts.

William Lloyd Garrison Papers, Boston Public Library.

William Lloyd Garrison Papers, Massachusetts Historical Society, Boston, Massachusetts.

Walter Q. Gresham Papers, Library of Congress.

Benjamin Harrison Papers, Library of Congress.

Nils P. Haugen Papers, Wisconsin State Historical Society, Madison, Wisconsin.

Rutherford B. Hayes Papers, Rutherford B. Hayes Library, Fremont, Ohio.

Burke A. Hinsdale Papers, Michigan Historical Collections, University of Michigan, Ann Arbor, Michigan.

Timothy O. Howe Papers, Wisconsin State Historical Society, Madison, Wisconsin.

Elisha W. Keyes Papers, Wisconsin State Historical Society, Madison, Wisconsin.

Samuel J. Kirkwood Papers, Iowa State Department of History and Archives, Des Moines, Iowa.

John F. Lacey Papers, Iowa State Department of History and Archives, Des Moines, Iowa.

Henry Cabot Lodge Papers, Massachusetts Historical Society, Boston, Massachusetts.

John A. Logan Papers, Illinois State Historical Library, Springfield, Illinois.

John A. Logan Papers, Library of Congress.
John D. Long Papers, Massachusetts Historical Society, Boston, Massachusetts.
Edward McPherson Papers, Library of Congress.
Louis T. Michener Papers, Library of Congress.
Justin S. Morrill Papers, Library of Congress.
Levi P. Morton Papers, New York Public Library.
Whitelaw Reid Papers, Library of Congress.
Jeremiah Rusk Papers, Wisconsin State Historical Society, Madison, Wisconsin.
Carl Schurz Papers, Library of Congress.
John Sherman Papers, Library of Congress.
William Henry Smith Papers of the Indiana Historical Society, Microfilm, Rutherford B. Hayes Library, Fremont, Ohio.
William Henry Smith Papers, Ohio State Historical Society, Columbus, Ohio.
John C. Spooner Papers, Library of Congress.
Fanny Garrison Villard Papers, Harvard University Library, Cambridge, Massachusetts.

PUBLIC DOCUMENTS

Congressional Record, 1875, 1877–1893.
Richardson, James D. (ed.). *A Compilation of the Messages and Papers of the Presidents.* Vols. X–XIII. New York: Bureau of National Literature, 1897.
U. S. Bureau of the Census. *Tenth Census of the United States: 1880.* Vol. I. Washington: Government Printing Office, 1883.
U. S. Congress, Senate. *Report and Testimony of the Select Committee of the United States Senate to Investigate the Causes of the Removal of the Negro from the Southern States to the Northern States.* Senate Report 693. 46 Congress, 2 Session. 3 vols. Washington: Government Printing Office, 1880.
U. S. Congress, Senate. *Report of the Committee on the Judiciary on the Municipal Election at Jackson, Mississippi.* Senate Report 1887. 50 Congress, 1 Session. Washington: Government Printing Office, 1888.
U. S. Congress, Senate. *Report of the Special Committee to Inquire into Alleged Election Outrages at Danville, Virginia.* Senate Report 579. 48 Congress, 1 Session. 2 vols. Washington: Government Printing Office, 1884.
U. S. Congress, Senate. *Report of the Special Committee to Inquire into*

the Mississippi Election of 1883. Senate Report 512. 48 Congress, 1 Session. 2 vols. Washington: Government Printing Office, 1884.

U. S. Congress, Senate. *Report of the United States Committee to Inquire into Alleged Frauds and Violence in the Elections of 1878.* Senate Report 855. 45 Congress, 3 Session. 2 vols. Washington: Government Printing Office, 1879.

NEWSPAPERS

Atlanta Constitution, 1879, 1890.
Boston Daily Advertiser, 1883.
Brooklyn Standard Union, 1890.
Chicago Tribune, 1877–1893.
Cincinnati Commercial, 1877–1883.
Cincinnati Commercial Gazette, 1883–1893.
Cincinnati Enquirer, 1877–1893.
Cincinnati Gazette, 1877–1883.
Cleveland Gazette, 1886–1893.
Concord Evening Monitor, 1877–1893.
Hartford Courant, 1877–1893.
Indianapolis Journal, 1888.
Des Moines *Iowa State Register,* 1877–1893.
Newark Daily Advertiser, 1877–1893.
New Orleans Picayune, 1879.
New Orleans Times, 1879.
New Orleans Times-Democrat, 1889.
New Orleans Weekly Pelican, 1889.
New York Age, 1887–1893.
New York Commercial Advertiser, 1877–1893.
New York Commercial Bulletin, 1879–1893.
New York Daily Bulletin, 1877–1878.
New York Evening Post, 1877–1893, 1903.
New York Freeman, 1884–1887.
New York Globe, 1883–1884.
New York Herald, 1877–1893.
New York Journal of Commerce, 1877–1893.
New York Mail and Express, 1890.
New York Shipping and Commercial List, 1877.
New York Sun, 1890, 1892.
New York Times, 1877–1893, 1957–1960.
New York Tribune, 1877–1893, 1903.
New York World, 1877–1893.

Philadelphia Inquirer, 1890.
Philadelphia North American, 1877–1893.
Philadelphia Press, 1877–1893.
Portland Oregonian, 1877–1893.
Richmond State, 1889.
St. Paul Pioneer Press, 1877–1893.
Springfield Daily Republican, 1877–1893.
Washington Bee, 1883–1893.
Washington National Republican, 1877–1888.

PERIODICALS

American Almanac, 1883–1884, 1889.
American Catholic Quarterly Review, 1888.
American Grocer, 1890.
Appletons' Annual Cyclopaedia, 1877–1893.
Bradstreet's, 1883.
Bulletin of the American Iron and Steel Association, 1877–1893.
Commercial and Financial Chronicle, 1877–1879.
Contemporary Review, 1883.
Cosmopolitan, 1892.
Current History, 1958.
Forum, 1886–1893.
Harper's Weekly, 1865–1893.
Independent, 1877–1893.
Nation, 1865–1893.
North American Review, 1877–1893.
Public Opinion, 1886–1893.
Railway Age, 1879.
Review of Reviews, 1892.
Tribune Almanac, 1883–1890.

REPORTS

Proceedings of the Republican National Convention of 1876. Concord: Republican Press Association, 1876.
Proceedings of the Republican National Convention of 1880. Chicago: Jno. B. Jeffrey Printing & Publishing House, 1881.
Proceedings of the Republican National Convention of 1884. Chicago: Rand, McNally & Company, 1884.
Proceedings of the Republican National Convention of 1888. Chicago: Rand, McNally & Company, 1888.

Proceedings of the Republican National Convention of 1892. Minneapolis: Chas. W. Johnson, 1903.

Twelfth Annual Report of the Cincinnati Board of Trade and Transportation for Commercial Year Ending January 1, 1881. Cincinnati: Bloch & Company, 1881.

Williams' Cincinnati Directory, 1880. Cincinnati: Cincinnati Directory Office, 1880.

PAMPHLETS

A *Soldier of Conscience, Edward Perkins Clark.* Brooklyn: The Eagle Press, 1903.

Clark, Edward P. *A Bill to Promote Mendicancy.* New York: The Evening Post Publishing Company, 1886–1890.

Letters of Mr. William E. Chandler Relative to the So-Called Southern Policy of President Hayes Together with a Letter to Mr. Chandler of Mr. William Lloyd Garrison. Concord: Monitor and Statesman Office, 1878.

UNPUBLISHED WORKS

Abramowitz, Jack. "Accomodation and Militancy in Negro Life, 1876–1916." Unpublished Ph. D. dissertation, Columbia University, 1950.

Cochran, William Cox. "Political Experiences of Major General Jacob Dolson Cox." Unpublished manuscript in Rutherford B. Hayes Library, Fremont, Ohio, 1940. 2 vols.

De Santis, Vincent P. "Republican Efforts to Break Up the Democratic South, 1877–1892." Unpublished Ph. D. dissertation, Johns Hopkins University, 1952.

Fishel, Leslie H. "The North and the Negro, 1865–1900: A Study in Race Discrimination." Unpublished Ph. D. dissertation, Harvard University, 1953. 2 vols.

Gray, Edgar Laughlin. "The Career of William Henry Smith, Politician-Journalist." Unpublished Ph. D. dissertation, Ohio State University, 1950.

Hantke, Richard Watson. "The Life of Elisha William Keyes." Unpublished Ph. D. dissertation, University of Wisconsin, 1942.

Hollis, Daniel Walker. "The Force Bill of 1890." Unpublished Master's thesis, Columbia University, 1947.

Kleinpell, Eugene H. "James M. Comly, Journalist-Politician." Unpublished Ph. D. dissertation, Ohio State University, 1936.

Krebs, Frank John. "Hayes and the South." Unpublished Ph. D. dissertation, Ohio State University, 1950.

McLachlan, James S. "The Genteel Reformers, 1865–1884." Unpublished Master's thesis, Columbia University, 1958.

Ross, Sam. "A Biography of Lucius Fairchild of Wisconsin." Unpublished Ph. D. dissertation, University of Wisconsin, 1955.

Strauss, Grace. "Northern Opinion of the South, 1880–1900, As Revealed in the Magazines." Unpublished Master's thesis, Columbia University, 1939.

Thompson, Edwin Bruce. "Benjamin Helm Bristow, Symbol of Reform." Unpublished Ph. D. dissertation, University of Wisconsin, 1940.

White, Edward Arthur. "The Republican Party in National Politics, 1888–1891." Unpublished Ph. D. dissertation, University of Wisconsin, 1941.

ARTICLES

Bacote, Clarence A. "Negro Officeholders in Georgia under President McKinley," *Journal of Negro History*, XLIV (July, 1959), 217–239.

Bage, Elvena S. "President Garfield's Forgotten Pronouncement," *Negro History Bulletin*, XIV (June, 1951), 195–197, 206, 214.

Davis, T. Frederick. "The Disston Land Purchase," *Florida Historical Quarterly*, XVII (January, 1939), 200–210.

De Santis, Vincent P. "Benjamin Harrison and the Republican Party in the South," *Indiana Magazine of History*, LI (December, 1955), 279–302.

———. "Negro Dissatisfaction with Republican Policy in the South, 1882–1884," *Journal of Negro History*, XXXVI (April, 1951), 148–159.

———. "President Arthur and the Independent Movements in the South in 1882," *Journal of Southern History*, XIX (August, 1953), 346–363.

———. "President Garfield and the 'Solid South,'" *North Carolina Historical Review*, XXXVI (October, 1959), 442–465.

———. "President Hayes's Southern Policy," *Journal of Southern History*, XXI (November, 1955), 476–494.

———. "Republican Efforts to 'Crack' the Democratic South," *Review of Politics*, XIV (April, 1952), 244–264.

———. "The Republican Party and the Southern Negro, 1877–1897," *Journal of Negro History*, XLV (April, 1960), 71–87.

Dozer, Donald Marquand. "Benjamin Harrison and the Presidential Campaign in 1892," *American Historical Review*, LIV (October, 1948), 49–77.

Fishel, Leslie H. "The Negro in Northern Politics, 1870–1900," *Mississippi Valley Historical Review*, XLII (December, 1955), 466–489.

Going, Allen J. "The South and the Blair Bill," *Mississippi Valley Historical Review*, XLIV (September, 1957), 267–290.

Halsell, Willie D. "James R. Chalmers and 'Mahoneism' in Mississippi," *Journal of Southern History*, X (February, 1944), 37–58.

————. "Republican Factionalism in Mississippi, 1882–1884," *Journal of Southern History*, VII (February, 1941), 84–101.

————. "The Appointment of L. Q. C. Lamar to the Supreme Court," *Mississippi Valley Historical Review*, XXVIII (December, 1941), 399–412.

Hesseltine, William B. "Economic Factors in the Abandonment of Reconstruction," *Mississippi Valley Historical Review*, XXII (September, 1935), 191–210.

Link, Arthur S. "Theodore Roosevelt and the South in 1912," *North Carolina Historical Review*, XXIII (July, 1946), 313–324.

Mowry, George E. "The South and the Progressive Lily White Party of 1912," *Journal of Southern History*, VI (May, 1940), 237–247.

Pringle, Henry F. "Theodore Roosevelt and the South," *Virginia Quarterly Review*, IX (January, 1933), 14–25.

"Remarks on this Exodus by Frederick Douglass," *Journal of Negro History*, IV (January, 1919), 56–57.

Van Deusen, John G. "Did Republicans 'Colonize' Indiana in 1879?" *Indiana Magazine of History*, XXX (December, 1934), 335–346.

————. "The Exodus of 1879," *Journal of Negro History*, XXI (April, 1936), 111–129.

Volwiler, Albert T. (ed.). "Tariff Strategy and Propaganda in the United States, 1887–1888," *American Historical Review*, XXXVI (October, 1930), 76–96.

Wellborn, Fred. "The Influence of the Silver-Republican Senators, 1889–1891," *Mississippi Valley Historical Review*, XIV (March, 1928), 462–480.

Williams, Frank B., Jr. "Public Reaction to the Poll Tax as a Suffrage Requirement in Mississippi, 1890–1905," *Journal of Mississippi History*, XVII (October, 1955), 229–248.

AUTOBIOGRAPHIES, MEMOIRS, AND PUBLISHED
COLLECTIONS OF LETTERS AND DOCUMENTS

Bancroft, Frederic, and Dunning, William A. (eds.). *The Reminiscences of Carl Schurz.* 3 vols. New York: The McClure Company, 1908.

Bancroft, Frederic (ed.). *Speeches, Correspondence and Political Papers of Carl Schurz.* 6 vols. New York and London: G. P. Putnam's, 1913.

Blaine, James G. *Twenty Years of Congress, From Lincoln to Garfield.* 2 vols. Norwich, Connecticut: The Henry Bill Publishing Company, 1886.

Brown, George Rothwell (ed.). *Reminiscences of Senator William M. Stewart.* New York and Washington: The Neale Publishing Company, 1908.

Boutwell, George S. *Reminiscences of Sixty Years in Public Affairs.* New York: McClure, Phillips & Company, 1902.

Carpenter, Frank G. *Carp's Washington.* New York: McGraw-Hill Book Company, 1960.

Cullom, Shelby M. *Fifty Years of Public Service.* Chicago: A. C. McClurg & Company, 1911.

Depew, Chauncey M. *My Memories of Eighty Years.* New York: Charles Scribner's Sons, 1924.

Evarts, Sherman (ed.). *The Arguments and Speeches of William Maxwell Evarts.* 3 vols. New York: The Macmillan Company, 1919.

Foner, Philip S. (ed.). *The Life and Writings of Frederick Douglass.* 4 vols. New York: International Publishers, 1955.

Foraker, Joseph B. *Notes of a Busy Life.* 2 vols. Cincinnati: Stewart and Kidd, 1917.

Haskell, Daniel C. (ed.). *The Nation Index, 1865–1917.* 2 vols. New York: The New York Public Library, 1953.

Hedges, Charles (ed.). *Speeches of Benjamin Harrison, February 1888 to February 1892.* New York: United States Book Company, 1892.

Hinsdale, Burke A. (ed.). *The Works of James Abram Garfield.* 2 vols. Boston: James R. Osgood & Company, 1882.

Hinsdale, Mary (ed.). *The Garfield-Hinsdale Letters, Correspondence between James Abram Garfield and Burke Aaron Hinsdale.* Ann Arbor: University of Michigan Press, 1949.

Hoar, George Frisbie. *Autobiography of Seventy Years.* 2 vols. New York: Charles Scribner's Sons, 1903.

Kelley, William D. *The Old South and the New.* New York and London: G. P. Putnam's, 1887.

Lodge, Henry Cabot. *Early Memories.* New York: Charles Scribner's Sons, 1913.

———. (ed.). *Selections from the Correspondence of Theodore Roosevelt and Henry Cabot Lodge, 1884–1918.* 2 vols. New York: Charles Scribner's Sons, 1925.

Morison, Elting E. (ed.). *The Letters of Theodore Roosevelt.* 8 vols. Cambridge: Harvard University Press, 1951–1954.

Norton, Charles Eliot (ed.). *Letters of James Russell Lowell.* New York: Harper & Brothers, 1893.

————. (ed.). *Orations and Addresses of George William Curtis.* 3 vols. New York: Harper & Brothers, 1894.

Norton, Sara, and De Wolfe, Mark Anthony (eds.). *Letters of Charles Eliot Norton.* 2 vols. Boston and New York: Houghton Mifflin Company, 1913.

Ogden, Rollo (ed.). *Life and Letters of Edwin Lawrence Godkin.* 2 vols. New York: The Macmillan Company, 1907.

Payne, Daniel Alexander. *Recollections of Seventy Years.* Nashville: House of the A. M. E. Sunday School Union, 1888.

Platt, Thomas Collier. *Autobiography.* New York: B. W. Dodge & Company, 1910.

Porter, Kirk H., and Johnson, Donald Bruce (eds.). *National Party Platforms, 1840–1956.* Urbana: University of Illinois Press, 1956.

Sherman, John. *Recollections of Forty Years.* 2 vols. Akron: The Werner Company, 1895.

Stoddard, Henry L. *As I Knew Them, Presidents and Politics from Grant to Coolidge.* New York and London: Harper & Brothers, 1927.

Thorndike, Rachel Sherman (ed.). *The Sherman Letters, Correspondence between General and Senator Sherman from 1837 to 1891.* New York: Charles Scribner's Sons, 1894.

Tourgee, Albion W. *An Appeal to Caesar.* New York: Fords, Howard & Hulbert, 1884.

Volwiler, Albert T. (ed.). *The Correspondence between Benjamin Harrison and James G. Blaine, 1882–1893.* Philadelphia: The American Philosophical Society, 1940.

Wakefield, Eva Ingersoll (ed.). *The Letters of Robert G. Ingersoll.* New York: Philosophical Library, 1951.

Autobiography of Andrew Dickson White. 2 vols. New York: The Century Company, 1904.

Williams, Charles R. (ed.). *Diary and Letters of Rutherford B. Hayes.* 5 vols. Columbus: Ohio State Archaeological and Historical Society, 1922–1925.

MONOGRAPHS AND BIOGRAPHIES

Barnard, Harry. *Rutherford B. Hayes and His America.* Indianapolis: The Bobbs-Merrill Company, 1954.

Barrows, Chester L. *William M. Evarts, Lawyer, Diplomat, Statesman.* Chapel Hill: University of North Carolina Press, 1941.

Beale, Howard K. *The Critical Year, A Study of Andrew Johnson and Reconstruction.* New York: Harcourt, Brace and Company, 1930.

Bentley, George R. *A History of the Freedmen's Bureau.* Philadelphia: University of Pennsylvania Press, 1955.

Blake, Nelson Morehouse. *William Mahone of Virginia, Soldier and Political Insurgent.* Richmond: Garrett and Massie, 1935.

Blum, John Morton. *The Republican Roosevelt.* Cambridge: Harvard University Press, 1954.

Bowers, Claude G. *Beveridge and the Progressive Era.* Boston: Houghton Mifflin Company, 1932.

Buck, Paul H. *The Road to Reunion, 1865–1900.* Boston: Little, Brown and Company, 1938.

Caldwell, Robert G. *James A. Garfield, Party Chieftain.* New York: Dodd, Mead & Company, 1931.

Casson, Henry. *'Uncle Jerry', The Life of General Jeremiah M. Rusk.* Madison: Junius W. Hill, 1895.

Cate, Wirt A. *Lucius Q. C. Lamar, Secession and Reunion.* Chapel Hill: University of North Carolina Press, 1935.

Chester, Giraud. *Embattled Maiden, The Life of Anna Dickinson.* New York: G. P. Putnam's, 1951.

Chidsey, Donald Barr. *The Gentleman from New York, A Life of Roscoe Conkling.* New Haven: Yale University Press, 1935.

Clancy, Herbert J. *The Presidential Election of 1880.* Chicago: Loyola University Press, 1958.

Commager, Henry Steele. *The American Mind.* New Haven: Yale University Press, 1950.

Conkling, Alfred R. *The Life and Letters of Roscoe Conkling, Orator, Statesman, Advocate.* New York: Charles L. Webster and Company, 1889.

Connelley, William E. *The Life of Preston B. Plumb, 1837–1891.* Chicago: Browne and Howell Company, 1913.

Coolidge, Louis A. *An Old-Fashioned Senator, Orville H. Platt of Connecticut.* New York and London: G. P. Putnam's Sons, 1910.

Cortissoz, Royal. *The Life of Whitelaw Reid.* 2 vols. New York: Charles Scribner's Sons, 1921.

Cramer, Clarence H. *Royal Bob, The Life of Robert G. Ingersoll.* Indianapolis: The Bobbs-Merrill Company, 1952.

Current, Richard Nelson. *Pine Logs and Politics, A Life of Philetus Sawyer, 1816–1900.* Madison: State Historical Society of Wisconsin, 1950.

De Santis, Vincent P. *Republicans Face the Southern Question, The New Departure Years, 1877–1897.* Baltimore: Johns Hopkins Press, 1959.

Durden, Robert F. *James Shepherd Pike, Republicanism and the American Negro, 1850–1882.* Durham: Duke University Press, 1957.

Foulke, William Dudley. *The Life of Oliver P. Morton.* 2 vols. Indianapolis: The Bowen-Merrill Company, 1899.

Fuess, Claude Moore. *Carl Schurz, Reformer.* New York: Dodd, Mead & Company, 1932.

Garraty, John A. *Henry Cabot Lodge, A Biography.* New York: Alfred A. Knopf, 1953.

Gillett, Frederick H. *George Frisbie Hoar.* Boston and New York: Houghton Mifflin Company, 1934.

Groves, Charles S. *Henry Cabot Lodge, The Statesman.* Boston: Small, Maynard & Company, 1925.

Hamilton, Gail. *Biography of James G. Blaine.* Norwich, Connecticut: The Henry Bill Company, 1895.

Hamlin, Charles Eugene. *The Life and Times of Hannibal Hamlin.* Cambridge: Riverside Press, 1899.

Haworth, Paul L. *The Hayes-Tilden Election.* Indianapolis: The Bobbs-Merrill Company, 1927.

Hedges, James B. *Henry Villard and the Railways of the Northwest.* New Haven: Yale University Press, 1930.

Hendrick, Burton J. *The Life of Andrew Carnegie.* New York: Doubleday, Doran and Company, 1932.

Hinsdale, Burke A. *President Garfield and Education.* Boston: James R. Osgood & Company, 1881.

Howe, George Frederick. *Chester A. Arthur, A Quarter-Century of Machine Politics.* New York: Dodd, Mead & Company, 1934.

Jarrell, Hampton M. *Wade Hampton and the Negro, The Road Not Taken.* Columbia: University of South Carolina Press, 1949.

Josephson, Matthew. *The Politicos, 1865–1896.* New York: Harcourt, Brace and Company, 1938.

Knoles, George Harmon. *The Presidential Campaign and Election of 1892.* Stanford University: Stanford University Press, 1942.

Lambert, John R. *Arthur Pue Gorman.* Baton Rouge: Louisiana State University Press, 1953.

Lambert, Oscar Doane. *Stephen Benton Elkins, American Foursquare, 1841–1911.* Pittsburgh: University of Pittsburgh Press, 1955.

Lee, Gordon Canfield. *The Struggle for Federal Aid, First Phase, A History of the Attempts to Obtain Federal Aid for Common Schools,*

1870–1890. New York: Bureau of Publications, Teachers College, Columbia University, 1949.

Logan, Rayford W. *The Negro in American Life and Thought, The Nadir, 1877–1901.* New York: Dial Press, 1954.

————. *The Negro in the United States.* Princeton: D. Van Nostrand, 1957.

Lowitt, Richard. *A Merchant Prince of the Nineteenth Century, William E. Dodge.* New York: Columbia University Press, 1954.

McCall, Samuel W. *The Life of Thomas Brackett Reed.* Boston and New York: Houghton Mifflin Company, 1914.

McElroy, Robert M. *Levi Parsons Morton, Banker, Diplomat, and Statesman.* New York and London: G. P. Putnam's Sons, 1930.

Mayes, Edward. *Lucius Q. C. Lamar, His Life, Times, and Speeches, 1825–1893.* Nashville: Publishing House of the Methodist Episcopal Church South, 1895.

Merriam, George S. *The Life and Times of Samuel Bowles.* New York: The Century Company, 1885.

Milne, Gordon. *George William Curtis and the Genteel Tradition.* Bloomington: Indiana University Press, 1956.

Muzzey, David Saville. *James G. Blaine, A Political Idol of Other Days.* New York: Dodd, Mead & Company, 1934.

Nevins, Allan. *Grover Cleveland, A Study in Courage.* New York: Dodd, Mead & Company, 1932.

————. *The Evening Post, A Century of Journalism.* New York: Boni and Liveright, 1922.

Oberholtzer, Ellis Paxson. *A History of the United States Since the Civil War.* 5 vols. New York: The Macmillan Company, 1917–1937.

Olcott, Charles S. *The Life of William McKinley.* 2 vols. Boston and New York: Houghton Mifflin Company, 1916.

Orcutt, William Dana. *Burrows of Michigan and the Republican Party, A Biography and a History.* 2 vols. New York: Longmans, Green and Company, 1917.

Parker, William Belmont. *The Life and Public Services of Justin Smith Morrill.* Boston and New York: Houghton Mifflin Company, 1924.

Pearson, Charles Chilton. *The Readjuster Movement in Virginia.* Vol. IV of *Yale Historical Publications.* New Haven: Yale University Press, 1917.

Peck, Harry Thurston. *Twenty Years of the Republic, 1885–1905.* New York: Dodd, Mead & Company, 1906.

Perkins, Jacob R. *Trails, Rails and War, The Life of General G. M. Dodge.* Indianapolis: The Bobbs-Merrill Company, 1929.

Pleasants, Samuel A. *Fernando Wood of New York*. New York: Columbia University Press, 1948.

Pringle, Henry F. *The Life and Times of William Howard Taft, A Biography*. 2 vols. New York and Toronto: Farrar & Rinehart, 1939.

———. *Theodore Roosevelt, A Biography*. New York: Harcourt, Brace and Company, 1931.

Quarles, Benjamin. *Frederick Douglass*. Washington: Associated Publishers, 1948.

Randall, James G. *The Civil War and Reconstruction*. Boston: D. C. Heath and Company, 1937.

Rhodes, James Ford. *A History of the United States from the Compromise of 1850*. 9 vols. New York: The Macmillan Company, 1900–1928.

Richardson, Leon Burr. *William E. Chandler, Republican*. New York: Dodd, Mead & Company, 1940.

Robinson, William Alexander. *Thomas B. Reed, Parliamentarian*. New York: Dodd, Mead & Company, 1930.

Royall, William L. *History of the Virginia Debt Controversy, The Negro's Vicious Influence in Politics*. Richmond: George M. West, 1897.

Sage, Leland L. *William Boyd Allison, A Study in Practical Politics*. Iowa City: State Historical Society of Iowa, 1956.

Schriftgiesser, Karl. *The Gentleman from Massachusetts, Henry Cabot Lodge*. Boston: Little, Brown and Company, 1944.

Sievers, Harry J. *Benjamin Harrison, Hoosier Statesman*. New York: University Publishers, 1959.

Smith, Theodore Clark. *The Life and Letters of James Abram Garfield*. 2 vols. New Haven: Yale University Press, 1925.

Stephenson, Nathaniel Wright. *Nelson W. Aldrich, A Leader in American Politics*. New York: Charles Scribner's Sons, 1930.

Thomas, Harrison Cook. *The Return of the Democratic Party to Power in 1884*. New York: n. p., 1919.

Thompson, Edwin Bruce. *Matthew Hale Carpenter, Webster of the West*. Madison: State Historical Society of Wisconsin, 1954.

Tindall, George Brown. *South Carolina Negroes, 1877–1900*. Columbia: University of South Carolina Press, 1952.

Trefousse, Hans L. *Ben Butler, The South Called Him Beast!* New York: Twayne Publishers, 1957.

Wall, Joseph Frazier. *Henry Watterson, Reconstructed Rebel*. New York: Oxford University Press, 1956.

Walters, Everett. *Joseph Benson Foraker, An Uncompromising Republican*. Columbus: Ohio State Archaeological and Historical Society, 1948.

Warren, Charles. *The Supreme Court in United States History*. 2 vols. Boston: Little, Brown and Company, 1926.

Wellman, Manly Wade. *Giant in Gray, A Biography of Wade Hampton of South Carolina*. New York: Charles Scribner's Sons, 1949.

Wharton, Vernon Lane. *The Negro in Mississippi, 1865–1890*. Vol. XXVIII of the *James Sprunt Studies in History and Political Science*. Chapel Hill: University of North Carolina Press, 1947.

William Lloyd Garrison, 1805–1879, The Story of His Life Told by His Children. 4 vols. New York: The Century Company, 1885–1889.

Williams, Charles R. *The Life of Rutherford Birchard Hayes*. 2 vols. Boston and New York: Houghton Mifflin Company, 1914.

Williams, T. Harry. *Lincoln and the Radicals*. Madison: University of Wisconsin Press, 1941.

Woodson, Carter G. *A Century of Negro Migration*. Washington: Association for the Study of Negro Life and History, 1918.

Woodward, C. Vann. *Origins of the New South, 1877–1913*. Vol. IX of *A History of the South*. Edited by Wendell Holmes Stephenson and E. Merton Coulter. Baton Rouge: Louisiana State University Press, 1951.

————. *Reunion and Reaction, The Compromise of 1877 and the End of Reconstruction*. Boston: Little, Brown and Company, 1951.

————. *The Strange Career of Jim Crow. The James W. Richards Lectures in History, 1954*. New York: Oxford University Press, 1955.

Woolfolk, George R. *The Cotton Regency, The Northern Merchants and Reconstruction, 1865–1880*. New York: Bookman Associates, 1958.

Younger, Edward. *John A. Kasson, Politics and Diplomacy from Lincoln to McKinley*. Iowa City: State Historical Society of Iowa, 1955.

Notes

1. A PRESIDENT, A POLICY, AND A PARTY

1. Howard K. Beale, *The Critical Year, A Study of Andrew Johnson and Reconstruction* (New York, 1930), *passim.*

2. C. Vann Woodward, *Reunion and Reaction, The Compromise of 1877 and the End of Reconstruction* (Boston, 1951), pp. 14–15.

3. James Ford Rhodes, *History of the United States from the Compromise of 1850* (New York, 1906), VII, 14; Matthew Josephson, *The Politicos, 1865–1896* (New York, 1938), pp. 3–8, 15–18, 20–22.

4. Woodward, *Reunion and Reaction*, p. 7; Josephson, *Politicos*, p. 206.

5. Rhodes, *History of the U.S.*, VII, 282–284; Josephson, *Politicos*, pp. 223–225.

6. *Proceedings of the Republican National Convention of 1876* (Concord, N.H., 1876), p. 56.

7. George S. Merriam, *The Life and Times of Samuel Bowles* (New York, 1885), II, 278–279.

8. New York *Tribune*, October 30, 1876.

9. Quoted in Josephson, *Politicos*, p. 224.

10. New York *Tribune*, September 1, August 12, October 17, 1876.

11. *Proceedings of the Republican National Convention of 1876*, p. 117.

12. Rutherford B. Hayes to James G. Blaine, Columbus, September 14, 1876, in Gail Hamilton, *Biography of James G. Blaine* (Norwich, Conn., 1895), p. 422.

13. Paul Haworth, *The Hayes-Tilden Election* (Indianapolis, 1927), pp. 45–49; Rhodes, *History of the U.S.*, VII, 291–293.

14. Quoted in Charles R. Williams, *Life of Rutherford Birchard Hayes* (Boston, 1914), I, 493-494.

15. Zachariah Chandler to Edward Wade, Washington, December 1, 1876, Vol. 7, Chandler Papers, Library of Congress; William E. Chandler to Hayes, Washington, February 9, 1877, Hayes Papers, Rutherford B. Hayes Library, Fremont, Ohio.

16. James A. Garfield to Hayes, Washington, December 12, 1876, Hayes Papers, Rutherford B. Hayes Library, Fremont, Ohio; William Henry Smith to Hayes, December 7, 1876, and Medill quoted in Smith to Henry V. Boynton, December 22, 1876, letterbook in Box 22, Smith Papers, Ohio State Historical Society, Columbus.

17. Jacob D. Cox to Carl Schurz, Toledo, January 26, 1877, Vol. 29, Schurz Papers, Library of Congress; Hayes Diary, February 25, 1877, in Charles R. Williams (ed.), *Diary and Letters of Rutherford Birchard Hayes* (Columbus, 1922-1926), III, 420-421.

18. Harry Barnard, *Rutherford B. Hayes and His America* (Indianapolis, 1954), pp. 287, 295; Woodward, *Reunion and Reaction,* pp. 150-156.

19. Woodward, *Reunion and Reaction, passim.*

20. James D. Richardson (ed.), *A Compilation of the Messages and Papers of the Presidents* (New York, 1897), X, 4395-4396.

21. Josephson, *Politicos,* pp. 237-238; Donald Barr Chidsey, *The Gentleman from New York, A Life of Roscoe Conkling* (New Haven, 1935), p. 237; Woodward, *Reunion and Reaction,* p. 216.

22. John A. Logan to Mary Logan, Washington, March 8, 1877, Logan Papers, Library of Congress.

23. George Frisbie Hoar, *Autobiography of Seventy Years* (New York, 1903), II, 7.

24. *Congressional Record,* 45 Cong., Special sess. of Senate (March 6, 1877), 6; David S. Muzzey, *James G. Blaine, A Political Idol of Other Days* (New York, 1934), pp. 130-134.

25. Timothy O. Howe to Grace T. Howe, Washington, March 6, 1877, Box 2, Howe Papers, Wisconsin State Historical Society, Madison.

26. Garfield Diary, March 11, 1877, Garfield Papers, Library of Congress.

27. Springfield *Daily Republican,* March 10, 1877.

28. New York *Tribune,* March 22, 1877.

29. Chicago *Tribune,* March 22, 1877.

30. Hampton M. Jarrell, *Wade Hampton and the Negro, The Road Not Taken* (Columbia, S.C., 1949), p. 114; Williams, *Life of Rutherford*

Birchard Hayes, II, 51–53; Woodward, *Reunion and Reaction,* pp. 219–221.

31. New York *Tribune,* February 27, and March 1, 1877; New York *Commercial Advertiser,* March 6, 1877. For earlier efforts of businessmen to hasten sectional reconciliation see William B. Hesseltine, "Economic Factors in the Abandonment of Reconstruction," *Mississippi Valley Historical Review,* XXII (September, 1935), 191–210.

32. For Chicago, *Congressional Record,* 44 Cong., 2 sess. (January 22, 1877), 817; for Detroit, *ibid.* (January 20, 1877), 794; for Philadelphia, *ibid.* (January 24, 1877), 929; for Kansas City and Burlington, *ibid.* (January 26, 1877), 983; for New York, Cincinnati, and Pittsburgh, New York *Tribune,* March 1, March 2, February 27, 1877.

33. *Congressional Record,* 44 Cong., 2 sess. (January 2, 1877), 406, 411–412, 438; (December 23, 29, 1876), 39, 374; (January 8, 12, 1877), 472, 588.

34. New York *Shipping and Commercial List,* February 24, 1877; *Commercial and Financial Chronicle,* XXIV (January 20, 1877), 50.

35. Garfield Diary, January 19, 1877, Garfield Papers.

36. Hamilton Fish to John A. Dix, Washington, Vol. 118, Fish Papers, Library of Congress.

37. Lucien B. Caswell to Elisha W. Keyes, Washington, January 22, 1877, and Angus Cameron to Keyes, Washington, January 30, 1877, Box 43, Keyes Papers, Wisconsin State Historical Society, Madison.

38. *Congressional Record,* 44 Cong., 2 sess. (January 25, 1877), 942.

39. New York *Daily Bulletin,* January 20, 1877.

40. New York *Commercial Advertiser,* March 8, 1877.

41. Brown Brothers to William M. Evarts, New York, March 29, 1877, in New York *Times,* April 9, 1877.

42. John A. Scudder, President, St. Louis Merchants Exchange, to Hayes, St. Louis, March 29, 1877; C. W. Simmons, President, St. Louis Cotton Exchange, to Hayes, March 29, 1877; Jesse Spalding to David Davis, Chicago, March 12, 1877; Henry Pomerene, President, Cleveland Board of Trade, to Hayes, Cleveland, March 10, 1877; Theodore Cook, Cincinnati Chamber of Commerce, to Hayes, Cincinnati, March 9, 1877; William J. White, President, Philadelphia Exchange Company, to Hayes, Philadelphia, March 19, 1877, Hayes Papers.

43. New York *Commercial Advertiser,* March 6, 1877; *Commercial and Financial Chronicle,* XXIV (April 7, 1877), 309.

44. Cyrus Clay Carpenter to James S. Clarkson, Washington, March 16, 1877, Box 1, Clarkson Papers, Iowa State Department of History and Archives, Des Moines.

45. James G. Blaine to the Editor of the Boston *Herald*, Augusta, Maine, April 10, 1877, Vol. 1, Blaine Papers, Library of Congress.

46. Benjamin F. Wade to U. H. Painter, Jefferson, Ohio, April 9, 1877, in New York *Tribune*, April 24, 1877.

47. Samuel J. May to William Lloyd Garrison, Leicester, April 28, 1877, Vol. 39, Garrison Papers, Boston Public Library.

48. New York *Herald*, March 27, and April 3, 1877.

49. New York *Tribune*, April 6, 1877.

50. Oliver P. Morton to Southern Republicans, Indianapolis, May 24, 1877, in New York *Times*, May 26, 1877; Grant quoted in Chicago *Tribune*, April 7, 1877.

51. New York *Tribune*, April 16, 1877; Hartford *Courant*, May 1, 1877.

52. Woodward, *Reunion and Reaction*, pp. 225–226.

53. Newark *Daily Advertiser*, July 5, 1877.

54. Chandler to Edward McPherson, Waterloo, New Hampshire, August 22, 1877, Vol. 26, McPherson Papers, Library of Congress.

55. Elisha W. Keyes to J. Bintliff, October 11, 1877, copy, Keyes Papers.

56. James F. Wilson to James S. Clarkson, Fairfield, Iowa, June 7, 1877, Box 2, Clarkson Papers, Library of Congress; Samuel J. Kirkwood to William B. Allison, Washington, May 7, 1877, Box 103, Allison Papers, and Sherman to Kirkwood, Washington, May 14, 1877, Box 5, Kirkwood Papers, Iowa State Department of History and Archives, Des Moines. Kirkwood, of course, was referring to Hampton's assertion that Republicans would not be persecuted if the troops were withdrawn.

57. New York *World*, February 6, 1893; Leland L. Sage, *William Boyd Allison, A Study in Practical Politics* (Iowa City, 1956), pp. 148, 150.

58. Chicago *Tribune*, June 28, 1877; New York *World*, February 6, 1893.

59. New York *Herald*, September 6, 1877.

60. New York *Tribune*, September 6, 1877.

61. New York *Herald*, September 26, 1877.

62. Hartford *Courant*, August 2, 1877.

63. Josephson, *Politicos*, pp. 243–248; George William Curtis to Charles Eliot Norton, Ashfield, Massachusetts, September 30, 1877, Curtis Papers, Harvard University Library.

64. New York *Commercial Advertiser*, October 10, November 1, 1877. Among the Republicans sponsoring the meeting were John Jay, Whitelaw Reid, editor and owner of the New York *Tribune*, William W. Astor, the capitalist and journalist, Dorman B. Eaton, the civil service advocate,

Theodore Roosevelt, Sr., Francis B. Thurber, the grocer, and bankers Levi P. Morton, Jesse Seligman, and J. Pierpont Morgan.

65. New York *Tribune,* June 27, 1877; Woodward, *Reunion and Reaction,* p. 228.

66. New York *Tribune,* July 12, August 17, 21, 23, 24, 1877.

67. Hayes Diary, August 26, 1877, in Williams (ed.), *Diary and Letters of Rutherford Birchard Hayes,* III, 442.

68. New York *Tribune,* September 18, 20, and 24, 1877; *Independent,* XXIX (September 27, 1877), 18; Woodward, *Reunion and Reaction,* p. 229.

69. Hayes Diary, September, 1877, in Williams (ed.), *Diary and Letters of Rutherford Birchard Hayes,* III, 443; Smith to Hayes, Chicago, September 27, 1877, Hayes Papers.

70. Washington *National Republican,* November 27, 1877; Newark *Daily Advertiser,* November 16, 1877; New York *Tribune,* May 21, 1877.

71. Woodward, *Reunion and Reaction,* pp. 232–235.

72. New York *Tribune,* October 22, 1877; Garfield Diary, October 20, 1877, Garfield Papers.

73. Hoar, *Autobiography,* II, 7; Vincent P. De Santis, *Republicans Face the Southern Question, The New Departure Years, 1877–1897* (Baltimore, 1959), p. 120.

74. Howe to Grace Howe, Washington, November 16, 1877, Box 2, Howe Papers; New York *Tribune,* November 19, 1877.

75. James D. Richardson (ed.), *Messages and Papers of the Presidents,* X, 4411–4412.

76. Cameron to Keyes, Washington, November 4, 1877, Box 45, Keyes Papers.

77. *Letters of Mr. William E. Chandler Relative to the So-Called Southern Policy of President Hayes Together with a Letter to Mr. Chandler of Mr. William Lloyd Garrison* (Concord, N.H., 1878), 4–5, 7–8, 14–16; Leon Burr Richardson, *William E. Chandler, Republican* (New York, 1940), pp. 211–214.

78. Zachariah Chandler to William Chandler, December 28, 1877, in L. B. Richardson, *William E. Chandler,* p. 219; Garrison to Chandler, Boston, January 21, 1878, in *Letters of Mr. William E. Chandler Relative to the So-Called Southern Policy of President Hayes,* 47; Whitelaw Reid to Chandler, February 28, 1878, Letterbook 31, Reid Papers, Library of Congress.

79. Cameron to Keyes, Washington, March 20, 1878, Box 48, Keyes Papers.

80. *Congressional Record,* 45 Cong., 2 sess. (March 25, 1878), 2000–2008.

81. New York *World,* April 17, 1878.

82. Schurz to Henry Cabot Lodge, Washington, April 6, 1878, Lodge Papers, Massachusetts Historical Society.

83. New York *Herald,* January 5, 1878.

84. Smith to A. C. McClurg, August 23, 1878, letterbook in Box 22, Smith Papers.

85. Garfield to John A. Kasson, Washington, February 20, 1878, Vol. III, Charles Aldrich Collection, Iowa State Department of History and Archives, Des Moines; Richard Smith to William Henry Smith, Cincinnati, February 23, 1878, William Henry Smith Collection of the Indianapolis Historical Society, Microfilm, Hayes Library; Richard Smith to Hayes, Cincinnati, June 8, 1878, Hayes Papers; Fish to Kasson, New York, March 4, 1878, Vol. III, Aldrich Collection.

2. DISILLUSIONMENT AND UNITY

1. New York *Herald,* October 17, 1878; Manly Wade Wellman, *Giant in Gray, A Biography of Wade Hampton of South Carolina* (New York, 1949), pp. 300–301; New York *Tribune,* October 16, 1878.

2. Charles Devens to Charles E. Mayes, Washington, October 3, and Devens to Hayes, Washington, October 4, 1878, Rutherford B. Hayes Papers, Hayes Library, Fremont, Ohio; New York *Tribune,* December 30 and 31, 1878. Federal laws provided for imprisonment from six months to six years and for fines from $500 to $5,000 for those found guilty.

3. *Nation,* XXVII (October 31, 1878), 263.

4. *Appletons' Annual Cyclopaedia,* XVII (1877), 398, 476, 524, 561–562, 620, 633, 768; XVIII (1878), 451–452, 515, 536, 567, 623, 667, 684.

5. Springfield *Daily Republican,* October 17, 1878; *Nation,* XXVII (October 10, 1878), 218.

6. New York *Times,* October 20, 1878.

7. Hayes to James M. Comly, Washington, October 29, 1878, Comly Papers, Ohio State Historical Society, Columbus.

8. Vincent P. De Santis, "President Hayes's Southern Policy," *Journal of Southern History,* XXI (November, 1955), 491–492.

9. Chicago *Tribune,* November 15, 1878; Portland *Oregonian,* Novem-

ber 14, 1878; New York *Tribune,* November 19, 1878; Springfield *Daily Republican,* November 23, 1878.

10. *Independent,* XXX (November 21, 1878), 14.

11. New York *Herald,* November 13, 1878.

12. *Independent,* XXX (November 28, 1878), 15.

13. William E. Chandler to William Lloyd Garrison, Washington, February 6, 1879, Vol. 40, Garrison Papers, Boston Public Library. Chandler was referring, of course, to the President's salary.

14. Washington *National Republican,* November 13, 1878; Chicago *Tribune,* November 13, 1878; New York *Tribune,* November 13, 1878.

15. Washington *National Republican,* November 19, 1878. The standard biography of Evarts is Chester L. Barrows, *William M. Evarts, Lawyer, Diplomat, Statesman* (Chapel Hill, N.C., 1941).

16. St. Paul *Pioneer-Press,* November 15 and 16, 1878; New York *Herald,* November 16, 1878.

17. James D. Richardson (ed.), *A Compilation of the Messages and Papers of the Presidents* (New York, 1897), X, 4445-4447.

18. *Congressional Record,* 45 Cong., 3 sess. (December 2, 1878), 7; New York *Times,* December 3, 1878.

19. James G. Blaine to Chandler, Augusta, Maine, November 12, 1878, Vol. 46, Chandler Papers, Library of Congress.

20. *Congressional Record,* 45 Cong., 3 sess. (December 2, 1878), 2.

21. *Ibid.,* (December 11, 1878), 84-86.

22. *Ibid.,* 86.

23. *Ibid.,* (December 17, 1878), 243.

24. "Report of the United States Senate Committee to Inquire into Alleged Frauds and Violence in the Elections of 1878," *Senate Reports,* 45 Cong., 1 sess., No. 855, I, xxiv-xxvi, xlv-xlvi. The Democrats did not submit a minority report.

25. *Congressional Record,* 45 Cong., 3 sess. (December 9, 1878), 59.

26. *Ibid.,* (January 7, 1879), 342.

27. *Ibid.,* (January 20, 1879), 567.

28. *Ibid.,* (February 4, 1879), 954-957.

29. *Ibid.,* (February 5, 1879), 1021, 1029-1030.

30. *Ibid.,* (February 26, 1879), 1912.

31. William Lloyd Garrison to the Editor of the New York *Tribune,* Boston, December 19, 1878, in New York *Tribune,* January 4, 1879; *William Lloyd Garrison, 1805-1879, The Story of His Life Told by His Children* (New York, 1889), IV, 295.

32. New York *Tribune,* January 2, 1879.

33. *Congressional Record,* 46 Cong., 1 sess. (April 14, 1879), 418; (April 24, 1879), 801–807, and (April 25, 1879), 837.

34. *Ibid.,* (April 17, 1879), 504–511, and (April 21, 1879), 593–600.

35. Garfield Diary, March 6, 1879, Garfield Papers, Library of Congress.

36. Richardson (ed.), *Messages and Papers of the Presidents,* X, 4475–4484.

37. William A. Wheeler to Hayes, Malone, New York, May 5, 1879, and Shelby M. Cullom to Hayes, Springfield, May 5, 1879, Hayes Papers.

38. *Appletons' Annual Cyclopaedia,* XIX (1879), 521, 580–581, 603, 679, 703, 723, 851.

39. New York *Tribune,* July 24, and 25, 1879.

40. New York *Evening Post,* September 18, 1879.

41. For Sheridan, see Chicago *Tribune,* September 25, 1879; for Blaine and Sherman, see New York *Tribune,* September 29, and October 13, 1879.

42. For Conkling, see Springfield *Daily Republican,* October 9, 1879. For Sherman, New York *Tribune,* October 27 and 28; for Evarts, October 22, and for Foster, Burrows, and Choate, October 25, 1879.

43. William B. Hesseltine, *Ulysses S. Grant, Politician* (New York, 1935), pp. 426–431.

44. Cincinnati *Commercial,* November 19, 1879; New York *Herald,* November 15, 1880.

45. New York *Evening Post,* November 24, 1879; Chicago *Tribune,* April 27, 1880.

46. Atlanta *Constitution,* November 5, 1879; Washington *National Republican,* October 27, 1879; Portland *Oregonian,* November 18, 1879; Cincinnati *Commercial,* January 18, 1880.

47. New York *Times,* November 13, 1879.

48. For Key, see Springfield *Daily Republican,* November 12, 1879; for Schumaker, Washington *National Republican,* November 21, 1879.

49. Richardson (ed.), *Messages and Papers of the Presidents,* X, 4512–4513.

50. New York *Times,* January 1, 2, 3, 7, March 23, April 10, 11, 13, 14, 16, 1880.

51. Chicago *Tribune,* April 27, 1880; George S. Boutwell, "General Grant and a Third Term," *North American Review,* CXXX (April, 1880), 383.

52. Springfield *Daily Republican,* November 12, 1879.

53. Hesseltine, *Ulysses S. Grant,* pp. 437–439; *Proceedings of the*

Republican National Convention . . . 1880 (Chicago, 1881), *passim.*
54. New York *Tribune,* September 29, 1880.

3. EXODUS

1. James D. Richardson (ed.), *A Compilation of the Messages and Papers of the Presidents* (New York, 1897), X, 4366; William B. Hesseltine, *Ulysses S. Grant, Politician* (New York, 1935), pp. 417–418.
2. New York *Herald,* July 26, 1878; Chicago *Tribune,* February 15, and March 20, 1879.
3. Rutherford B. Hayes to Rev. Mr. Sturks, Washington, January 14, 1878, in New York *Times,* January 15, 1878.
4. *Congressional Record,* 45 Cong., 3 sess. (January 16, 1879), 483; Rayford W. Logan, *The Negro in American Life and Thought, The Nadir, 1877–1901* (New York, 1954), p. 128.
5. Washington *National Republican,* March 22, 1879.
6. Chicago *Tribune,* February 15, 1879. James Blaine Hedges, *Henry Villard and the Railways of the Northwest* (New Haven, 1930), pp. 22, 49, calls Windom "an old-time friend of the Northern Pacific." Throughout the 1870's he was instrumental in obtaining land grants and other important concessions for the road.
7. *Congressional Record,* 45 Cong., 3 sess. (February 7, 1879), 1077–1082, 1088.
8. Vernon Lane Wharton, *The Negro in Mississippi, 1865–1890* (Vol. XXVIII in the *James Sprunt Studies in History and Political Science,* Chapel Hill, N.C., 1947), pp. 112, 114; John G. Van Deusen, "The Exodus of 1879," *Journal of Negro History,* XXI (April, 1936), 111–112; Portland *Oregonian,* June 24, 1879. In all, between 25,000 and 30,000 Negroes migrated to Kansas.
9. "Report and Testimony of the Select Committee of the United States Senate to Investigate the Causes of the Removal of the Negro from the Southern States to the Northern States," *Senate Reports,* 46 Cong., 2 sess., No. 693, I, 277; William Windom to James A. Garfield, Washington, April 2, 1879, Vol. 60, Garfield Papers, Library of Congress; New York *Times,* April 7, 1879.
10. Zachariah Chandler to H. Willis, Washington, April 9, 1879, Vol. 40, William Lloyd Garrison Papers, Boston Public Library.
11. New York *Tribune,* April 12, 1879; New York *Herald,* April 11, 1879; for Plumb and Ingalls, see New York *Herald,* April 4 and 22, 1879; Hayes Diary, May 25, 1879, in Charles R. Williams (ed.), *Diary and*

Letters of Rutherford Birchard Hayes (Columbus, 1922–1926), III, 553–554.

12. New York *Herald,* April 7, 1879.

13. William Lloyd Garrison to the Editor of the Boston *Traveller,* April 24, 1879, in *William Lloyd Garrison, 1805–1879, The Story of His Life Told by His Children* (New York, 1889), IV, 303.

14. *Congressional Record,* 46 Cong., 1 sess. (April 21, 1879), 620.

15. Van Deusen, "The Exodus of 1879," 126; John P. St. John to the Friends of the Colored People, Topeka, June 26, 1879, broadside in Rutherford B. Hayes Papers, Hayes Library, Fremont, Ohio.

16. Cincinnati *Commercial,* June 18, 1879; New York *Times,* April 25, 1879; Garrison to Fanny Garrison Villard, Roxbury, April 25, 1879, Fanny Villard Papers, Harvard University; Garrison to William Lloyd Garrison, Jr., New York, May 7, 1879, William Lloyd Garrison Papers, Massachusetts Historical Society; William Lloyd Garrison, Jr., to Mary B. Claflin, Boston, November 12, 1880, William Claflin Papers, Hayes Library.

17. *Senate Reports,* 46 Cong., 2 sess., No. 693, III, 433. On Conway see Thomas W. Conway to John A. Logan, Brooklyn, June 21, 1884, Vol. 1, Logan Papers, Illinois State Historical Society, Springfield; George R. Bentley, *A History of the Freedmen's Bureau* (Philadelphia, 1955), pp. 55, 187–188, 215; George Ruble Woolfolk, *The Cotton Regency, The Northern Merchants and Reconstruction, 1865–1880* (New York, 1958), p. 106.

18. Springfield *Daily Republican,* April 9, 1879; New York *Times,* April 26, 1879. Butler's latest biographer is Hans L. Trefousse, *Ben Butler, The South Called Him Beast!* (New York, 1957). For Ingersoll's generosity see Robert G. Ingersoll to J. M. Adams, secretary of the National Emigration Aid Society, May 14, 1879, in Eva Ingersoll Wakefield (ed.), *The Letters of Robert G. Ingersoll* (New York, 1951), pp. 682–683.

19. This incident occurred in April, 1864, when during the capture of the Tennessee post Confederate soldiers killed over five hundred of the seven hundred man garrison, most of whom were Negroes. Southern losses amounted to only twenty men. After the battle General Nathan Bedford Forrest, the Confederate commander, boasted that the river in front of the fort was red with blood for 200 yards. Lincoln acted cautiously, but Senate investigators concluded that the massacre was part of a Southern plot to discourage the enlistment and use of colored troops by the North. See T. Harry Williams, *Lincoln and the Radicals* (Madison, 1941), pp. 343–348; James G. Randall, *The Civil War and Reconstruction* (New York, 1937), pp. 506–507.

20. *Senate Reports,* 46 Cong., 2 sess., No. 693, III, 435; New Orleans *Times,* May 14, 1879.

21. Conway to Hayes, St. Louis, May 16, 1879, Hayes Papers; Conway to Zachariah Chandler, St. Louis, May 15, 1879, Vol. 7, Chandler Papers, Library of Congress.

22. New Orleans *Picayune,* May 27, 1879; Conway to Hayes, Washington, May 24, 1879, Hayes Papers.

23. *Senate Reports,* 46 Cong., 2 sess., No. 693, III, 438; Conway to Edward McPherson, Boston, June 18, 1879, Vol. 28, McPherson Papers, Library of Congress; New York *Tribune,* June 3 and 25, 1879; New York *Times,* June 10, 1879.

24. New York *Commercial Bulletin,* April 17, 1879; *Commercial and Financial Chronicle,* XXVIII (April 12, 1879), 363–364; *Railway Age,* IV (June 5, 1879), 266.

25. New York *Journal of Commerce,* July 8, 1879.

26. *Senate Reports,* 46 Cong., 2 sess., No. 693, III, 435.

27. New York *Tribune,* June 25, 1879.

28. Benjamin H. Bristow to John Murray Forbes, New York, October 1, 1879, Forbes Papers, Massachusetts Historical Society; Williams quoted in New York *Tribune,* October 23, 1879; John Sherman to Warren T. Hendrick, September 29, 1879, Letterbook 4, Sherman Papers, Library of Congress.

29. *Journal of Negro History,* IV (January, 1919), 56–57. See also Benjamin Quarles, *Frederick Douglass* (Washington, 1948), pp. 287–288.

30. Chicago *Tribune,* December 9, 1879; Springfield *Daily Republican,* December 19, 1879.

31. *Appletons' Annual Cyclopaedia,* XVI (1876), 411.

32. Louisville *Courier-Journal,* quoted in New York *Tribune,* November 28, 1879; *Nation,* XXIX (December 18, 1879), 413; Cincinnati *Enquirer,* October 27, 1879.

33. *Congressional Record,* 46 Cong., 2 sess. (December 11, 1879), 80, and (December 15, 1879), 104.

34. *Ibid.,* (December 18, 1879), 156.

35. *Ibid.,* 164–165.

36. *Ibid.,* 159, 156, 170. Fourteen Republicans (nine from the Midwest and five from New England), twelve Democrats (nine from the South, two from the Midwest, and one from New Jersey), and one Conservative passed the resolution. Six Southern Democrats, one Southern Republican, and one Democrat each from Connecticut, Delaware, Illinois, Oregon, and California opposed the resolution. The Middle Atlantic states seemed the least concerned with the issue. Neither of the Senators from New

York or Pennsylvania bothered to vote, while only one each from New Jersey and Delaware cast ballots. Plumb and Ingalls did not vote, but the two Democrats from Indiana voted yes.

37. *Senate Reports*, 46 Cong., 2 sess., No. 693, II, 1–36.

38. *Ibid.*, I, 85–86; John G. Van Deusen, "Did the Republicans 'Colonize' Indiana in 1879?" *Indiana Magazine of History*, XXX (December, 1934), 336–337. Van Deusen's article, based solely upon the testimony accumulated by the Voorhees committee, concludes that the Republicans were completely innocent.

39. *Senate Reports*, 46 Cong., 2 sess., No. 693, III, 440–445.

40. Conway to Zachariah Chandler, St. Louis, May 15, 1879, Vol. 7, Chandler Papers.

41. *Senate Reports*, 46 Cong., 2 sess., No. 693, III, 440–445.

42. Sherman to B. D. Fearing, November 1, 1879, Letterbook 4, Sherman Papers.

43. J. M. Adams to Sherman, Washington, November 18, 1879, *ibid.*

44. *Senate Reports*, 46 Cong., 2 sess., No. 693, I, ii–viii, ix–xxv.

45. *Congressional Record*, 46 Cong., 2 sess. (June 4, 1880), 4141–4143, and (June 14, 1880), 4518–4524.

46. Ellis Paxson Oberholtzer, *A History of the United States Since the Civil War* (New York, 1931), IV, 534; Quarles, *Frederick Douglass*, p. 289.

4. GARFIELD: THE SEARCH FOR A SOUTHERN POLICY

1. *Congressional Record*, 45 Cong., 3 sess. (December 10, 1878), 75; Herbert J. Clancy, *The Presidential Election of 1880* (Chicago, 1958), p. 175.

2. Robert Granville Caldwell, *James A. Garfield, Party Chieftain* (New York, 1931), pp. 265–270.

3. Kirk H. Porter and Donald Bruce Johnson (eds.), *National Party Platforms, 1840–1956* (Urbana, 1956), p. 62.

4. Newark *Daily Advertiser*, July 13, 1880.

5. Hayes Diary, July 21, 1880, in Charles R. Williams (ed.), *Diary and Letters of Rutherford Birchard Hayes* (Columbus, 1922–1926), III, 615.

6. John A. Logan to James A. Garfield, Washington, July 15, 1880, Vol. 84, Garfield Papers, Library of Congress.

7. Theodore Clark Smith, *The Life and Letters of James Abram Gar-*

field (New Haven, 1925), II, 1007–1017; Thomas Collier Platt, *Autobiography* (New York, 1910), p. 128; Garfield to John Sherman, Mentor, Ohio, July 31, 1880, Vol. 227, Sherman Papers, Library of Congress.

8. Alfred R. Conkling, *The Life and Letters of Roscoe Conkling, Orator, Statesman, Advocate* (New York, 1889), p. 612; George Frederick Howe, *Chester A. Arthur, A Quarter-Century of Machine Politics* (New York, 1934), pp. 117–120; Robert McElroy, *Levi Parsons Morton, Banker, Diplomat, Statesman* (New York, 1930), pp. 108–112.

9. New York *Commercial Advertiser*, August 6, 1880; John Sherman, *Recollections of Forty Years* (Akron, 1895), II, 780; *Nation*, XXXI (August 12, 1880), 103.

10. St. Paul *Pioneer-Press*, August 8, 1880.

11. *Ibid.*, August 7, 1880.

12. *Nation*, XXXI (August 19, 1880), 126; Jay A. Hubbell to Garfield, Washington, August 23, 1880, Vol. 89, Garfield Papers.

13. New York *Tribune*, September 18, 1880.

14. New York *Journal of Commerce*, August 31, September 24, 1880, and July 25, 1881; New York *Commercial Bulletin*, October 14, 1880. Unfortunately, since New York Republican leaders like Conkling, Platt, Arthur, and Morton left only insignificant manuscript collections, it is impossible to ascertain more than the general business reaction to their tactics.

15. Cincinnati *Commercial*, October 2, 1880; Cincinnati *Gazette*, September 7 and 22, 1880.

16. Cincinnati *Enquirer*, October 2, 3, and 5, 1880; Cincinnati *Gazette*, October 4, 1880.

17. Cincinnati *Gazette*, October 4, 1880.

18. *Twelfth Annual Report of the Cincinnati Board of Trade and Transportation for the Year Ending 1880* (Cincinnati: Bloch and Company, 1881), *passim; Williams' Cincinnati Directory, 1880* (Cincinnati, 1880), pp. 11, insert opposite 72, 223, insert opposite 420, 421, 640, 971, and insert opposite 974; Cincinnati *Gazette*, October 4, 1880; Cincinnati *Enquirer*, October 3 and 4, 1880. Other Republican firms objecting to the bloody shirt tactics were: the George Fox Starch Manufacturing Company; Robert Morris and Company, printers; the Globe Rolling Mill Company, iron producers with two large plants; T. & J. W. Gaff, distillers of bourbon and rye whiskies; and Schmidlapp and Company, distillers and wholesale liquor dealers.

19. Cincinnati *Gazette*, October 2, 1880. Accompanying the account of Conkling's speech is a list of 161 prominent Republicans who attended the meeting and served on the welcoming committee.

20. Cincinnati *Enquirer,* October 11, 1880.

21. Garfield to Sherman, Mentor, September 25, 1880, Vol. 230, Sherman Papers.

22. Leon Burr Richardson, *William E. Chandler, Republican* (New York, 1940), pp. 260–261.

23. Matthew Josephson, *The Politicos, 1865–1896* (New York, 1938), p. 300.

24. Frank John Krebs, "Hayes and the South" (Ph. D. dissertation, Ohio State University, 1950), 250; Gordon Canfield Lee, *The Struggle for Federal Aid, First Phase, A History of the Attempts to Obtain Federal Aid for the Common Schools, 1870–1890* (New York, 1949), pp. 42, 54–55, 57, 58–59, 81–86.

25. Porter and Johnson (eds.), *National Party Platforms,* p. 61.

26. Williams (ed.), *Diary and Letters of Rutherford B. Hayes,* III, 591; James D. Richardson (ed.), *A Compilation of the Messages and Papers of the Presidents* (New York, 1897), X, 4431, 4458, 4531, 4578; Lee, *Struggle for Federal Aid,* pp. 73–74; New York *Tribune,* August 12, 1880; *Harper's Weekly,* XXIV (September 25, 1880), 611.

27. New York *Tribune,* October 21, 1880.

28. Albion W. Tourgee, "Aaron's Rod in Politics," *North American Review,* CXXXII (February, 1881), 143, 153, 156; Burke A. Hinsdale, *President Garfield and Education* (Boston, 1881), pp. 229, 247; Newark *Daily Advertiser,* July 13, 1880.

29. Albion W. Tourgee to Garfield, Philadelphia, December 14, 1880, Vol. 116, Garfield Papers.

30. Garfield to Burke A. Hinsdale, Mentor, December 18, 1880, Box II, Hinsdale Collection, Michigan Historical Collections, Ann Arbor; Hinsdale to Garfield, December 21, 1880, Vol. 118, Garfield Papers.

31. Garfield to Hinsdale, Mentor, December 30, 1880, copy, Box II, Hinsdale Collection; Mary L. Hinsdale (ed.), *The Garfield-Hinsdale Letters, Correspondence between James Abram Garfield and Burke Aaron Hinsdale* (Ann Arbor, 1949), pp. 469–470.

32. Tourgee, "Aaron's Rod in Politics," 139–162; Tourgee to Garfield, Philadelphia, December 23, 1880, Vol. 118, Garfield Papers.

33. New York *Times,* January 15, 1881.

34. *Ibid.,* January 18, 1881.

35. *Ibid.,* December 12, 1880.

36. James D. Richardson (ed.), *Messages and Papers of the Presidents,* X, 4598–4599; Rayford W. Logan, *The Negro in American Life and Thought, The Nadir, 1877–1901* (New York, 1954), pp. 38–43; Elvena

S. Bage, "President Garfield's Forgotten Pronouncement," *Negro History Bulletin*, XIV (June, 1951), 195–197, 206, 214.

37. Burke A. Hinsdale, *President Garfield and Education*, pp. 173–174; New York *Times*, March 31, 1881. See especially Albion W. Tourgee, *An Appeal to Caesar* (New York, 1884), pp. 9–20. Tourgee wrote his book, which is a detailed plea for national aid to education, in fulfillment of a pledge to Garfield.

38. Nelson Morehouse Blake, *William Mahone of Virginia, Soldier and Political Insurgent* (Richmond, 1935), pp. 182, 198; Charles Chilton Pearson, *The Readjuster Movement in Virginia* (Vol. IV of *Yale Historical Publications*, New Haven, 1917), p. 135; Vincent P. De Santis, "President Hayes's Southern Policy," *Journal of Southern History*, XXXI (November, 1955), 485–486; William Henry Smith to J. Stanley Brown, April 25, 1881, letterbook in Box 22, Smith Papers, Ohio State Historical Society, Columbus; Vincent P. De Santis, "Republican Efforts to Break Up the Democratic South, 1877–1892" (Ph. D. dissertation, Johns Hopkins University, 1952), 64.

39. Garfield to Hinsdale, Washington, December 20, 1879, Box II, Hinsdale Papers.

40. Blake, *William Mahone*, pp. 206, 211; Pearson, *The Readjuster Movement*, p. 138.

41. Garfield Diary, December 29, 1880, Garfield Papers; Preston B. Plumb to Garfield, Emporia, November 12, 1880, Vol. 108, *ibid.;* George Frisbie Hoar to John D. Long, Washington, April 5, 1881, Long Papers, Massachusetts Historical Society; New York *Times*, April 11, 1881.

42. Daniel H. Chamberlain to Garfield, New York, December 28, 1880, and January 24, 1881; Garfield to Chamberlain, Mentor, January 15, 1881, and February 3, 1881, in New York *Times*, October 7, 1883.

43. Garfield Diary, April 29, 1881, Garfield Papers.

44. Washington *National Republican*, April 7, 1881.

45. Garfield to Henry L. Dawes, Washington, May 2, 1881, Dawes Papers, Library of Congress.

46. Smith, *Life and Letters of James A. Garfield*, II, 1117.

47. Philadelphia *North American*, June 2, 1881.

5. POLITICS AS USUAL

1. Chicago *Tribune*, December 20, 1881.

2. *Nation*, XXXIII (December 29, 1881), 461; Hayes Diary, December

29, 1881, in Charles R. Williams (ed.), *Diary and Letters of Rutherford Birchard Hayes* (Columbus, 1922–1926), IV, 59.

3. See, for example, S. J. Wright to Chester A. Arthur, Charleston, February 17, 1882, in Presidential Box 8, Attorney General's File 5W, National Archives.

4. Benjamin H. Brewster to Dallas Sanders, Assistant United States District Attorney at Charleston, Washington, March 18, 1882, in Department of Justice Instructions Book L, *ibid.*

5. Philadelphia *Press*, March 24, 1882; Samuel W. Melton to Brewster, Charleston, March 22, 1882, Box 652, Attorney General's File 5W.

6. Hartford *Courant*, April 1, 1882.

7. New York *Tribune*, May 11, 1882.

8. Brewster to United States Marshal A. Blythe, in New York *Times*, June 7, 1882.

9. Melton to William E. Chandler, Charleston, May 18, 1883, Vol. 63, Chandler Papers, Library of Congress.

10. *Ibid.*

11. Daniel Alexander Payne, *Recollections of Seventy Years* (Nashville, 1888), pp. 286–289; New York *Times*, March 30, and April 13, 1882; Springfield *Daily Republican*, April 14, 1882; Jacksonville *Daily Florida Union*, April 6, 1882, clipping in Vol. I of "Southern Affairs," Chester A. Arthur Personal Scrapbooks, Columbia University Library.

12. Department of Justice Instructions Books L and M, Attorney General's File 5W. These volumes cover 1881 through 1883.

13. Chicago *Tribune*, September 10, 1882; John W. Niles to John Sherman, January 17, 1888, Vol. 424, Sherman Papers, Library of Congress; *Congressional Record*, 48 Cong., 1 sess. (December 5, 1883), 31, and (December 6, 1883), 45; *ibid.*, 48 Cong., 2 sess. (January 26, 1885), 996.

14. Niles to Arthur, Bailey, Arkansas, September 14, 1883, in Presidential Box 8, Attorney General's File 5W; Brewster to Niles, September 28, 1883, in Department of Justice Letterbook P, Attorney General's File 5W.

15. New York *Herald*, October 18, 1883.

16. Niles to Sherman, January 17, 1888, Vol. 424, Sherman Papers.

17. Civil Rights Cases, 109 U.S. 3 (1883); Charles Warren, *The Supreme Court in United States History* (Boston, 1926), II, 612–615; Rayford W. Logan, *The Negro in American Life and Thought, The Nadir, 1877–1901* (New York, 1954), pp. 45–46, 97.

18. New York *Evening Post*, October 16, 1883; Chicago *Tribune*, October 17, 1883; New York *Journal of Commerce*, October 31, 1883.

19. For Ingersoll, see Washington *National Republican*, October 17, 1883, and Frank G. Carpenter, *Carp's Washington* (New York, 1960), p. 65; Samuel J. Kirkwood to William B. Allison, Iowa City, February 12, 1884, Box 247, Allison Papers, Iowa State Department of History and Archives, Des Moines; for Sherman, see New York *Tribune*, November 20, 1883; Louis T. Michener to Walter Q. Gresham, Shelbyville, Indiana, October 27, 1883, Vol. 15, Gresham Papers, Library of Congress.

20. New York *Globe*, October 20, 1883.

21. Chicago *Tribune*, October 26 and 29, 1883; Cincinnati *Enquirer*, October 23, 1883; Philip Foner, *The Life and Writings of Frederick Douglass* (New York, 1955), IV, 392–403; Benjamin Quarles, *Frederick Douglass* (Washington, 1948), pp. 290–291; Clarence H. Cramer, *Royal Bob, The Life of Robert Ingersoll* (Indianapolis, 1952), pp. 90, 235; Philadelphia *Press*, October 17, 1883; Harry J. Sievers, *Benjamin Harrison, Hoosier Statesman* (New York, 1959), p. 231.

22. James D. Richardson (ed.), *A Compilation of the Messages and Papers of the Presidents* (New York, 1897), XI, 4775.

23. Congressional Record, 48 Cong., 1 sess. (December 4, 1883, to January 21, 1884), 11–12, 18, 133–137, 249, 288, 517. Bills were introduced by Senators James F. Wilson and George F. Edmunds, and by Representatives Thomas Ryan, Joseph Keifer, and William W. Brown.

24. George Frederick Howe, *Chester A. Arthur, A Quarter-Century of Machine Politics* (New York, 1934), pp. 215–216; Leon Burr Richardson, *William E. Chandler, Republican* (New York, 1940), pp. 312, 345; and the following *Journal of Southern History* articles: Vincent P. De Santis, "President Arthur and the Independent Movements in the South in 1882," XIX (August, 1953), 352–353; Willie D. Halsell (ed.), "Republican Factionalism in Mississippi, 1882–1884," VII (February, 1941), 85; Willie D. Halsell, "James R. Chalmers and 'Mahoneism' in Mississippi," X (February, 1944), 38–39.

25. Nelson Morehouse Blake, *William Mahone of Virginia* (Richmond, 1935), pp. 215–216; De Santis, "President Arthur and the Independent Movements in the South in 1882," 347.

26. New York *Times*, November 20, 1881; William L. Royall, *History of the Virginia Debt Controversy, The Negro's Vicious Influence in Politics* (Richmond, 1897), pp. 46–47.

27. C. Vann Woodward, *Origins of the New South, 1877–1913* (Vol. IX of *A History of the South*, ed. by Wendell Holmes Stephenson and E. Merton Coulter, Baton Rouge, 1951), p. 101; Royall, *History of the Virginia Debt Controversy*, p. 53; Vincent P. De Santis, *Republicans*

Face the Southern Question, The New Departure Years, 1877–1897 (Baltimore, 1959), p. 154.

28. Boston *Herald*, undated clipping, and Mobile *Daily Register*, January 27, 1882, clipping, in Vol. I of "Southern Affairs," Chester A. Arthur Personal Scrapbooks.

29. New York *Globe*, March 10, and September 1, 1883.

30. Cincinnati *Commercial*, November 13, 1881.

31. Washington *National Republican*, May 26, 1883; Newark *Daily Advertiser*, November 18, 1881; Hartford *Courant*, January 30, 1884; Cincinnati *Commercial Gazette*, November 20, 1883; *Independent*, XXXV (September 13, 1883), 18; Chicago *Tribune*, May 3, 1882.

32. *Nation*, XXXVI (May 17, 1883),418; St. Paul *Pioneer-Press*, September 1, 1882; *Bradstreet's*, VIII (October 27, 1883), 258.

33. Ulysses S. Grant to James D. Brady, New York, October 4, 1881, in New York *Times*, October 20, 1881.

34. John J. Ingalls to J. Ambler Smith, Washington, June 16, 1881, in New York *Times*, July 2, 1881.

35. Royall, *History of the Virginia Debt Controversy*, pp. 53–54.

36. Philadelphia *North American*, June 2, 1881.

37. James M. Donnan, Secretary of the Republican State Central Committee of Virginia, to Lucius Fairchild, Richmond, August 18, 1883, Box 45, Fairchild Papers, Wisconsin State Historical Society, Madison; Washington *National Republican*, March 29, 1883; Chicago *Tribune*, September 21, 1882.

38. New York *Times*, September 3, 1882.

39. Chicago *Tribune*, September 19, 1882.

40. New York *Times*, September 27, 1882; Chicago *Tribune*, September 27, 1882.

41. New York *Tribune*, September 30, 1882.

42. Hartford *Courant*, September 28, 1882; Chicago *Tribune*, September 28, 1882.

43. Chandler to James G. Blaine, New York, October 2, 1882, Vol. 56, Chandler Papers.

44. Washington *National Republican*, October 10, 1882, clipping in Vol. II of "Southern Affairs," Chester A. Arthur Personal Scrapbooks. The remarks of Mahone himself, made in an interview with the New York *Times* (November 21, 1881) in which he spoke of Garfield's reluctance to aid the Readjusters, cast considerable doubt upon the validity of Gorham's story.

45. Philadelphia *Press*, September 1, 1882, to November 30, 1882,

passim. On Mahone, see September 2, 1882, and on Chalmers, see September 1, 1882.

46. New York *Tribune,* October 17, 1882.

47. *Ibid.,* October 26, 1882.

48. Chandler to the Editor of the New York *Tribune,* Washington, October 31, 1882, in New York *Tribune,* November 2, 1882.

49. *Ibid.,* December 15, 1883.

50. Chandler to Whitelaw Reid, Washington, December 17, 1883, Reid Papers, Library of Congress.

51. Chandler to Reid, December 20, 1883, *ibid.*

52. *Harper's Weekly,* XXVII (May 26, 1883), 322; Leon Burr Richardson, *William E. Chandler,* p. 312; New York *Tribune,* May 14, 1883.

53. New York *Times,* May 29, 1883.

54. Chandler to John F. Dezendorf, Washington, May 17, 1883, in New York *Times,* May 23, 1883.

55. Dezendorf to Chandler, May 22, 1883, in New York *Tribune,* May 24, 1883.

56. Leon Burr Richardson, *William E. Chandler,* p. 312; New York *Tribune,* October 25, 1883.

57. De Santis, "President Arthur and the Independent Movements in the South in 1882," 359–361; Vincent P. De Santis, "Negro Dissatisfaction with Republican Policy in the South, 1882–1884," *Journal of Negro History,* XXXVI (April, 1951), 152.

58. De Santis, "President Arthur and the Independent Movements in the South in 1882," 361–362; Blake, *William Mahone of Virginia,* p. 224.

59. Chicago *Tribune,* September 28 and 29, 1882.

60. New York *Globe,* March 3, 1883; Washington *Bee,* March 10, 1883.

61. New York *Times,* August 12, 1883.

62. T. Thomas Fortune to the Editor of the New York *Times,* New York, August 13, 1883, in New York *Times,* August 14, 1883.

63. De Santis, "Negro Dissatisfaction with Republican Policy in the South, 1882–1884," 155–156; *Nation,* XXXVII (October 4, 1883), 284.

64. Fortune to the Editor of the New York *Evening Post,* November 2, 1883, in New York *Evening Post,* November 3, 1883.

65. New York *Times,* August 30, 1883.

66. Harrison Cook Thomas, *The Return of the Democratic Party to Power in 1884* (New York, 1919), p. 130; Charles Chilton Pearson, *The Readjuster Movement in Virginia* (Vol. IV of *Yale Historical Publications,* New Haven, 1917), p. 136; John F. Carl to John Sherman, Danville, November 6, 1883, Vol. 305, Sherman Papers, Library of Congress.

67. Pearson, *Readjuster Movement*, p. 136; Boston *Journal*, undated clipping in Vol. II of "Southern Affairs," Chester A. Arthur Personal Scrapbooks; *American Almanac . . . 1883* (New York, 1883), p. 262; *American Almanac . . . 1884* (New York, 1884), p. 262.

68. Thomas, *Return of the Democratic Party*, p. 130; Springfield *Daily Republican*, December 15, 1883.

69. Boston *Daily Advertiser*, November 16, 1883.

70. New York *Times*, February 18, 1884.

71. *Congressional Record*, 48 Cong., 1 sess. (January 23, 1884), 588–589, and (January 29, 1884), 715–716; John Sherman, *Recollections of Forty Years* (Akron, 1895), II, 869–873.

72. Washington *National Republican*, November 17, 1883, January 25, and March 12, 1884.

73. "Report of the Special Committee to Inquire into the Mississippi Election of 1883," *Senate Reports*, 48 Cong., 1 sess., No. 512, I, xxxv–xxxvi, and II, lxxiii.

74. "Report of the Special Committee to Inquire into Alleged Election Outrages at Danville, Virginia," *Senate Reports*, 48 Cong., 1 sess., No. 579, I, xlii, and II, lxxiii.

75. Pearson, *Readjuster Movement*, p. 168; *Appletons' Annual Cyclopaedia*, XXIX (1884), 798.

76. William Mahone to William B. Allison, Petersburg, Virginia, November 17, 1887, Box 258, Allison Papers; New York *Evening Post*, August 30, 1884.

77. Frederick Douglass to Friends Hayden and Watson, Paris, November 19, 1886, in Foner, *Life and Writings of Frederick Douglass*, IV, 447.

6. MANUFACTURERS, MUGWUMPS, AND MERCHANTS

1. New York *Times*, July 19, 1884.

2. Newark *Daily Advertiser*, July 19, 1884; Chicago *Tribune*, July 19, 1884.

3. David Saville Muzzey, *James G. Blaine, A Political Idol of Other Days* (New York, 1934), p. 313; Oscar Doane Lambert, *Stephen Benton Elkins, American Foursquare, 1841–1911* (Pittsburgh, 1955), p. 100; Harrison Cook Thomas, *The Return of the Democratic Party to Power in 1884* (New York, 1919), p. 196.

4. Springfield *Daily Republican*, October 3, 1884.

5. *Tribune Almanac . . . 1885* (New York, 1885), p. 85.

6. Muzzey, *James G. Blaine,* p. 314; Thomas, *Return of the Democratic Party,* p. 224; New York *Tribune,* October 17 and 21, 1884.

7. Thomas, *Return of the Democratic Party,* pp. 214–215; New York *Tribune,* October 22 and 24, 1884.

8. See Henry Steele Commager, *The American Mind* (New Haven, 1950), pp. 317–319; Paul Buck, *The Road to Reunion, 1865–1900* (Boston, 1937), pp. 94–96; Matthew Josephson, *The Politicos, 1865–1896* (New York, 1938), p. 159, for further information on the Mugwumps.

9. Howard K. Beale, *The Critical Year, A Study of Andrew Johnson and Reconstruction* (New York, 1930), pp. 70–73; Josephson, *Politicos,* pp. 21–22.

10. Frederic Bancroft and William A. Dunning (eds.), *The Reminiscences of Carl Schurz* (New York, 1908), III, 319–322, 329. See Carl Schurz to James A. Garfield, Washington, September 22, 1880, Vol. 64, Schurz Papers, Library of Congress.

11. *Harper's Weekly,* IX (May 20, 1865), 306. The most recent study of Curtis is Gordon Milne, *George William Curtis and the Genteel Tradition* (Bloomington, 1956).

12. *Harper's Weekly,* XVI (June 22, 1872), 482–483; XXI (April 14, 1877), 282; XXII (September 21, 1878), 747, and XXIII (September 27, 1879), 762; XXIV (July 24, 1880), 466; XXVI (August 26, 1882), 530.

13. Edwin L. Godkin to Charles Eliot Norton, February 28, 1865, in Rollo Ogden (ed.), *Life and Letters of Edwin Lawrence Godkin* (New York, 1907), II, 45–47.

14. *Nation,* III (November 29, 1866), 430–431; IV (February 14, 1867), 130–131; XII (March 23, 1871), 192–193, and (March 20, 1871), 212–213. Godkin's articles are identified in Daniel C. Haskell (ed.), *The Nation Index, 1865–1917* (New York, 1953), II, 184–194.

15. Edwin L. Godkin, "Southern States Since the War," *Contemporary Review,* XLIV (November, 1883), 696.

16. Springfield *Daily Republican,* July 1, 1884.

17. *Ibid.,* July 23, 1884.

18. Henry C. Lea to Edward McPherson, Delaware Water Gap, October 18, 1884, in New York *Evening Post,* October 28, 1884.

19. Buck, *Road to Reunion,* p. 25.

20. Springfield *Daily Republican,* September 2, 1884; New York *Evening Post,* October 4, 1884.

21. Springfield *Daily Republican,* September 4, 1884.

22. Allan Nevins, *Grover Cleveland, A Study in Courage* (New York, 1932), pp. 181–182; Royal Cortissoz, *The Life of Whitelaw Reid* (New York, 1921), II, 96–99; Muzzey, *James G. Blaine,* pp. 295–296, 316–318.

23. *Harper's Weekly,* XXVIII (November 22, 1884), 763, and (November 29, 1884), 794.

24. George Frisbie Hoar to Henry Cabot Lodge, Worcester, November 12, 1884, Lodge Papers, Massachusetts Historical Society.

25. New York *Tribune,* November 19, 1884.

26. *Nation,* XXXIX (November 27, 1884), 447; *Harper's Weekly,* XXVIII (November 29, 1884), 780–781; Springfield *Daily Republican,* November 20, 1884. The quoted passages are from the *Nation.*

27. *Nation,* XL (February 26, 1885), 168.

28. Murat Halstead, "The Revival of Sectionalism," *North American Review,* CXL (March, 1885), 235–250.

29. John Sherman, *Recollections of Forty Years* (Akron, 1895), II, 920; New York *Tribune,* July 5, 1885.

30. Washington *National Republican,* September 10, 1885; New York *Tribune,* September 25, 1885.

31. New York *Tribune,* October 1, 1885.

32. Springfield *Daily Republican,* October 1, and July 1, 1885. The Massachusetts election in 1885 was for local offices.

33. Thomas Wentworth Higginson to the Editor of the Boston *Advertiser,* Springfield *Daily Republican,* October 5, 1885.

34. New York *Tribune,* October 15, 1885.

35. Springfield *Daily Republican,* October 12, 1885.

36. *Ibid.,* July 1, 1885.

37. New York *Evening Post,* October 7, 1885.

38. Theodore Bacon and others to the Independent Voters of New York State, in New York *Evening Post,* October 26, 1885.

39. Schurz to Alfred T. White, New York, October 12, 1885, in New York *Evening Post,* October 16, 1885.

40. Joseph B. Foraker to James F. Gluck, November 13, 1885, copy, Foraker Papers, Historical and Philosophical Society of Ohio, Cincinnati.

41. See, for example, Cincinnati *Commercial Gazette,* November 14, 1884.

42. Cincinnati *Enquirer,* November 20 and 21, 1884; *Twelfth Annual Report of the Cincinnati Board of Trade for the Year Ending January 1, 1881* (Cincinnati, 1881), *passim.* This Board of Trade report contains drawings which indicate the size of many important firms. Since these commercial complaints developed *after* the election, they obviously were more than just a part of a Democratic campaign maneuver. It was only natural, however, for the *Enquirer* to try to capitalize on the fears of businessmen.

43. Cincinnati *Enquirer,* November 20, 21, and 30, 1884.

44. Joseph Benson Foraker, *Notes of a Busy Life* (Cincinnati, 1916), I, 176–177.

45. *Ibid.*, I, 176–182. Ohio, traditionally a closely contested state, had 79,900 Negroes in 1880, compared to only 65,104 for New York. *Appletons' Annual Cyclopaedia*, XXI (1881), 849.

46. Foraker, *Notes of a Busy Life*, I, 192–200; Everett Walters, *Joseph Benson Foraker, An Uncompromising Republican* (Columbus, 1948), p. 33; Sherman, *Recollections*, II, 925–931; Charles S. Olcott, *The Life of William McKinley* (Boston, 1916), I, 222–223; New York *Tribune*, July 2, and August 27, 1885; Washington *National Republican*, September 5, 1885.

47. Cincinnati *Enquirer*, October 11, 1885.

48. *Ibid.*, October 4, 1885.

49. Foraker, *Notes of a Busy Life*, I, 209; Walters, *Joseph Benson Foraker*, p. 35; *Tribune Almanac . . . 1886* (New York, 1886), p. 62.

50. William E. Chandler, "National Control of Elections," *Forum*, IX (August, 1890), 712.

51. Concord *Evening Monitor*, June 10, 1887.

52. John C. Spooner to Joseph Ulman, December 5, 1887, Letterbook 4, Spooner Papers, Library of Congress.

53. John R. Lynch to Chandler, Washington, June 15, 1887, in Concord *Evening Monitor*, June 21, 1887.

7. PROTECTION FOR THE NEGRO OR FOR INDUSTRY?

1. Washington *Bee*, August 28, 1886.

2. Philadelphia *North American*, October 18, 21, and 28, 1886.

3. Philadelphia *Press*, October 28, 1886.

4. James M. Swank to Nelson W. Aldrich, Philadelphia, May 7, 1884, Box 15, and November 20, 1888, Box 23, Aldrich Papers, Library of Congress; Swank to William B. Allison, Philadelphia, February 5, 1886, Box 256, Allison Papers, Iowa State Department of History and Archives, Des Moines; Swank to Nils P. Haugen, Philadelphia, February 28, 1888, Box 7, Haugen Papers, Wisconsin State Historical Society, Madison; Swank to John Sherman, Philadelphia, October 29, 1886, Vol. 384, Sherman Papers, Library of Congress. See also Albert T. Volwiler, "Tariff Strategy and Propaganda in the United States, 1887–1888," *American Historical Review*, XXXVI (October, 1930), 76–78.

5. Swank to Justin Morrill, Philadelphia, December 1, 1886, Vol. 37, Morrill Papers, Library of Congress.

6. Philadelphia *Press*, November 28, and December 11, 1886.

7. Portland *Oregonian*, January 3, 1885; New York *Commercial Advertiser*, November 10, 1885; Washington *National Republican*, April 6, 1887; New York *Tribune*, November 23, 1886.

8. Macon *Telegraph*, Augusta *Chronicle*, and Boston *Herald*, quoted in Portland *Oregonian*, August 15, 1887; Allan Nevins, *Grover Cleveland, A Study in Courage* (New York, 1932), p. 339.

9. For White, see Portland *Oregonian*, August 15, 1887; for Burwell and Ammidown, see Philadelphia *Press*, December 26, 1886, and April 7, 1887.

10. Cincinnati *Enquirer*, March 7, 1887.

11. Chicago *Tribune*, March 25, and April 1, 1887; John Sherman, *Recollections of Forty Years* (Akron, 1895), II, 975-978.

12. Sherman, *Recollections*, II, 978.

13. *Ibid.*, II, 978-980.

14. Philadelphia *Press*, March 25, 1887.

15. Kansas City *Times*, quoted in *Public Opinion*, III (April 16, 1887), 10; New York *Times*, March 29, 1887.

16. Chicago *Tribune*, March 20, 1887; *Bulletin of the American Iron and Steel Association*, XXI (March 30, 1887), 82. The latest study of Watterson is Joseph Frazier Wall, *Henry Watterson, Reconstructed Rebel* (New York, 1956).

17. Quoted in Chicago *Tribune*, April 1, 1887.

18. Cincinnati *Enquirer*, quoted in Philadelphia *Press*, March 28, 1887; New York *Herald*, April 2, 1887; Philadelphia *Press*, April 2, 1887.

19. Philadelphia *Press*, March 31, 1887.

20. New York *Tribune*, June 2, 1887.

21. *Nation*, XLIV (June 9, 1887), 479; New York *Herald*, July 19, 1887.

22. Cincinnati *Enquirer*, June 16, 1887.

23. Sherman, *Recollections*, II, 984; Philadelphia *Press*, June 25, 1887; Sherman to Colonel A. W. Willis, Washington, February 16, 1888, in New York *Times*, March 3, 1888.

24. Hartford *Courant*, September 16, 1887.

25. William E. Chandler to Edward McPherson, Concord, New Hampshire, February 19, 1887, Vol. 38, McPherson Papers, Library of Congress.

26. *Congressional Record*, 50 Cong., 2 sess. (December 12, 1887), 29,

(January 10, 1888), 341, and (January 12, 1888), 406; Leon Burr Richardson, *William E. Chandler, Republican* (New York, 1940), pp. 390–391.

27. "Report of the Committee on the Judiciary on the Municipal Election at Jackson, Mississippi," *Senate Reports*, 50 Cong., 1 sess., No. 1887, I, 1–11, II, 1–24.

28. Nevins, *Grover Cleveland*, p. 339; Thomas M. Cooley Diary, November 27, 1887, Cooley Papers, Michigan Historical Collections, Ann Arbor. Cooley was a Republican jurist from Michigan who at this time was a member of the Interstate Commerce Commission.

29. John C. Spooner to George C. Gentry, January 10, 1888, Letterbook 4, Spooner Papers, Library of Congress; Joseph B. Foraker to Albion W. Tourgee, January 7, 1888, copy, Foraker Papers, Historical and Philosophical Society of Ohio, Cincinnati.

30. Spooner to R. J. Flint, January 10, 1888, Letterbook 4, Spooner Papers; Cincinnati *Commercial Gazette*, January 1, 1888.

31. Charles Foster to John Sherman, Fostoria, Ohio, January 5, 1888, Vol. 421, Sherman Papers, Library of Congress. Foster's interview with Lamar had been held at the suggestion of James A. Garfield, then president-elect.

32. Chandler to Whitelaw Reid, Washington, December 26 and 30, 1887, Reid Papers, Library of Congress; Willie D. Halsell, "The Appointment of L. Q. C. Lamar to the Supreme Court," *Mississippi Valley Historical Review*, XXVIII (December, 1941), 402.

33. New York *Tribune*, January 2, 3, 4, 5, 9, and 12, 1888.

34. For Stewart, see Springfield *Daily Republican*, January 10, 1888; for Sawyer, see New York *Times*, January 4, 1888, and Richard Nelson Current, *Pine Logs and Politics, A Life of Philetus Sawyer, 1816–1900* (Madison, 1950), pp. 207–209.

35. Edward Mayes, *Lucius Q. C. Lamar, His Life, Times, and Speeches, 1825–1893* (Nashville, 1895) p. 534; George Rothwell Brown (ed.), *Reminiscences of Senator William M. Stewart* (New York and Washington, 1908), pp. 308–309; New York *Times*, January 17, 1888.

36. New York *Commercial Advertiser*, January 17, 1888.

37. Nevins, *Grover Cleveland*, pp. 379–381.

38. *Iowa State Register*, January 15, 1888.

39. New York *Evening Post*, January 21, 1888; *Nation*, XLVI (January 26, 1888), 64–65; Stephen B. Elkins to James S. Clarkson, January 22, 1888, Box 2, Clarkson Papers, Library of Congress.

40. *Iowa State Register*, February 8, 1888.

41. Grenville Dodge to Chandler, New York, January 30, 1888, and

February 9, 1888, letterbook in Box 391, Dodge Papers, Iowa State Department of History and Archives, Des Moines.

42. Clarkson to Dodge, Des Moines, February 6, 1888, Box 21, *ibid.*

43. Chandler to Dodge, Washington, February 27, 1888, *ibid.*

44. Chicago *Tribune,* February 12, 1888; Benjamin Harrison to Stephen B. Elkins, Indianapolis, February 13, 1888, Elkins Papers, West Virginia University Library, Morgantown; New York *Times,* February 12, 1888.

45. James S. Clarkson, "Permanent Republican Clubs," *North American Review,* CXLVI (March, 1888), 261.

46. New York *World,* February 3, 1888; Hartford *Courant,* March 23, 1888; Portland *Oregonian,* January 27, 1888.

47. Russell Alger to Foraker, Detroit, February 8, 1888, Foraker Papers; for Hanson, see Philadelphia *Press,* quoted in *Bulletin of the American Iron and Steel Association,* XXIII (February 15, 1888), 49.

48. John J. Ingalls, "Fetichism in the Campaign," *North American Review,* CXLVI (June, 1888), 656; Chandler to John E. Bruce, Washington, April 30, 1888, in New York *Age,* May 12, 1888.

49. Kirk H. Porter and Donald Bruce Johnson (eds.), *National Party Platforms, 1840-1956* (Urbana, 1956), pp. 79-83.

50. Spooner to J. V. Quarles, October 10, 1888, Letterbook 6, Spooner Papers; Spooner to Henry C. Payne, October 11, 1888, *ibid.*

51. *Congressional Record,* 50 Cong., 1 sess. (June 12, 1888 to October 4, 1888), 5316, 6500, 7818, 7865-7881, 8282-8295, 8980-9010.

52. Foraker to Murat Halstead, August 17, 1888, copy, Foraker Papers; Concord *Evening Monitor,* August 10, 1888.

53. Clarkson to Foraker, New York, August 20, 1888, Foraker Papers.

54. Foraker to C. L. Edwards, September 10, 1888, copy, *ibid.*

55. Giraud Chester, *Embattled Maiden, The Life of Anna Dickinson* (New York, 1951), pp. 240-243.

56. Anna E. Dickinson to Susan Dickinson, Indianapolis, September 23, 1888, Dickinson Papers, Library of Congress; Chester, *Embattled Maiden,* pp. 247-252, 270-272.

57. Jacob Sloat Fassett to Reid, New York, September 26, 1888, Reid Papers.

58. For Harrison letter, see New York *Tribune,* September 12, 1888; Harrison to Russell Alger, Indianapolis, September 12, 1888, Alger Papers, William L. Clements Library, Ann Arbor, Michigan.

59. Charles Hedges (ed.), *Speeches of Benjamin Harrison* (New York, 1892), pp. 12-16, 62; Cincinnati *Commercial Gazette,* November 15, 1888; Harry J. Sievers, *Benjamin Harrison, Hoosier Statesman* (New York, 1959), p. 361.

60. New York *Age,* October 13, 1888.

61. New York *Herald,* November 25, 1888.

62. For Sherman, see New York *World,* September 15, 1888; for Morton, see *ibid.,* October 3, 1888.

63. *Ibid.,* September 21, 1888; *Bulletin of the American Iron and Steel Association,* XXII (November 7, and 14, 1888), 333; Swank to Morrill, Philadelphia, April 20, 1888, Vol. 38, Morrill Papers.

64. New York *Tribune,* November 9, 1888; James G. Blaine to Harrison, Augusta, Maine, November 9, 1888, Vol. 46, Harrison Papers, Library of Congress.

65. New York *Tribune,* November 9, 1888.

66. *Appletons' Annual Cyclopaedia,* XXVIII (1888), 828.

67. *Ibid.*

8. THE END OF A DREAM

1. Indianapolis *Journal,* November 8, 1888; New York *Times,* November 12, 1888.

2. Indianapolis *Journal,* November 16, 1888.

3. Chicago *Tribune,* December 2, 1888.

4. Arthur E. Bateman to Benjamin Harrison, New York, December 17, 1888, Vol. 51, Harrison Papers, Library of Congress; New York *Tribune,* January 5, 1889; for Blaine, see the Philadelphia *Press,* February 13, 1889.

5. Chicago *Tribune,* December 5, 1888.

6. New York *Herald,* December 23, 1888. Quoted is Gallinger's account of the conversation.

7. New York *Tribune,* October 8 and 19, 1878; Harry Barnard, *Rutherford B. Hayes and His America* (Indianapolis, 1954), pp. 474–478. There is no adequate sketch of Woolley. Unfortunately, he is today a forgotten figure.

8. John Sherman to Joseph B. Foraker, Mansfield, Ohio, September 26, 1886, Foraker Papers, Historical and Philosophical Society of Ohio, Cincinnati; Charles W. Woolley to Sherman, Cincinnati, September 19, 1888, copy, Vol. 41, Harrison Papers. Significantly, the only existing copy of this letter is in the Harrison Papers.

9. Allan Nevins, *Grover Cleveland, A Study in Courage* (New York, 1932), pp. 389–394, 432–433.

10. Although this letter is frequently referred to in Woolley's letters, all copies of it have been destroyed.

11. Woolley to Colonel R. E. Rivers, Cincinnati, December 3, 1888, copy, Vol. 463, Sherman Papers, Library of Congress.

12. Harrison to A. B. Williams, editor of the Greenville, South Carolina, *Daily News*, Indianapolis, November 14, 1888, in New York *Herald*, November 28, 1888.

13. Woolley to Sherman, Cincinnati, December 8, 1888, Vol. 463, Sherman Papers; Joseph E. Brown to Woolley, Atlanta, November 30, 1888, copy, *ibid*. Unfortunately, Sherman destroyed the letter from Harrison, although he kept the one from Brown.

14. *Congressional Record*, 50 Cong., 2 sess. (January 21, 1889), 1026.

15. See the letters from Woolley to Sherman in the Sherman Papers dated Cincinnati, no date, Vol. 463; Washington, December 24, 1888, Vol. 465; Cincinnati, January 16, 1889, Vol. 465.

16. The Allison bill passed the Senate by a strict party vote of 32 to 30. *Congressional Record*, 50 Cong., 2 sess. (January 22, 1889), 1105.

17. New York *Tribune*, December 19, 1888.

18. Springfield *Daily Republican*, January 27, 1889; Rufus B. Bullock to the Editor of the Chicago *Tribune*, Albion, New York, December 25, 1888, in Chicago *Tribune*, December 28, 1888.

19. Springfield *Daily Republican*, January 27 and February 14, 1889; New York *Tribune*, February 12, 1889.

20. Petition, J. B. Hyde to Benjamin Harrison, the Cabinet, and Republican Senators, Grenville County, South Carolina, January, 1889, Box 1, Jeremiah Rusk Papers, Wisconsin State Historical Society, Madison.

21. Foraker to Harrison, Columbus, November 24, 1889, Vol. 48, Harrison Papers, Library of Congress; Chandler to Harrison, Washington, December 22, 1888, Vol. 52, *ibid*.

22. John J. Ingalls to E. A. Angier, Atchison, Kansas, November 12, 1888, in Chicago *Tribune*, November 20, 1888; New York *World*, December 3, 1888.

23. *Congressional Record*, 50 Cong., 2 sess. (January 18, 1889, to January 25, 1889), 920, 922, 1162, 1177; (February 20, 1889), 2083, and (February 22, 1889), 2188–2189; (January 8, 1889), 576.

24. *Ibid.*, 49 Cong., 2 sess. (January 26, 1887), 1038, and 50 Cong., 2 sess. (February 13, 1889), 1824–1856.

25. James D. Richardson (ed.), *A Compilation of the Messages and Papers of the Presidents* (New York, 1897), XII, 5443–5444; Rayford W. Logan, *The Negro in American Life and Thought, The Nadir, 1877–1901* (New York, 1954), pp. 53–54.

26. New York *Herald*, March 17, 1889.

27. *Ibid.*, March 23, 1889; Portland *Oregonian*, March 27, 1889; Hart-

ford *Courant*, March 19, 1889; New York *Tribune*, March 18, 1889.

28. Chicago *Tribune*, March 15, and April 10, 1889.

29. *Ibid.*, April 10, 1889.

30. New York *Herald*, April 10, 11, and 12, 1889.

31. Springfield *Daily Republican*, April 14, 1889.

32. Quoted in *Public Opinion*, VII (April 27, 1889), 44.

33. Springfield *Daily Republican*, April 26, 1889; New York *Times*, January 29, 1891.

34. New York *Age*, May 4, 1889.

35. Concord *Evening Monitor*, May 8, 1889.

36. Chandler to the Editor of the New York *Tribune*, Washington, May 4, 1889, in New York *Tribune*, May 6, 1889.

37. Springfield *Daily Republican*, June 11, 1889.

38. St. Paul *Pioneer-Press*, June 22, 1889.

39. New York *World*, June 7, 1889.

40. New York *Press*, quoted in *Public Opinion*, VII (June 15, 1889), 204; Washington *Bee*, July 6, 1889; Concord *Evening Monitor*, July 8, 1889.

41. Hartford *Courant*, August 22, 1889.

42. New York *Times*, August 6, 1889.

43. Telegram, Henry C. Minor to Benjamin Harrison, New Orleans, August 10, 1889, Vol. 84, Harrison Papers. For Coleman's tactics see Chicago *Tribune*, November 15 and 16, 1888.

44. New York *Times*, August 22, 1889.

45. New Orleans *Times-Democrat*, August 28, 29, and 30, 1889.

46. Springfield *Daily Republican*, August 15, 1889; Minor to Thomas A. Cage, President of the Republican Convention of the Third District of Louisiana, Houma, Louisiana, August 9, 1889, in New Orleans *Weekly Pelican*, August 17, 1889.

47. *Appletons' Annual Cyclopaedia*, XXIX (1889), 519. The third district of Louisiana had always been strongly Democrat. In 1888 the Democratic candidate for Congress received 18,854 votes and the Republican candidate 6,331. See *American Almanac . . . 1889* (New York and Washington, 1889), p. 222.

48. For Burrows, see New Orleans *Times-Democrat*, September 3, 1889; for Minor, see Springfield *Daily Republican*, September 8, 1889.

49. New Orleans *Weekly Pelican*, September 7, 1889.

50. Springfield *Daily Republican*, August 23, and September 5, 1889.

51. *Ibid.*, September 6, 1889.

52. New York *Herald*, July 30, 1889; New York *Times*, August 21, and September 1, 1889.

53. James S. Clarkson to Harrison, Washington, June 28, 1889, Vol. 89, Harrison Papers; Clarkson to Harrison, June 29, 1889, Vol. 91, *ibid.*

54. New York *Age,* July 27, 1889; New York *Herald,* July 20, and October 14, 1889.

55. Springfield *Daily Republican,* August 24 and 25, 1889.

56. New York *Times,* August 2, 1889.

57. New York *World,* August 22, 1889; Manly Wade Wellman, *Giant in Gray, A Biography of Wade Hampton of South Carolina* (New York, 1949), pp. 310–311.

58. Nelson Morehouse Blake, *William Mahone of Virginia, Soldier and Political Insurgent* (Richmond, 1936), pp. 246–248.

59. Richmond *State,* September 24, and October 18, 1889; New York *Times,* October 19, 1889.

60. New York *Herald,* October 14, 1889.

61. Richmond *State,* September 23, 1889; New York *Herald,* October 4, 14, and 19, 1889.

62. Clarkson to Harrison, Warm Sulphur Springs, Virginia, October 3, 1889, Vol. 88, Harrison Papers.

63. Concord *Evening Monitor,* October 9, 1889.

64. New York *Tribune,* October 28, 1889.

65. Blake, *William Mahone,* p. 250; *Appletons' Annual Cyclopaedia,* XXIX (1889), 820.

66. *Tribune Almanac . . . 1890* (New York, 1890), 85–86.

67. New York *World,* quoted in Springfield *Daily Republican,* November 8, 1889; New York *Age,* November 9, 1889; New York *Times,* November 6, 1889.

9. THE LINES OF SECTIONAL BATTLE ARE DRAWN

1. Chicago *Tribune,* December 13, 1889.

2. *Congressional Record,* 51 Cong., 1 sess. (December 12, 1889), 155, 157, and (January 23, 1890), 802.

3. *Ibid.,* (January 7, 1890), 419–420, and (January 16, 1890), 622. For the Windom resolution see Chapter 3.

4. *Ibid.,* (January 16, 1890), 628–630, and (January 23, 1890), 802–807.

5. Cleveland *Gazette,* March 22, 1890; Portland *Oregonian,* January 6, 1890; Newark *Daily Advertiser,* January 17, 1890.

6. *Congressional Record*, 48 Cong., 1 sess. (April 7, 1884), 2724; 49 Cong., 1 sess. (March 5, 1886), 2105; 50 Cong., 1 sess. (February 15, 1888), 1223; Allen J. Going, "The South and the Blair Bill," *Mississippi Valley Historical Review*, XLIV (September, 1957), 288; Gordon Canfield Lee, *The Struggle for Federal Aid, First Phase, A History of the Attempts to Obtain Federal Aid for Common Schools, 1870–1890* (New York, 1949), pp. 160–162. The vote in the Senate in 1884 was 33 to 11, with two Republicans voting no; in 1886, 36 to 11, with five Republicans against; in 1888, 39 to 29, with twelve Republicans in opposition. For a discussion of earlier Republican efforts in education, see above, pp. 86–94.

7. *Congressional Record*, 48 Cong., 1 sess. (December 5, 1883), 36, and (March 18, 1884), 2000; Edward McPherson to the Editor of the Philadelphia *Record*, in *Bulletin of the American Iron and Steel Association*, XXIII (August 23, 1889), 235; Lee, *Struggle for Federal Aid*, p. 90.

8. *Congressional Record*, 48 Cong., 1 sess. (March 19, 1884), 2062, 2069, and (March 20, 1884), 2100; Going, "The South and the Blair Bill," 267.

9. *Ibid.*, (March 24, 1884), 2208–2209.

10. Chicago *Tribune*, March 22, 1884; Joseph R. Hawley to Carl Schurz, Washington, December 4, 1887, Vol. 93, Schurz Papers, Library of Congress; H. S. Van Eaton to the Editor of the Summit (Miss.) *Sentinel*, Washington, April 14, 1886, in Washington *National Republican*, May 12, 1886; Henry W. Blair to Whitelaw Reid, Washington, March 8, 1886, Reid Papers, Library of Congress.

11. Concord *Evening Monitor*, July 14, 1888; *Congressional Record*, 49 Cong., 1 sess. (March 3 and 5, 1886), 1989–1991, 2105; New York *World*, September 12, 1888.

12. James D. Richardson (ed.), *A Compilation of the Messages and Papers of the Presidents* (New York, 1897), XII, 5489–5490.

13. New York *Evening Post*, April 7, 1884.

14. Born in 1847 in Huntington, Massachusetts, Clark was graduated from Yale University in 1870 and served as managing editor of the Springfield *Daily Republican* from 1872 to 1879. After working for the Philadelphia *Times*, the Philadelphia *Press*, the Milwaukee *Sentinel*, and the New York *World*, he came to the *Evening Post*, on which he remained until his death in 1903. See New York *Tribune*, February 17, 1903, *A Soldier of Conscience, Edward Perkins Clark* (Brooklyn, 1903), pp. 7–13; Allan Nevins, *The Evening Post, A Century of Journalism* (New York, 1922), p. 526.

15. Edward P. Clark to John D. Long, New York, March 23, April 3

and 13, 1886, March 16, April 14, May 23, and December 21, 1887, Long Papers, Massachusetts Historical Society; Edward P. Clark, *A Bill to Promote Mendicancy* (New York, 1886–1890), *passim;* Clark to Daniel S. Lamont, New York, January 6, 1888, Vol. 190, Grover Cleveland Papers, Library of Congress.

16. Clark to Grover Cleveland, New York, February 26, 1887, Vol. 148, Grover Cleveland Papers.

17. Clark to James B. Angell, New York, February 14, 1889, Box 13, Angell Papers, Michigan Historical Collections, Ann Arbor. There is no evidence in the Benjamin Harrison Papers, Library of Congress, that Angell followed Clark's advice.

18. *Congressional Record,* 51 Cong., 1 sess. (February 11, 1890), 1199.

19. John Jay to Whitelaw Reid, New York, February 15, 1888, Reid Papers; Jay to William M. Evarts and Frank Hiscock, New York, March 18, 1890, in New York *Tribune,* March 19, 1890.

20. New York *Evening Post,* February 16, 1903.

21. Indianapolis *News,* quoted in New York *Evening Post,* February 20, 1903.

22. Quoted in *A Soldier of Conscience, Edward Perkins Clark,* p. 57.

23. *Congressional Record,* 50 Cong., 1 sess. (February 15, 1888), 218. A worldwide anti-Jesuit movement was taking place about this time. The order was expelled from Germany in 1872 and from France in 1880.

24. *Ibid.,* 51 Cong., 1 sess. (February 20, 1890), 1546–1547. The New York *Mail and Express,* March 10, 1890, and Jay, in his letter to Evarts and Hiscock previously cited, also stressed the opposition of these Catholic journals to the Blair bill.

25. John Gilmary Shea, "Federal Schemes to Aid Common Schools in the Southern States," *The American Catholic Quarterly Review,* XIII (April, 1888), 345–359.

26. Lee, *Struggle for Federal Aid,* pp. 156–157; New York *Tribune,* March 21, 1890.

27. Lee, *Struggle for Federal Aid,* p. 156.

28. New York *Mail and Express,* March 22, 1890.

29. Henry Cabot Lodge, *Early Memories* (New York, 1913), pp. 113, 282.

30. John A. Garraty, *Henry Cabot Lodge, A Biography* (New York, 1953), pp. 12–13; Lodge, *Early Memories,* p. 289.

31. Lodge, *Early Memories,* pp. 116–118, 123, 126, 133, 291.

32. Garraty, *Henry Cabot Lodge,* p. 60; Henry Cabot Lodge to John D. Long, Boston, January 2, 1880, Long Papers.

33. New York *Herald,* November 30, 1889; *Nation,* XLIX (November 7, 1889), 359. Lodge was not motivated by a desire to hold on to a slipping constituency. He was immensely popular in his district, his 1888 plurality of more than 5,000 votes being over seven times his 1886 plurality. See Charles S. Groves, *Henry Cabot Lodge, The Statesman* (Boston, 1925), p. 16.

34. Lodge to Nathan Goff, November 14, 1889, Lodge Papers, Massachusetts Historical Society; Lodge to Wellington Wells, December 20, 1889, *ibid.*

35. New York *Herald,* November 30, 1889; Samuel W. McCall, *The Life of Thomas Brackett Reed* (Boston and New York, 1914), p. 162.

36. New York *Herald,* December 24, 1889; Lodge to W. W. Clapp, December 27, 1889, Lodge Papers.

37. Newark *Daily Advertiser,* February 13, 1890.

38. Nils P. Haugen to John T. Hay, May 19, 1890, copy, Haugen Papers, Wisconsin State Historical Society, Madison; Haugen to R. G. Andrews, April 20, 1890, copy, *ibid;* John F. Lacey to Will Lacey, Washington, January 26, 1890, and February 22, 1890, Box 22, Lacey Papers, Iowa State Department of History and Archives, Des Moines.

39. William E. Chandler to Thomas B. Reed, Washington, April 28, 1890, Vol. 81, Chandler Papers, Library of Congress; Chicago *Tribune,* May 11, 1890; John C. Spooner to George Farham, May 8, 1890, Letterbook 12, Spooner Papers, Library of Congress.

40. In order, the bills of Sherman, Spooner, Chandler, Hoar, Kelley, Lodge, and Rowell are in *Congressional Record,* 51 Cong., 1 sess. (December 4, 1889), 96; (December 4, 1889), 100; (December 4, 1889), 102; (April 24, 1890), 3760, 6079; (March 7, 1890), 2325; (March 15, 1890), 2285; (May 8, 1890), 4362.

41. Philadelphia *Press,* April 27, 1890.

42. *Congressional Record,* 51 Cong., 1 sess. (June 26, 1890), 6538; Concord *Evening Monitor,* June 17, 1890; Daniel Walker Hollis, "The Force Bill of 1890," (M. A. thesis, Columbia University, 1947), 43–46.

43. McCall, *Life of Thomas Brackett Reed,* pp. 175–176; New York *Times,* June 17 and 18, 1890. Unfortunately, the exact details and vote of the caucus were not recorded.

44. *Congressional Record,* 51 Cong., 1 sess. (June 19, 1890), 6286; John R. Lambert, *Arthur Pue Gorman* (Baton Rouge, 1953), pp. 145–148.

45. The important Republicans who still believed that they could break up the Solid South with the tariff issue will be discussed in the next chapter.

46. Richardson (ed.), *Messages and Papers of the Presidents*, XII, 5490–5491.

47. New York *Age*, December 7, 1889.

48. Washington *Bee*, February 1, 1890.

49. New York *Tribune*, August 16, 1890. The standard biography of Burrows is William Dana Orcutt, *Burrows of Michigan and the Republican Party* (New York, 1917), 2 vols.

50. New York *World*, September 15, 1888; Cincinnati *Enquirer*, July 8, 1890.

51. Grenville Dodge to William E. Chandler, New York, January 30, 1888, letterbook in Box 391, Dodge Papers, Iowa State Department of History and Archives, Des Moines.

52. Dodge to William Boyd Allison, New York, July 15, 1890, letterbook in Box 395, *ibid.*

53. James S. Clarkson, "Permanent Republican Clubs," *North American Review*, CXLVI (March, 1888), pp. 260–261.

54. *Iowa State Register*, April 29, 1890; Chicago *Tribune*, April 28, 1890.

55. Philadelphia *Press*, May 24, 1890; Clarkson to Louis T. Michener, Washington, May 29, 1890, Box 1, Michener Papers, Library of Congress; Leland L. Sage, *William Boyd Allison, A Study in Practical Politics* (Iowa City, 1956), p. 245.

56. Philadelphia *Press*, April 27, 1890; *Iowa State Register*, April 29, 1890.

57. Thomas B. Reed, "Federal Control of Elections," *North American Review*, CL (June, 1890), 673–677, 680.

58. For McMillan, see *Congressional Record*, 51 Cong., 1 sess. (June 25, 1890), 6507–6508; for Hemphill, see *ibid.* (June 26, 1890), 6548–6552; for Flower and Covert, see *ibid.* (June 27, 1890), 6595, 6599–6601.

59. *Ibid.*, (June 25, 1890), 6538–6544.

60. For Ewart, see *ibid.*, (June 28, 1890), 6688–6692; for Coleman, see *ibid.*, (June 30, 1890), 6772–6773.

61. *Ibid.*, (July 2, 1890), 6940–6941; Leon Burr Richardson, *William E. Chandler, Republican* (New York, 1940), p. 410; McCall, *Life of Thomas Brackett Reed*, pp. 175–176; Rayford W. Logan, *The Negro in American Life and Thought, The Nadir, 1877–1901* (New York, 1954), p. 64; Vincent P. De Santis, *Republicans Face the Southern Question, The New Departure Years, 1877–1897* (Baltimore, 1959), p. 206.

62. New York *Evening Post*, July 3, 1890.

10. FACTIONS

1. Thomas B. Reed to William E. Chandler, Washington, July 10, 1890, Vol. 81, Chandler Papers, Library of Congress; Henry Cabot Lodge to Chandler, Nahant, Massachusetts, July 10, 1890, *ibid.;* Chandler to Lodge, Waterloo, New Hampshire, July 7, 1890, Lodge Papers, Massachusetts Historical Society.

2. Edwin L. Godkin, "The Republican Party and the Negro," *Forum*, VII (May, 1889), 252–256.

3. *Harper's Weekly*, XXXIV (July 16, 1890), 574, and (August 9, 1890), 614; Benjamin H. Bristow to Walter Q. Gresham, New York, July 15, 1890, Vol. 38, Gresham Papers, Library of Congress.

4. New York *Commercial Bulletin*, July 25, 1890; New York *Commercial Advertiser*, July 16, 1890; New York *Journal of Commerce*, July 2, 1890.

5. "Business Men and the Force Bill," *American Grocer*, XLIV (July 23, 1890), 9.

6. Atlanta *Constitution*, July 20, 1890.

7. *Ibid.*, July 22, 1890. The paper was referring to the proposal of Mayor Fernando Wood to establish an independent New York in 1860. See Samuel A. Pleasants, *Fernando Wood of New York* (New York, 1948).

8. John B. Gordon to the Editor of the New York *Herald*, Atlanta, July 21, 1890, in New York *Herald*, July 22, 1890.

9. Concord *Evening Monitor*, July 23, 1890; Newark *Daily Advertiser*, July 24, 1890; Philadelphia *Press*, July 24, 1890; New York *Herald*, July 23, 1890.

10. New York *Times*, August 8, 1890; New York *Evening Post*, August 8, 1890.

11. *Congressional Record*, 51 Cong., 1 sess. (August 8, 1890), 8306–8307; New York *Herald*, August 9, 1890; Springfield *Daily Republican*, August 9, 1890.

12. *Congressional Record*, 51 Cong., 1 sess. (July 28, 1890), 7792; 43 Cong., 2 sess. (February 4, 1875), 981.

13. Atlanta *Constitution*, July 29, 1890. On the surface the *Constitution* hardly seems a reliable source for a story on Ingalls, but it was carrying a press association release.

14. Springfield *Daily Republican*, July 21, 1890; Cameron quoted in

Public Opinion, IX (August 16, 1890), 428; Karl Schriftgiesser, *The Gentleman from Massachusetts, Henry Cabot Lodge* (Boston, 1944), p. 107.

15. George Frisbie Hoar to John Sherman, Washington, August 26, 1890, Vol. 526, Sherman Papers, Library of Congress.

16. William E. Chandler, "National Control of Elections," *Forum,* IX (August, 1890), 711–713, 718.

17. Grenville Dodge to G. B. Pray, Great South Bay, July 29, 1890, letterbook in Box 395, Dodge Papers, Iowa State Department of History and Archives, Des Moines.

18. John C. Spooner to Henry Fink, July 27, 1890, Letterbook 13, Spooner Papers, Library of Congress.

19. James G. Blaine to Joseph H. Manley, Bar Harbor, September 3, 1892, in New York *Herald,* September 7, 1892; Blaine to Mrs. Henry Cabot Lodge, Ellsworth, Maine, August 31, 1890, Lodge Papers.

20. Brooklyn *Standard Union,* July 14, 1890. During the struggle over the Force bill Halstead signed most of his editorials.

21. Chandler to the Editor of the New York *Mail and Express,* Waterloo, New Hampshire, July 17, 1890, in New York *Mail and Express,* July 19, 1890.

22. Brooklyn *Standard Union,* July 21, 1890.

23. New York *Times,* July 24, 1890; New York *Evening Post,* July 29, 1890; *Congressional Record,* 51 Cong., 1 sess. (July 31, 1890), 7835–7836, 7942, and (August 2, 1890), 8048.

24. New York *Times,* August 9, 1890.

25. Philadelphia *Press,* July 2, 1890; Philadelphia *Inquirer,* August 5, 1890; Spooner to Alexander Meggett, June 17, 1890, Letterbook 15, Spooner Papers.

26. Portland *Oregonian,* August 13, 1890; Philadelphia *Inquirer,* August 13, 1890; *Congressional Record,* 51 Cong., 1 sess. (August 12, 1890), 8466.

27. Philadelphia *Press,* August 14, 1890; New York *World,* August 16, 1890.

28. New York *Sun,* August 13, 1890; New York *Tribune,* August 14, 1890; New York *Herald,* August 18, 1890; William D. Kelley, *The Old South and the New* (New York, 1888), pp. 23–27; T. Frederick Davis, "The Disston Land Purchase," *Florida Historical Quarterly,* XVII (January, 1939), 200–210.

29. New York *Tribune,* August 14, 1890.

30. New York *Evening Post,* August 8, 1890.

31. New York *Times,* August 20, 1890.

32. Blaine to Benjamin Harrison, Washington, August 30, 1890, Vol. 111, Harrison Papers, Library of Congress; Blaine to Mrs. Henry Cabot Lodge, Ellsworth, August 31, 1890, Lodge Papers.

33. Portland *Oregonian*, August 15, 1890.

34. Philadelphia *Press*, August 16, 1890.

35. Springfield *Daily Republican*, August 2, 5, 7, 16, and September 2, 1890.

36. Philadelphia *Press*, August 16, 1890.

37. New York *Tribune*, August 16, 1890.

38. *Ibid.*, August 15, 1890.

39. Philadelphia *Press*, August 16, 1890; Nathaniel Wright Stephenson, *Nelson W. Aldrich, A Leader in American Politics* (New York, 1930), p. 438.

40. New York *Tribune*, August 23, 1890.

41. George F. Edmunds to Justin Morrill, Washington, September 9, 1890, Vol. 40, Morrill Papers, Library of Congress; Louis A. Coolidge, *An Old-Fashioned Senator, Orville Platt of Connecticut* (New York, 1910), pp. 232–234; Henry Cabot Lodge, "The Federal Election Bill," *North American Review*, CLI (September, 1890), 257–266.

42. Washington *Bee*, September 20, 1890.

43. New York *Tribune*, September 9, 1890; New York *Commercial Advertiser*, September 5, 1890.

44. Matthew Josephson, *The Politicos, 1865–1896* (New York, 1938), pp. 464–465.

45. Bristow to Gresham, New York, November 6, 1890, Vol. 38, Gresham Papers; Stephen B. Elkins to Whitelaw Reid, New York, November 14, 1890, Reid Papers, Library of Congress.

46. James D. Richardson (ed.), *A Compilation of the Messages and Papers of the Presidents* (New York, 1897), XII, 5562–5564.

47. *Congressional Record*, 51 Cong., 2 sess. (December 6, 1890), and (February 26, 1891), 3403; (December 10, 1890), 297; (December 16, 1890), 502.

48. Chicago *Tribune*, December 15, 1890; Spooner to Horace Rublee, December 28, 1890, Letterbook 14, Spooner Papers.

49. Fred Wellborn, "The Influence of the Silver-Republican Senators, 1889–1891," *Mississippi Valley Historical Review*, XIV (March, 1928), 475–476.

50. *Congressional Record*, 51 Cong., 2 sess. (January 5, 1891), 912–913; William A. Robinson, *Thomas B. Reed, Parliamentarian* (New York, 1930), p. 239; Edward Arthur White, "The Republican Party in National Politics, 1888–1891" (Ph. D. Dissertation, University of Wis-

consin, 1941), 471. Detesting free coinage of silver even more than the Force bill, Eastern Republican Senators, many of whom in August, 1890, had upheld the Quay resolution, as a bloc opposed Stewart's maneuver.

51. *Congressional Record,* 51 Cong., 2 sess. (January 14, 1891), 1323–1324; (January 20, 1891), 1564; (January 22, 1891), 1739–1740; Robert McElroy, *Levi Parsons Morton, Banker, Diplomat, Statesman* (New York, 1930), pp. 187–194. For the story of Cameron's speculations see Philadelphia *North American,* January 22, 24, 1891.

52. New York *Tribune,* January 28, 1891.

53. George Frisbie Hoar, "The Fate of the Election Bill," *Forum,* XI (April, 1891), 132–133.

54. For Dodge, see *Iowa State Register,* February 14, 1891; James S. Clarkson to John E. Bruce, Washington, March 21, 1891, Bruce Papers, Schomburg Collection of the New York Public Library.

11. THE "GOOD FELLOW" BUSINESS

1. The best treatments of the Republican party's attitude toward the Negro after 1890 are: C. Vann Woodward, *Origins of the New South, 1877–1913* (Vol. IX of *A History of the South* ed. by Wendell Holmes Stephenson and E. Merton Coulter, Baton Rouge, 1951), pp. 462–469, 478; Vincent P. De Santis, *Republicans Face the Southern Question, The New Departure Years, 1877–1897* (Baltimore, 1959), pp. 227–262; Rayford W. Logan, *The Negro in the United States* (Princeton, 1957), pp. 49–50, 60–61, 65–66; Rayford W. Logan, *The Negro in American Life and Thought, The Nadir, 1877–1901* (New York, 1954), pp. 87–96; John Morton Blum, *The Republican Roosevelt* (Cambridge, Mass., 1954), pp. 43–47; Henry F. Pringle, "Theodore Roosevelt and the South," *Virginia Quarterly Review,* IX (January, 1933), 14–25; George E. Mowry, "The South and the Progressive Lily White Party of 1912," *Journal of Southern History,* VII (May, 1940), 237–247; Arthur S. Link, "Theodore Roosevelt and the South in 1912," *North Carolina Historical Review,* XXIII (July, 1946), 313–324; Henry F. Pringle, *William Howard Taft, A Biography* (New York, 1939), I, 347, 390; Clarence A. Bacote, "Negro Officeholders in Georgia under President McKinley," *Journal of Negro History,* XLIV (July, 1959), 217–239.

2. William E. Chandler to T. Thomas Fortune, Waterloo, New Hampshire, September 2, 1891, Vol. 83, Chandler Papers, Library of Congress. Chandler's charge that Negroes had helped draft the Mississippi

Constitution was correct. See New York *Commercial Advertiser,* September 20, 1890.

3. Chandler to Fortune, Waterloo, September 2, 1891, Vol. 83, Chandler Papers; Magnus L. Robinson to Chandler, Alexandria, April 26, 1892, and May 2, 1892, Vol. 86, *ibid.*

4. Newark *Daily Advertiser,* August 13, 1891; Chicago *Tribune,* May 20, 1892.

5. Frederick Douglass, "Lynch Law in the South," *North American Review,* CLV (July, 1892), 21-24.

6. Benjamin Harrison to Mrs. H. Davis, Washington, April 1, 1892, copy, Vol. 138, Harrison Papers, Library of Congress.

7. James D. Richardson (ed.), *A Compilation of the Messages and Papers of the Presidents* (New York, 1897), XII, 5645-5646.

8. Joseph B. Foraker, *Notes of a Busy Life* (Cincinnati, 1917), I, 450-451.

9. Kirk H. Porter and Donald Bruce Johnson (eds.), *National Party Platforms, 1840-1956* (Urbana, 1956), pp. 92-93.

10. Allan Nevins, *Grover Cleveland, A Study in Courage* (New York, 1932), p. 491.

11. Harry Thurston Peck, *Twenty Years of the Republic, 1885-1905* (New York, 1906), pp. 296-297.

12. New York *Sun,* July 5 and 12, 1892.

13. Philadelphia *Press,* July 2, 1892.

14. Grover Cleveland to J. W. Campbell, Buzzard's Bay, Massachusetts, July 7, 1892, in New York *Times,* July 14, 1892; Cleveland to Basil B. Gordon, Buzzard's Bay, July 9, 1892, in New York *Times,* July 19, 1892.

15. Brooklyn *Times,* July 25, 1892, in *Public Opinion,* XIII (July 30, 1892), 397; Pittsburgh *Commercial-Gazette,* July 29, 1892, in *Public Opinion,* XIII (August 6, 1892), 420.

16. Joseph R. Hawley to Harrison, Washington, August 3, 1892, Vol. 145, Harrison Papers.

17. New York *Times,* September 6, 1892.

18. Chicago *Tribune,* September 7, 1892; *Iowa State Register,* September 7, 1892.

19. James G. Blaine, "The Presidential Election of 1892," *North American Review,* CLV (November, 1892), 519-520; Murat Halstead, "Review of Current Events," *Cosmopolitan,* XII (January, 1892), 373-374.

20. *Nation,* LX (August 25, 1892), 135; New York *Herald,* September 23, 1892.

21. *Nation,* LX (August 25, 1892), 135.

22. New York *Herald,* August 21, 1892.

23. New York *Sun,* September 27, 1892.

24. New York *Times,* October 26, 1892.

25. New York *World,* October 27, 1892; *Iowa State Register,* November 1, 1892.

26. *Annual Address of James S. Clarkson, President of the National Republican League. Sixth Annual Convention of the League. Held at Louisville, Kentucky, May 10, 1893,* p. 6, in Box 1, Clarkson Papers, Library of Congress.

27. George Harmon Knoles, *The Presidential Campaign and Election of 1892* (Stanford, 1942), p. 178.

28. New York *Herald,* September 19, 1892; *Review of Reviews,* VI (November, 1892), 405.

29. Frederic Bancroft (ed.), *Speeches, Correspondence and Political Papers of Carl Schurz* (New York, 1913), V, 119–120.

30. New York *Sun,* November 9, 1892.

31. *Review of Reviews,* VI (December, 1892), 517–520.

32. For Harrison, see New York *World,* November 12, 1892; for Douglass, see Cleveland *Gazette,* November 26, 1892; James S. Clarkson to John E. Bruce, New York, December 2, 1892, Bruce Papers, Schomburg Collection of the New York Public Library.

33. Allan Nevins, *Grover Cleveland, A Study in Courage* (New York, 1932), pp. 498–499, 505; Matthew Josephson, *The Politicos, 1865–1896* (New York, 1938), pp. 508–509.

34. Richardson (ed.), *Messages and Papers of the Presidents,* XII, 5766–5767.

35. Chicago *Tribune,* February 4, 1893.

36. *Iowa State Register,* February 4, 1893; New York *World,* February 5, 1893; New York *Sun,* February 5, 1893. The cremation of the Texas Negro is described in the New York *World,* February 2, 1893.

37. New York *World,* February 6, 1893; Chicago *Tribune,* February 4, 1893.

38. Clarkson to the Editor of the New York *World,* in New York *World,* February 8, 1893.

39. *Ibid.,* February 7, 1893.

40. *Iowa State Register,* February 19, 1893; *Congressional Record,* 52 Cong., 2 sess. (February 22, 1893), 2008.

41. *Annual Address of James S. Clarkson, President of the National Republican League. Sixth Annual Convention of the League. Held at Louisville, Kentucky, May 10, 1893,* pp. 6–8, in Box 1, Clarkson Papers.

42. *Iowa State Register,* May 12, 1893.

43. John C. Spooner to Clarkson, April 16, 1893, Letterbook 17, Spooner Papers, Library of Congress; William S. Ball to Spooner, Chicago, July 5, 1893, *ibid.*

44. Leon Burr Richardson, *William E. Chandler, Republican* (New York, 1940), p. 443.

45. George Frisbie Hoar to Bruce, Washington, February 25, 1895, Bruce Papers.

46. Foraker, *Notes of a Busy Life,* I and II, *passim.*

47. Logan, *The Negro in American Life and Thought,* p. 87.

48. Charles S. Olcott, *The Life of William McKinley* (Boston, 1916), I, 226.

12. THE PARTY AND THE NEGRO

1. It has been called this by Rayford W. Logan, *The Negro in American Life and Thought, The Nadir, 1877–1901* (New York, 1954).

2. This is the theme of Paul H. Buck, *The Road to Reunion, 1865–1900* (Boston, 1937).

3. See Dewey W. Grantham, Jr., "Politics Below the Potomac," *Current History,* 35 (November, 1958), 263–265; New York *Times,* September 11 and 13, 1960.

4. New York *Times,* September 29, and October 4, 1960.

5. *Ibid.,* October 6, 1957, and December 11, 1960.

6. Cincinnati *Enquirer,* November 20, 1884; New York *Times,* December 6, 1960.

7. New York *Times,* September 13, 1960.

Index

(Hayes, Rutherford B., *cont.*)
28, 35; withdraws troops from South, 28–29; Republican attitudes toward, 33–38, 40–44; tours New England and South, 38–39; first annual message, 41; on Stalwart attacks, 43; dismayed by Bourbon atrocities, 47; admits Bourbons deceived him, 49–50; denounces Southern frauds, 50–51; vetoes riders, 57; attacks South, 58–59; annual message of 1879, 61; rejects scheme to settle Negroes in Santo Domingo, 64; supports Negro exodus, 67; promises to protect Negroes fleeing northward, 69; accused of fostering exodus, 73; on bloody shirt, 79; favors aid to common schools, 87; opposes Readjusters, 95; on Arthur, 100; compared with Arthur, 106; attack on, 117–118; and South, 253–254

Hemphill, John J., 212

Higginson, Thomas Wentworth: on Republicans and Negro, 11; changing attitude toward Negro, 129–130; on Negro vote, 132–133; Long denounces, 133

Hill, Benjamin, 43, 74

Hill, David B., 256; in 1892 election, 242–243; *Review of Reviews* on, 245

Hines, H. C., 138

Hinsdale, Burke A.: correspondence with Garfield and Tourgee on education, 88–91; Garfield's remarks to, on education, 93–94

Hiscock, Frank: and Blair bill, 200;

introduces anti-Lodge bill petition, 220–221

Hoar, George Frisbie, 233; ridicules businessmen, 31; supports Hayes, 40; proposal to aid common schools, 87; endorses Readjusters, 96; denounces Mugwumps, 130, 131, 133; on Southern frauds, 132, 176; opposes deportation of Negroes, 191; introduces election bill, 204; defends Lodge bill, 222; denounces Plumb, 229; on opponents of Force bill, 234, 235; on Southern question, 249

Holloway, William R.: denies Republicans fostered Negro migration to Indiana, 74; desires Negro colonization in Indiana, 75

Homestead (Pa.) strike, 246

Houk, Leonidas C.: on Republicanism in the South, 171; and Mississippi Constitution of 1890, 232

Howe, Timothy O., 28, 42–43

Hubbell, Jay A., 82

Huntsville *Independent,* 179

Illinois, Sherman in, 151–152

Independent: attacks Bourbon frauds, 48–49; supports Mahone, 108

Independents. See Mugwumps

Independents, Southern. See Readjusters

Indiana: Negro migration to, 72–73; investigation of migration to, 73–77; Foraker speaks in, 163

Indianapolis *Journal,* 74; on Harrison and the South, 168–169

Indianapolis *News,* 197